SUSTAINABILITY
with style

Environmental, social and cultural lessons
learnt by a fashionista turned environmentalist

♡

LISA HEINZE

I take sustainability seriously. This book was printed on recycled paper from an FSC-certified provider that uses 30% post-consumer recycled material. It was also created via Print on Demand, meaning it's only printed once ordered, reducing excess production. You can help lessen the book's eco-impact even more by sharing it!

Cover art: Wingrove Design

Photography: Alicia Fox

ISBN: 978-0-9924542-1-0

To Tyler, for your unending passion, dedication, support and love.

Introduction to the Second Edition

Welcome to the second edition of *Sustainability with Style,* my story of eco-awareness and learning to leave a lighter footprint while still looking and feeling like myself.

The two years since releasing the first edition of *Sustainability with Style* have been a whirlwind as I continue to immerse myself in the world of environmentalism. I have had the privilege of meeting innumerable dedicated, expert greenies and social campaigners. I've attended oodles of sustainability events in Australia and America. I've eco-shopped my way around the globe. And I've seen firsthand the first effects of climate change in India, the Maldives, East Africa, America and Australia.

The wider sustainability community has remained hard at work over the past couple of years, too. Scientists and engineers continue to create new, innovative clean energy technologies and homes of the future; sustainable fashion options are increasing by the day; economists have developed carbon pricing schemes and are exploring new economic systems; environmental advocates have increased their pressure on governments; and the younger generations have, for better or worse, grown up with the knowledge that climate change is 'real' and we need to work toward solutions. As a result of witnessing the positive momentum in the community, I feel more confident than ever that we will overcome the challenges posed by climate change.

And what I know above all else is that the magic ingredient to solving our climate crisis is *you.*

Yep. You have the power to change the world.

You can make changes in your personal life starting right now, and you can demand the necessary changes at the government, society and community levels that can stop climate change in its tracks. Even better, you can remain your wonderful, unique, stylish self while you're doing all these world-changing activities.

Sound too good to be true?

Well it isn't! Welcome to the green club, I'm thrilled you've decided to join us. And I have made a couple very exciting changes in this second edition that should help make your transition to eco-fabulousness even easier.

The first change is that *Sustainability with Style* is available in print, as well as ebook, for the first time. All books will be printed on recycled paper from an FSC-certified provider that uses a minimum of 30% post-consumer recycled material. The paperback version is also created using Print on Demand, meaning no excess books will be printed.

The second big change, and included by popular demand, is the addition of a Sustainable Shopping Guide. I have provided you a glimpse into my wardrobe and make-up bag to give you a head start on your own stylish sustainability journey.

Throughout the book I have also updated statistics, brands and company information where relevant – the world of sustainability is changing at the speed of light! I also moved the chapter titled 'Cultural and social lessons' to the Appendix.

For now, I invite you along on my journey. I hope to inform and inspire you, and show you how you truly are the most important piece of our sustainability solution. You can make a real difference, and together we will be the answer to our climate change dilemma.

CONTENTS

Thank you

♡

There are so many people who helped this book become a reality, and I have been humbled by the support I have received.

A huge thank you to Guy Redden, my dissertation supervisor at the University of Sydney, for guiding me through the world of cultural studies and encouraging me to create this book; your belief in me made this entire endeavour possible.

I also want to give special thanks to Romilly Madew, my former boss at the Green Building Council of Australia, not only for enabling me to work a part-time schedule to complete the book, but also for being an amazing mentor and role model.

Thank you to my incredible editor, Carolyn Roark, who worked her magic and seemed to know exactly what I was trying to say when I couldn't quite get the words right.

I owe a debt of gratitude to many beautiful friends who offered support in a multitude of ways – Erica, Nat, Beth, Mark, Liz, Logan, Chris, Lee, Penny, Orjan, Luke, Jess, Bindu, Nick B, Nick T, Shane, Annette, Stella, Aileen, Susie, Lou, Craig, Briana, Karen, Suzie, Lynne, Emily, Anna, Prue, Ian, Bonnie, Carlie, Kelly, Yatu and those I'm sure to have forgotten – and to my family for their unconditional support and love, especially my mother who always encouraged me to follow my dreams.

A special thanks to Hemingway's café for the comfortable and inspiring writing location overlooking Manly beach, and to Barefoot coffee for the organic, Fairtrade caffeine fixes.

Most importantly, to my husband and eco-partner Tyler – words cannot express my love or my gratitude for your support throughout this, and every, journey. Thank you.

Prologue

I emerge from the surf refreshed and rejuvenated after taking my new bikini for an inaugural swim. Walking back to my towel I hear someone call, "Great bikini!" It's from a couple girls sunbathing on the beach.

"Thank you so much!" I say, beaming, and wander over.

"I love the thick band around the hips, it's a really flattering cut," says one of them.

"Yeah, thank you," I say, relieved that this mail-order suit looks as good in reality as it did on the website. "Actually, it's made from recycled plastic bottles," I can't resist telling my admirers.

"Are you serious?"

"Yep, instead of regular spandex polyester they used recycled plastic bottles to make the fabric, how cool is that?"

We chat for a couple more minutes then I walk back to my towel to bask in the sunshine and the glow of an amazing eco-purchase.

The suit really is a great fit and a flattering cut, and despite not having any underwire the top is very supportive. Of course getting a shout-out from a couple strangers on the beach is icing on the cake. It took me a little more effort than just visiting the surf shops in Manly, Sydney, Australia, where I call home, but I can't think of a better opportunity to share the eco-credentials of my clothing than when someone compliments its style. It looks like I'm officially an eco-fashionista!

I haven't always given so much thought to my purchases. I used to be more carefree – my biggest shopping concerns were making sure my friends didn't buy the same handbag as me and that I had the very latest style before it hit the magazines (let alone the department stores). But a few years ago I had a good hard look at myself – and not just while applying makeup – and realised I wanted to do more with my life than just stay up on the latest trends. I uncovered a renewed sense of responsibility toward the environment, and wanted to start leading by example. I started to shed my designer ambitions and headed toward greener pastures (pun intended).

This is my story of dedicating myself to a worthy cause: Mother Earth. I hope to not come across too 'preachy' or like some kind of eco-martyr. I merely want to tell my story – the good, the bad and the ugly of becoming an environmentalist – and provide some insight into aspects of our society and culture that hinder green living. My journey into environmentalism wasn't as easy as I'd expected, and I hope others can learn from my mistakes and be better prepared for the challenges they may face along their own green journeys. And while it's true that I changed more than I ever imagined possible, I have also figured out how to live sustainably with style; hopefully my story will help you uncover how you can incorporate sustainability into your life, too.

Part One

How to become a greenie

My coffee cup moment

"Morning Babe," Tyler gives my shoulders a little squeeze and pecks the top of my head as he pads across the living room to the sun-drenched Surry Hills kitchen. My gorgeous husband looks adorable in ancient purple sweatpants, relics from his high school football days. Ty starts up his espresso machine and I settle back to my tea and the *Good Weekend* section of the *Sydney Morning Herald*. To my delight, the usual quizzes, recipes, fashion tips and feature articles have an overarching 'green' theme. I consider myself as a bit of a greenie. I mean honestly, how could anyone watch *An Inconvenient Truth* and not make some green changes in her life? Ty and I have switched all our light bulbs to compact fluorescents, commute using public transportation, religiously separate our recycling and take our own bags to the grocery store. At this moment, I think we are really starting to pull our weight with this whole global warming thing, especially compared to most people I know.

I've just finished reading an article about purchasing organic produce (best tip: whatever food you eat the most of is what you should buy organic) when I glimpse a non-descript little blurb asking me, "Did you know . . . takeaway coffee cups are not recyclable?" *What?!* I gasp and blink – that cannot say what I think it says. I look down again, and sure enough the sentence is still there. Apparently, and somewhat ironically, the plastic lids of takeaway coffees are recyclable; it's the paper cup that is the troublemaker. Most have a thin layer of a waxy plastic coating to prevent leakage, which also prevents the cups from being recyclable.

"What's going on over there?" Ty asks, hearing my gasp.

"Honey, you'll never believe this – takeaway coffee cups aren't recyclable!" I'm sure the shock is written all over my face. As Ty takes in the news, and comes to read the article over my shoulder, I am mentally calculating how many times I have painstakingly separated the plastic lid from the paper cup and recycled each into their appropriate bins, sometimes even bringing the lid home with me because it can be so hard to find plastic recycling bins in the street.

"Huh," Ty grunts, "I guess that's a good excuse to start using my travel mug on the way to work."

I usually appreciate his sense of calm, but this morning it is borderline infuriating.

"Doesn't this surprise you? I'm totally shocked!"

"I don't know, I think maybe I've heard that before," he says as he turns his attention back to his espresso machine.

I hop on the internet for confirmation – there are a few mixed reports, but the majority of websites agree – billions of takeaway cups get sent to landfill every day (about 500 million each year in Australia, and 23 *billion* in the USA). I quickly learn it is even worse than I imagined, because the cups are predominantly made from virgin, not recycled, paper. In the USA the Food and Drug Administration (FDA) has strict guidelines on what type of materials can be used to serve food and beverages, requiring virgin paper for food containers. The complexity and weight of this new realisation crashes over me like waves in a storm – or more accurately, like piles of empty takeaway cups being poured into the landfill – I'm shocked into stillness.

It seems silly, I know. It's just a takeaway coffee cup. I don't even buy a coffee every day, so it's not really going to impact my daily routine too much, except that now I know. And now that I know, I can never buy one again. It's just so sad. I will really miss that carefree experience: the sudden desire for a coffee, the joy of knowing that the city is bursting at the seams with delicious cafes and talented baristas who can make my latte in minutes – delivered hot and steamy in a convenient, light, travel size cup.

Oh takeaway coffee cup, we had many good times together, but I can take your dirty little lies no longer...

"Everything alright over there?" Tyler interrupts my mental breakup with the takeaway coffee cup.

"I just can't believe I didn't know this about the cups, that's all. I thought I was doing the right thing, recycling the paper cup all this time. I feel like I've been duped."

"Well, now you do know, so you can start doing the right thing."

"That's the problem; I thought I *was* doing the right thing. What else don't I know about? What else are we doing that we don't realise is hurting the environment?"

Finally, silence from my other-half.

"And even worse, we actually claim to care about the environment. What about everyone else out there who doesn't seem to care as much as we do?"

"This from the girl who still throws her plastic yoghurt container into the rubbish bin."

"You know I'm working on that," I say, irritated, "I'm serious though, think about all those people you see walking through the city everyday with their takeaway coffee."

"Well, what can we do?"

I look him in the eye, suddenly extremely confident that I have access to the best tool to quickly disseminate this very important information:

"I'll put it on Facebook," I say with an optimistic grin.

☙∅♕♔⚱♫♀👁☙♀♡

I think the coffee cup statistics hit me so hard because I've already been asking some serious questions about my life. In fact, I remember an experience I had at work just the other week that really set off some alarm bells in my mind. . .

"We want to sell this line of face wash as 'better-for-you,' really play up its natural ingredients and appeal to the health-conscious consumer and those people looking for all-natural products." I am sitting in the über-modern offices of my client, a multi-national FMCG company ("fast-moving consumer goods" for those not in the biz), and my contact Luke is describing the latest product to come out of its beauty department to my boss Duncan and me. We work for one of Sydney's leading marketing and design agencies, and it is our job to make our clients' products irresistible to millions of Australian consumers.

As Luke continues his discourse of the company's core ethics and values, I give him the once-over and decide he *almost* has excellent taste. At first glance he is well put together – decent suit, colourful but not overbearing tie, shiny black shoes that look as though they just walked out of the store window, all topped off with a sharp haircut and just the right amount of styling product. But, upon closer inspection I decide he is a carbon copy of practically every other man in this office. Sure they all look fantastic, and probably turn plenty of heads when they're out on the town, but there is nothing individual or unique on display here. Rather, they appear to be adhering to some company uniform that encourages basic corporate attire with a splash of colour to demonstrate they are 'fun'. The more I think about it, Luke probably didn't give much thought to his fuchsia and plum checked tie; more likely he bulk purchased a dozen or so equally impersonal ties at the latest David Jones half-yearly sale. Don't think he isn't a great guy, though; at last year's agency Christmas party (more commonly known as the agency-sponsored booze fest) Luke was one of the last men standing and could hold his own on the dance floor.

Now before you write me off as completely shallow and materialistic, working for a graphic design agency, it is essential for me to understand my clients' aesthetics. Eventually I will have to present designs to these people, and showing concepts to a style-conscious fashionista is very different to presenting to a budget-focused corporate warrior. My assessment of Luke tells me the ultimate design can be modern, but not too cutting-edge, and I will have to use a lot of the corporate jargon he sprinkles so easily into conversation if I want to succeed. So, judgemental as it may seem, I have practiced this method for years and can fully vouch for it. I will debate with anyone who swears you can't judge a book by its cover.

I know my clients will be judging my appearance, too, and I must give them what they want to see. They need to believe that aesthetics are *very* important to me. For this meeting, I'm in super-skinny black One Teaspoon jeans, a Chanel-inspired structured black and white tweed jacket over a billowy white blouse, a chunky ring comprised of a sea-green stone carved into a rose, black patent leather Jimmy Choo stilettos and an oversized eggplant Coach tote. My long chestnut hair has a slight golden sparkle and a finely balanced wave (that tousled, beachy look – meant to look casual but actually takes an hour of styling and the right products to achieve), and my Napolean eyeliner, mascara and lip gloss were touched up before heading to this meeting. Nothing too over the top, I am aiming for classy with a just a hint of spunk. I must appear to be creative, carefree and trustworthy all at the same time – not always an easy balance to maintain.

Waiting in the lobby before our meeting it was easy to spot the other creative agency folks waiting to meet with their respective clients: dramatic hair style here, straight-off-the-catwalk look there, and of course the blazer with jeans as the standard on the men. We're all aiming to project the same message: that we are creative, smart and business savvy. It's not rocket science, we all know the importance of image; we make our living from it.

Luke wraps up the design brief, "So, make sure the packaging looks as natural as possible, maybe so it looks like it's on recycled or unbleached paper."

I snap back to the task at hand, "That sounds great Luke. It's fantastic to be able to promote something that's all-natural, and recycled paper is so hot right now," I am quite impressed at the company's decision to promote a natural lifestyle. My current project list comprises the artificial world of chocolate, lollies and alcohol, and the prospect of working on a lovely, natural body product is very appealing.

"No, you misunderstand. We want the packaging to *look* recycled – we can't actually afford to print all the packaging on recycled or raw paper stock. Do you know how expensive that is? Just design something to make it look natural."

"Oh, right…" I'm slightly taken aback.

Luke continues, "And make sure that any imagery of the flowers or plants are illustrations, not photographs. The legal team won't let us portray real flowers unless the product contains more than 10% natural ingredients."

"But I thought you said it was a product for consumers who want all-natural products?" I smile, desperately trying to mask my annoyance and frustration.

"That's who we're targeting to buy the product, yes."

"So, what exactly *is* in the face wash then?"

Luke confidently slides the ingredient list across the table. "We're using extract of cucumber and mint in one product, and avocado and oatmeal in the other," he says proudly and succinctly, silently challenging me to question him further.

I look down the list and sure enough see those ingredients…far below chemicals I can't pronounce, and hidden amongst artificial fragrances and colours. I open my mouth to speak but Duncan shoots me a warning look as he jumps in to thank Luke for his time, signalling the end of the design brief. I am free to ask as many questions as I want about colour, texture and budget, but this time I had prodded a bit too deep about the honesty of the product for the comfort of this client (not to mention my boss).

"Great brief, isn't it?" asks Duncan as I drive the company's cherry-red Mini Cooper through the Sydney streets back to our design studio.

I gaze out on another sparkling day as we cross the Sydney Harbour Bridge on the way to our loft-inspired office, and I can't help but feel let down. It isn't just the deceptive brief, because as far as design briefs go this is a pretty good one; at least there are some natural ingredients in the product. No, it's bigger than the brief; it's the life I have created in this magnificent town after arriving from the US a few years ago. I can't help but have this overwhelming feeling that, actually, despite what my mother (and Bert and Ernie) always said, it's what's on the *outside* that counts.

Image is everything, or so I have gleaned through my career in advertising and design, my friends with similar interests in fashion and shopping, and the successes I have gained by fitting the part. I mean, in order to even get this job I had to officially be 'checked out' by the owner of the company – he flies in from Melbourne to personally meet each potential employee before making a job offer to make sure she or he has the right look. At my first interview I was told, "Don't worry, Larry is going to *love* you!" He must have loved my white, immaculately tailored Marc Jacobs suit, fuchsia camisole and dangerously high heels, otherwise I may not be living in Sydney now, and I really love this town. Yet somewhere along the way I have placed myself in a situation where I am rewarded solely on image alone, and nothing below the surface, of either the projects I design or myself. And do you want to know the real dilemma? 95% of the time, it's really fun (the other 5% when these pessimistic thoughts start creeping in, not so much.)

"Earth to Lisa," Duncan jokes.

"Oh yeah, great brief," I finally reply. "It would be great to convince Luke to spend the dollars on recycled paper, though, so at least part of the product is natural. Plus, raw paper looks so premium and modern, they'll sell more if they use it."

I don't have the strength to tell Duncan what I really think about the brief – that it's completely misleading and a perfect example of why so many people hate advertisers. Existential crisis or not, a girl needs a job, so I continue chatting about the project all the way back to the office. Once we're in the studio I get to work researching other natural body products to understand our client's competition, silently wishing they were my clients so I didn't have to continue to sell half-truths to innocent consumers. At least I can buy some of these lovely natural products, expense them as 'research' and take them home when I'm done – I think a little Jurlique facial scrub and moisturizer will be just the thing to add some shimmer to my complexion. And my spirits.

At the end of my nine-hour day, I rush into Pizza e Birra and kiss my gorgeous husband hello. I'm late for our weeknight date, and I apologize, "things got a bit crazy at work at the end of the day – big surprise." My working late is not uncommon, and if we hadn't scheduled this date I would probably still be at the studio.

"That's okay," he says as he puts his iPhone away, "I just ordered us a bottle of wine." Seriously, best husband ever. "How was your day?"

"You don't want to know. You?"

"Good. I went to site and watched as they put in the new signal lights in North Sydney station, I learned heaps." I love that even though I think his job as a project engineer for the commuter train lines sounds so dull, he thinks it's the most exciting job in the world, and seems genuinely satisfied with his work. He also manages to have that elusive work-life balance we all crave but never seem to attain – it's inspirational (if not a little envy inducing).

After working through a Margherita pizza, salad, and nearly a whole carafe of Chianti, I am ready to talk.

"I just don't know what I'm doing at this job."

"What's going on now?" Ty sighs. It's not the first time he's heard complaints about my job. "Crazy deadline? Cranky designer?"

"No, it's not that – though I suppose it's all related. It's this new brief I got today; it really made me question what I'm doing. It's for this face wash that has some natural ingredients, but mostly chemical stuff, and the client wants us to make it look 'all-natural'. It's not really that natural or better for people or the environment, but it's my job to make it look like it is so a lot of people buy it. I don't really know how else to explain it, but I just feel like I need more. Like, I need to feel that what I'm doing is really making a difference. I'm so sick of selling junk food and lying to people – surely there's more I can offer the world than this?" I look to him hopefully for some reassurance.

"I told you a long time ago advertising was evil," he says, a bit more smugly than I appreciate.

It's true, though. Tyler was my university sweetheart, we met while we were both studying engineering, and when I bailed for business school to study advertising he voiced his opinion that marketing was evil. I didn't care at the time – it seemed so fun and glamorous, much more so than the factories and oil refineries I saw in my engineering-future.

"I wouldn't mind marketing something I could feel good about, I just don't want to sell junk anymore. And why is there so much of this junk out there in the world anyway? There are so many more important things to be worrying about and spending money on than faux-natural products and energy drinks."

"So quit then." He suggests this often.

"I can't quit, I don't even know what I would do."

"You love fashion – why don't you try and get a job in that area?"

I sigh; he clearly doesn't understand. "That's not the answer – that's still not something I could feel good about. Sure, it's more interesting than selling candy, but I think it'd only be a matter of time before . . ." I trail off.

"Before what?"

"Before I start feeling empty again."

⌐∅🍶🍷🥂🍸🍾🍺🥛🍵🍶🥄💡♡

So now here I am, starting a Facebook group about the hidden evil of takeaway coffee cups. I primarily use Facebook to stay in touch with friends and family back in the States, but I know these sites also have strong activist potential. In 2008 a group of young Egyptians created headlines around the globe by using Facebook to organise the first nationwide strike in Egypt. Within one week of creating the *6 April* Facebook group, approximately one in 12 Egyptian Facebook users had joined the group; the simultaneous protests were unlike anything the country had ever seen. The group expanded to a website and continued to organise various free speech and democracy movements, ultimately influencing the 2011 Egyptian Revolution. The potential of social media activism is limitless.

So, armed with an internet connection and a burning desire to spread my message, I put my faith in social media and zealously create a Facebook group to encourage people to take up reusable mugs and give up cardboard takeaway cups. I include some of my recently learned facts, send an invite to all my Facebook friends, and wait for the number of followers to start climbing. I fancy myself a bit of a photographer, too, so I plan on adding some impactful imagery as the group grows. I expect my friends will react as I did to the news that cups are non-recyclable and help me lead a takeaway coffee revolution. And really, if groups like *Bring back Who's Line is it Anyway* can gain 15,000 fans, surely a group as well-meaning as mine can rally at least a couple thousand?

A week passes and I've yet to even crack triple digits. It's going okay, some friends have joined the group and sent the link to other friends to join, but I'm only up to 26 members. My favourite addition to the Facebook group is my friend Lillian; she quickly joined and started using a vintage thermos on her daily commute, writing on the Facebook wall:

> **I have stopped buying a million take aways, and take my thermos of tea/coffee on the train instead! The tea/coffee tastes even better from my cute thermos... =)**

I feel a glimmer of hope that perhaps Facebook *can* save the planet, but I'm holding out for some exponential growth in the group numbers before I get too carried away.

Shortly after starting the group, I head to a barbeque with friends who live in and around Bondi, excited to discover if anyone's made the switch to reusable mugs.

Most people in our group are ex-pats or new transplants to Sydney. Generally we all have an active lifestyle – there are many surfers in the group – and we love to get out and about in Sydney, exploring all the city has to offer. Many of us also work within the culture industry in advertising, design, media and fashion. Chloe works in a design agency like me. Lillian is an artist and she and Zoe work in fashion. Noel and Barry each work for popular lifestyle brands, and Emma works for a large retail group. Sam and Sarah both work in digital media. Randall works for a women's magazine. Nigel recently started film school. And though Geoff and Tyler are both engineers, they are also both obsessed with music and constantly on the lookout for the latest gigs. On the surface everyone seems happy and content and why wouldn't we? Life is fantastic.

Like many people in our relatively carefree stage of life (pre-kids, pre-mortgage, decent jobs), we lead fairly self-indulgent lifestyles – we work hard and spend our hard-earned cash on the pursuit of pleasure (i.e., lots of us love shopping and frequenting the newest bars and restaurants). We aren't unique in that; research even suggests that young professionals in the culture industry are especially attracted to this lifestyle, that we identify "with hedonism and a consumption-based ethic of enjoyment that shapes both the appeal and performance of the job,"[1]. I don't want to paint the picture that we are completely self-centred conspicuous consumers, because the group is also very caring and aware of wider social issues, but we certainly don't go without. Whether it's chasing the latest gadgets and fashions, travelling the globe, or renting the odd DJ set or snowmaking machine for a party, we're always up for a good time. (Come to think of it, my grey suede ankle boots have never been the same since that snow party.) Needless to say, I'm looking forward to today.

Five minutes after we arrive, a sense of vertigo washes over me as I see Sam casually drinking from a takeaway coffee cup. Wasn't it just a week ago he was the first person to join *Use Your Own Mug*?! He comes up to kiss me hello, but I can't hear what he is saying, I am literally shell-shocked.

"Hey, are you alright?" Sam asks with concern.

"*What are you drinking?!*"

So much for handling this environmental thing with grace.

Sam looks at his cup and sheepishly laughs, "I didn't even think about it. On my way over here I felt like a coffee so stopped at The Paris and grabbed one." He shows no remorse. "But, hey, did you see how many people I invited to join the group?"

"Um, yeah, I did. Thanks. Just try and *actually* use your own mug next time, okay?"

I stumble away. I think I was polite enough, but really I wanted to scream at him, rip the cup out of his hand and hurl it to the ground! While it would be nice to be a benevolent green goddess, I did not start the group as an experiment to achieve a large number of members, I actually want people to give up takeaway cups. I thought Sam was a keen supporter of the cause based on his quickness to join and spread the word, but it appears that something else besides a commitment to the environment motivated him. Were other group members behaving similarly? Joining but not actually following through with eco-action? This activism business may be harder than I initially thought.

Learning from the experts

A few weeks pass after my run-in with Sam and, to my dismay, most friends either do not join the group or, like Sam, join but continue to happily sip on their takeaway cups. Besides feeling disappointed by the slow (and unreliable) growth of *Use Your Own Mug*, I am confused; my friends are educated, thoughtful individuals who believe climate change is real and something should be done about it. So why the refusal to make just one lifestyle change?

I decide to talk to Geoff; he's an environmental engineer and I hope he can shed some light on the subject, or at least lend a sympathetic ear to a frustrated new greenie.

"Well Lise, as far as I'm concerned, the science is already done," he grins, with his usual cheeky optimism, "scientists for the most part know and agree on the facts of climate change and what needs to be done."

"So what's the problem, then? Why aren't things changing?"

"That's the tricky part. What I think we need to do now is understand people better in order for change to happen."

We talk for a few more minutes, and after we say goodbye I reflect on our conversation and think Geoff has a really good point. I've been doing more research since learning about takeaway cups, and despite what some contrasting or 'balanced' reports in mainstream media would have us believe, the scientific community has been in consensus for a while that global warming is occurring and that it is caused by human activity[1]. Findings from the 2007 International Panel on Climate Change (IPCC), a scientific organisation created to review existing science on climate change, concluded that no peer reviewed, published articles have refuted the theory that human activity increases global warming[2]. Even leading climate change sceptic, Bjorn Lomborg, does not disagree that climate change is occurring and is caused by human activity; he simply questions the extent of the potential damage and advises a cautious approach that will not sacrifice the economy for the sake of the environment[3]. The latest IPCC report published in 2013 maintains this commitment to human-influenced climate change, and Co-Chair of the group, Thomas Stocker, has said: "As a result of our past, present and expected future emissions of CO_2, we are committed to climate change, and effects will persist for many centuries even if emissions of CO_2 stop."[4]

Complacency regarding environmental issues is not unique amongst my group of friends, this is a common occurrence throughout much of society. Research into this apparent public complacency toward climate change cites reasons that are many and varied, including financial concerns, confusion about the science, concerns about loss of convenience and quality, expectations that better solutions can be created, and conflict with a desire for economic growth[5]. There is also research that suggests because greenhouse gases are not visible to the human eye, and the effects of global warming don't primarily occur where pollution originates, most people have a poor understanding of their personal and community greenhouse gas output.[6] In one of the worst examples of irony I know, this research also highlights the political implications of climate change, since the greatest impact is likely to be in developing countries that didn't play a role in causing the problem.

This all makes sense, but I feel there must be more to environmental inaction than these reported reasons. Otherwise, it means that "the most severe problem we are facing today, more serious than the threat of terrorism" [7] is not being addressed because of our obsessions with convenience and money, and that old adage, 'out of sight, out of mind'. Are we all really so self-centred that we can't see the problems we create every time we start our cars, take a plastic bag at the shops or get a takeaway coffee? Are we simply uninformed and confused by the mixed messages, or is something else preventing us from changing? And more puzzling to me, if the climate research is correct (and the scientific community believes that it is), why isn't more being done by governments around the world?

I suspect that the *Good Living* article I read on coffee cups and *An Inconvenient Truth* are just the tip of the iceberg for my grasp of the entire climate change picture, and I have a lot yet to learn.

❤️ 🖋 👚 👶 🔌 🔪 👤 ⏱ ☕ 💡 ♡

"Aiming for that 'girl-next-door' look, are we?" Duncan cattily asks as I slide into my desk at the studio and swap my Converse for my stilettos.

I'm wearing jeans and a singlet, though I do have a killer Camilla and Marc blazer to layer on top, and I look uncharacteristically casual today – hair pulled back into a ponytail and only a quick swipe of mascara and dab of lip balm – quite different from my usual fully coiffed and made-up self. I've also recently coloured my hair all one colour, in an attempt to go au-naturale and save the earth from the chemicals of my quarterly hair highlighting session.

The real tragedy is that this look took twice as long to perfect than my usual routine.

"Ha ha, very funny Duncan. I was feeling a bit lazy this morning. Anyway, I don't have any client meetings today."

He gives me a disapproving once-over but doesn't say anything else. He doesn't have any meetings either, but still looks like he stepped off the pages of GQ.

It's true that I have no client meetings today, but more importantly, thanks to a friend calling in a favour, I've landed a meeting with the editor of an environmental magazine so I wanted to look as 'green' as possible. I've been feeling increasingly frustrated with the lack of interest in *Use Your Own Mug,* and the editor has graciously offered me an hour out of her busy schedule to share her knowledge on the subject of people joining the environmental movement. I'm hoping she'll share some insights that will help me convert my friends to the cause, and perhaps spread the message even further.

Somehow I make it through the morning at the studio and head off to meet her on my lunch break. I decide to leave my stilettos, blazer and oversized designer handbag at the office, just bringing my wallet and a notebook. As I hop on the bus across town, the butterflies racing through my body are way bigger than the nerves I feel before a big creative pitch. I hope I'm dressed appropriately! I'm fairly new to this environmentalist gig, but I'm pretty sure prancing into the meeting in my usual fashionista-attire will not garner the respect I am seeking. Hence the 'less-is-more' approach to my look today. Will the editor take one look at me and assume I'm not up to scratch, even for a newbie greenie?

I arrive at the inner-city warehouse office and walk up two steamy flights of stairs to the magazine's headquarters where I'm guided directly to the editor's desk.

"Hi, I'm Lisa, we spoke on the phone," I introduce myself, hoping I'm hiding my nerves.

"Oh hi!" she welcomes me with a warm smile and a handshake, "I thought we could go to the café up the road for our chat, they make the most delicious peppermint tea out of fresh leaves."

If my appearance doesn't meet her expectations, she is professional enough to not let it show, and we head out. I note her perfectly clear make-up free face, freckles dancing across her nose and cheeks and beautiful, free-flowing strawberry blonde curls. I think to myself, "If it weren't for her faded t-shirt and cork sandals I'd never have pegged her as a greenie, just a naturally pretty woman." And though her style is not necessarily one I wish to emulate, it has been a hot start to the Sydney summer and I find myself envying her shorts as we re-enter the humid city streets.

"This isn't necessarily the magazine's 'on the record' opinion, but I have been involved in the environmental movement for awhile, so

I'll share with you my opinion about how different people get involved," she says when I explain that I'm trying to understand why it's so hard to make the environmental movement mainstream, including amongst my friends.

Over our fresh peppermint tea and a couple divine organic raspberry oat muffins (if this is what being an environmentalist means, count me in!), she explains to me her perspective on greenies:

"I think there are roughly three aspects of the environment that attract people to be green," she draws a circle and then cuts it into three sections, with a big dot in the very centre where the sections intersect.

"The first group are those who do it for their love of nature – these tend to be the more traditional greenies, from the original environmental movement. They're motivated by a desire to protect the wilderness; they truly love nature and want to restore and defend it. As an example, this group is likely to contain people who are vegetarians because of animal rights.

"The second group," she labels this circle 'neo-greens', "is primarily concerned about their carbon footprint. They are much less natural than the previous group, and tend to use technology as a means to help them reduce their footprint through solar panels, driving a Prius, those types of things. They may not change their lifestyle drastically, though, and are at risk of not really reducing their impact. In fact, I know someone here who drives his Prius to work everyday even though it's only a 10-15 minute walk from his house; the overall impact on the environment would be less if he didn't own a car. Vegetarians in this group are more likely to be avoiding methane emissions from livestock than concerning themselves with animal rights.

"Finally, the third group," she labels this 'toxics', "attracts a lot of new mums or people affected by disease, people primarily concerned with toxins and pollution. This is the organic produce and natural body products group, the stereotypical earth mother is likely to be in this group."

"What is that dark centre dot?"

"That represents the hard core environmentalists. They may have entered through any one of the three categories, but now they embody aspects from each category and want to protect the earth at any cost." I suspect the editor probably falls into this category, and I look to that dot with aspiration – maybe one day. For now I remain in the aptly labelled 'neo-greens' group, and probably on the outer rim of that group, too.

"Is there is anything in particular you've noticed generate interest in the environment since you've been working in the field?" I ask.

"There were two events in recent years that did have a noticeable effect on how much people were talking about the environment," she reflects, "the release of *An Inconvenient Truth* (Al! You speak to so many of us!) and the Stern Report – they were both released around the same time and there was a noticeable increase in environmental noise at the time. Unfortunately now with the global financial crisis, there is noticeably less overall interest in the environment. You can tell that the media doesn't cover it as much and people are too concerned about their financial stability right now to also worry about the environment."

We talk a bit more and she describes articles in the magazine and information on readership (the vast majority of her magazine's readers are female, university-educated and own their home, and over three-quarters are aged between 25 and 54 – women saving the world!). After an hour I reluctantly thank her for her time, pay the bill and run to the bus stop: back to the day job.

On my bus ride back to the studio (I am SO late, I wish I could take a taxi, damn new environmental ethos!) I ponder the editor's comments. I really appreciate her explanation of different ways to join the environmental movement, as well as the notion that the economy has distracted people from the cause, but I don't feel that she's completely identified the barriers to joining the movement. I feel that there's something else that relates to identity and lifestyle that no one is specifically talking about, and it's the one that I keep bumping up against.

I'm already learning that certain aspects of my lifestyle will be challenged as I endeavour to lead a sustainable existence. I've already committed to stop colouring my hair after going back to my natural shade, and today I did something out of character by not wearing make-up and dressing down because I wanted to present myself in a 'green' light. Is this behaviour really sustainable? Coffee cups are one thing, but my appearance? Can't I be green and still be myself?

To put it quite crudely, my current perception of environmentalists involves dread-locked hippies, shapeless frocks and cork sandals. I truly love that there's a group of people who are happy in that lifestyle, but it definitely doesn't coincide with the fashionable and trendy image I've been perfecting over the past decade. The all-over colour was one thing, but I just don't know that I can trust my precious locks to an all-natural shampoo. And sure, I took a bus today and I ride the train to work, but what happens on Saturday night? My designer dresses and four-inch heels simply do not *go* with the bus.

My image impacts everything – my job, my friends, my hobbies – what will happen if I change it? Who will I be? Do others fear this potential identity loss as well, assuming as I do that green equals hippy? Is this why it's so hard for environmentalism to break into the mainstream?

As the bus approaches the design studio, I sense an immanent collision with this new green world I am entering. How can I integrate the person I have been, the one who I worked so hard to become through the right career, the right clothes and the right interests, with the one who is presenting herself to me now, the one who wants to make a difference at any cost? I am caught between two worlds, one that contains everything I have been aspiring toward, and all of my friends, and one that devalues everything I know. I cannot see an easy way to reconcile the two.

Luckily for the environment, I am stubborn. I am determined to continue on my path of becoming greener, and even more determined to prove that you can do it without resorting to an all-hemp wardrobe. I'll figure out a way to be green and still be myself, and hopefully bring a few others along for the ride into environmentalism.

There is one change I must make immediately, though. I've been moving toward this for quite some time, and today is the day.

"Well, that may have been the *longest* lunch break in the history of the studio," Duncan quips as I walk up the stairs. Man is he on fire today!

"Oh Duncan, I am going to miss you."

He looks at me quizzically.

"I quit."

Becoming an environmentalist

In the weeks following my resignation, the word quickly spreads. Duncan and the agency were gobsmacked with my decision to leave; now my friends, family, and everyone else I know are, too. I face a barrage of questions everywhere I go.

"Are you going to another agency?"

"Has Duncan finally pushed you over the edge?"

"Are you moving back to America?"

"Are you pregnant?"

"Can you afford to quit?"

"Are you going travelling?"

"What are you going to do now?"

That last one is the hardest to answer.

I tell most people that my heart just isn't in it anymore and that I want to use my skills for good rather than evil, and then I change the subject as quickly as possible. Most days I can't believe I actually got up the courage to quit! I avoid talking about it much, partly because I don't want to appear judgmental of my colleagues or my clients. But truthfully, I also have no idea what I'm going to do with myself. I definitely believe saving the environment is a noble cause, but last time I checked Mother Earth wasn't putting anyone on her payroll.

At least now that I've officially wrapped up at the agency I have a lot more time to focus on greening my life.

I've quickly discovered there's no shortage of books, websites and articles providing tips on how to do this. Everywhere I turn I find eco-guidebooks and articles titled *10 easy steps to green your life/groceries/holiday/etc*. The hardest part may actually be deciding where to begin. I've made a decent start, though. Even before I got serious about the environment I'd already discovered some easy changes: carrying a stainless steel water bottle and taking my own bags to the grocery store. We even switched to compact fluorescent light globes in our apartment; luckily they now come in warm white, which is much more flattering than the greenish-hue I remember from my high school bathrooms. Now that I've also started using my own mug and stopped colouring my hair I'm really on a roll.

I particularly love that going green is saving me money. The eco-globes used to be a bit pricier than traditional bulbs, but not anymore. And because they use less energy and last longer than traditional lights, I am saving money in the long run. Some estimates predict $100 of savings per globe over course of its life.[1] And who needs to spend $2 on a bottle of water when Australia's tap water is healthy, clean, delicious and *free*?

Plastic water bottles are a larger environmental menace than I had realised. Currently Australia recycles only 36% of PET plastic drink bottles used (America's rate is around 30%), which means over 373 million end up in the landfill each year[2]; even if the bottles are recycled, the energy required to produce, fill and transport them means that the embodied energy of one bottle of water can equate to filling the bottle a quarter of the way with oil. Yuck. On the other hand, reusable stainless steel water bottles definitely save you money in the long run, and are better for the environment if used long enough. *The New York Times* reported that after only 50 uses the climate is better off, and after 500 uses all aspects of the environment are better off (taking into account extraction of resources from the earth, manufacturing of the bottles, distribution and disposal[3]). I also have a large plastic refillable bottle, which I prefer to take hiking because it's lighter and fits more water, and I made sure it was 'BPA-free' before making my purchase. Bisphenol A (BPA) is a known hormone disrupter, and research has shown that it can leach out of plastic food containers[4]. The majority of food containers are BPA-free these days, but I definitely made sure it was noted on the bottle I purchased.

I also used to spend about $200 on hair colour every three months, so I'm saving plenty of cash in my decision to go au naturale. The transition has been okay. Thankfully my natural colour is a rich dark brown, though I admit I miss do miss having that perfect shade. I am learning to live without highlights (and lowlights, and glosses …).

And another milestone: I recently made my very first eco-clothing purchase.

I am technically on a shopping hiatus until my income returns, but I still like to hit the shops, just to keep my eye on the trends. I was making the rounds at Myer and while meandering through the unmentionables I saw a range of bamboo-based underwear. My curiosity was piqued. I had this image of scratchy, hessian sack-like frocks from 'natural' clothing stores seared into my mind; I never even considered the possibility of eco-shopping for clothing.

According to the tag, bamboo is the latest eco wonder-fabric: it grows rapidly, uses less water than cotton, doesn't require fertiliser and is less soil-damaging to harvest. I rubbed the incredibly smooth fabric between my fingers; it felt like a cross between silk and cotton. I had to have a pair! What better way to create a sexy eco-friendly image than bamboo knickers? Okay, they weren't exactly fashion forward, just a basic low-rise in off-white or black, but I was willing to forego frilly for the sake of my first environmentally friendly clothing purchase.

Since then I've been telling anyone who will listen about my latest green purchase. My conversations are all "bamboo this" and "bamboo that"; they're probably just happy not to be hearing about coffee cups anymore. I think I'm starting to get the hang of this environmentalist business.

⌣⌀🎎🐉⌂🏺♀🌕🐚💡♡

It's a scorcher today, and there's no other place to be than North Bondi for swimming, snorkelling, sunbaking and surfing. I'm looking forward to catching up with the Bondi crew. I'm also hoping for assurance that some of my friends have adopted eco-changes, because at this point it is clear that the *Use Your Own Mug* Facebook group is an official flop.

"Hey Lise, how's things?" Noel asks excitedly as he gets out of the water, "still trying to save the world?"

"Trying; it's not easy, mate," I laugh – Noel's Kiwi charm is always infectious. "Truthfully, I'm feeling a bit frustrated that more action's not taking place since we know all the facts."

"Yeah, no kidding. Did you hear about the island where everyone had to be relocated because of rising sea levels?"

"Yeah, I heard about that!" chimes in Nigel, "and I read somewhere that the number of cyclones has doubled in the past 30 years."

"Well, what do you guys think is the problem? Why are people so hesitant to act?" I ask, curious on their take on the matter; the so-called environmental experts haven't been able to crack it so I figure I'll go right to the source and gather general public opinion.

"Well I think, what's the point of my taking public transportation if the government won't take steps to improve the environment?" says Noel.

"Yeah, at least in the US Obama budgeted $500 million to support green jobs, that's not happening here," Geoff adds as he enters the discussion.

"I guess my opinion is that we as individuals need to demonstrate in our personal lives the environment is something we care about if we expect the government to make any changes," I suggest – putting my money on democracy and grassroots activism – "you know, 'Be the change you want to see in the world'?"

I'm met with blank stares. Timidly, I carry on, "Well, for instance, what do you guys do for the environment?"

At this point the conversation takes on a life of its own, with everyone chiming in:

"Yeah, I know I should be doing more."

"I'm sure someone will sort it out, I'm not really concerned."

"Australia's not the problem, we really need to worry about China and India, they're the big polluters."

"How can we even think about it with the GFC right now?"

"You know what the real problem is? Overpopulation, that's what we really need to be worried about."

"And what about food shortages? I saw this really moving documentary on the ABC about all these people who aren't even guaranteed one meal a day."

"I really admire how passionate you are about the environment, Lise, I wish I could be that passionate about something."

Each of them has a point – we should be concerned about overpopulation as well as poverty (from both the environmental and human rights perspectives), and I totally understand that the GFC is on everyone's minds. But it feels like these comments are avoidance techniques more than anything, enabling everyone to get out of telling me specifically what they do (or don't do) for the environment. That last comment was especially creative – praising me without giving away any personal information– nicely done. But why is everyone acting so strangely?

We dry ourselves off and mosey up to the Bondi House, and I'm happy to see Zoe when we arrive. I absolutely love Zoe; she works in fashion, has impeccable taste, a wardrobe to die for, and also happens to be very generous and very funny – I'd probably hate her if I didn't love her. She looks particularly glam for a hot Saturday afternoon, with immaculately applied makeup, a flawless bob cut and a *to-die-for* black silk Marc Jacobs blouse.

"Guess who I met today?" she asks casually, green eyes sparkling.

Knowing Zoe's job it could've been any number of fashion models or designers, "I don't know, who?"

"Patricia Field!" she squeals.

"*The* Patricia Field? You wouldn't tease a girl, would you?" It's a well-known fact I'm a tragic *Sex and the City* fan – I am thrilled for Zoe. And also incredibly envious.

"Yep, the one and only," Zoe takes out her phone and shows me a happy snap she took of herself with the flame-haired style maven. "We're running a *Sex and the City* promotion at work and we flew her in to drum up some excitement for us."

"Mission accomplished!"

After showing me a few more photos Zoe asks, "What have you been up to, anyway? I haven't seen you in ages."

"I wrapped up at work a couple weeks ago, and I'm still trying to stop people using takeaway cups."

"Oh yeah, I saw the Facebook thing. I don't really drink coffee, but that's such a great idea. I know Lillian is loving using her vintage thermos."

"I'm a bit disappointed in the low numbers," I confess, "I thought that I'd have more people joining the group, but I just can't seem to drum up a lot of interest. It's making me start to think people are not really that interested in the environment and I'm trying to figure out why." Zoe looks thoughtful as I confide my feelings of being a Facebook-failure. I take the opportunity to ask her, "Well, for example, what do you for the environment? Or, what do you find hard about doing environmental things?"

I assume she probably doesn't do much for the environment; I've never heard her talk about it, and she looks even less like a greenie than I do, so I am quite keen to hear what she has to say.

"Oh, you know, things like shower timers, recycling, taking the bus to work, putting on a jumper instead of turning on the heater, waiting for the dishwasher to be full, reusing containers, using cloth grocery bags. . ."

She sounds like one of those *Ten easy steps to green your life* lists with which I'm becoming so familiar. Does she really do all of those things? I know she takes the bus to work, but I don't recall seeing a timer in her shower. And maybe she puts on a jumper at home when she's cold, but I can't picture her covering up that black silk Marc Jacobs blouse to tote her own containers to the takeaway shop for dinner. I realise I am making a whole host of assumptions and am being very judgmental; she could very well be doing all of those things and just not making a big deal about it. Besides, it's not like my lifestyle is really much greener yet... but why is she acting so strange? She's avoiding eye contact with me and her tone is almost defensive. Is she being dishonest, or does talking about the environment just make her uncomfortable?

On the bus ride home I reflect on the day's eco-conversations. My friends are clearly well informed on the topic of climate change and other important social issues, and it was interesting to hear their thoughts on why more is not being done for the environment. But more interesting was the behaviour I witnessed – defensive, standoffish, embarrassed and exuding a false environmentalist persona – it was fascinating. These are my friends, whom I thought I knew as well as family, and they don't appear to be honestly sharing their habits or beliefs. I asked the questions with the belief that most aren't terribly green in their behaviour aside from recycling and use of public transportation to commute to and from work, but I never expected misleading information about their environmental actions or such awkward tension around the topic. I hope I'm able to work through this and understand where their hold-ups are in the environmental movement so that we can all start to lead greener lives; right now I'm feeling a little confused.

⌐⌐⌐⌐⌐⌐⌐⌐⌐⌐⌐⌐

"Hey Randall, how's it going?" I ask as I kiss him hello; Ty and I have met up with Randall and his wife Anika for dinner at a fabulous little bistro on Crown Street.

"Kisses!" he exclaims in his humorous mocking tone, "I'm great, wonderful, blah, blah. How are you?"

"Oh, you know, 'finding myself,' trying to save the planet, the usual," I reply. Randall's heard all about my crusade against disposable cups, he thought *Use Your Own Mug* was a great idea. He's a fellow American living in Sydney and remembers (as I do) seeing reusable mugs a lot more back home. After our initial chat he went out and bought one immediately, looking forward to drinking his coffee as he strolled through Hyde Park on his way to work. I'm eager to hear how he's finding it – after the confusion with the rest of the gang I could use a green good news story.

"How are you liking using your own mug?" I ask.

"I'm not using it," he admits, casting his eyes down at the table.

"What?!" I'm devastated!

Anika adds, "It's been sitting untouched in the kitchen cabinet for weeks."

"Well I was into it, right? Then I told my co-workers about the group, and they told me how daggy it would be for me to come to work with a reusable mug, and that if I dared take it downstairs to the building's café I would be laughed at."

"You're kidding?" I ask, reeling.

"No. Anyway, I'm starting to think it's too much of a hassle – you know, one more thing to organise in the morning."

I am beyond disappointed. Randall is a writer and editor at a popular Australian women's magazine, and as far as I'm concerned he's letting some shallow, short-sighted magazine writers influence

28

his dedication to the environment. Look, I'm sure they're nice people, but really, *laugh* at someone for using their own mug? Even the pre-greenie Lisa wouldn't be that shallow.

"Maybe you can start a new trend and make it cool. You are from New York. Can't you play that up a bit?" I plead, desperately wanting him to change his mind.

"Yeah, I'm not so sure that would work – sorry."

I want him on board with the cause, of course, but I was also hoping for his influence. Little would make me happier than knowing that people within that kind of image factory are carrying reusable mugs. Plenty of the magazines produced in his office claim it is 'cool to care' in their headlines, but from what I'm hearing tonight it's not cool to do anything personally if it has a negative impact on your own glamorous image.

I suppose I shouldn't be surprised, though. This is the same bunch who informed Randall they could spot the 'older' people in the office because they wear their sunglasses on their heads.

Randall's story is excellent motivation for me to work out how to live green and still be myself. I seriously doubt carrying around a reusable coffee mug will irreparably tarnish my image. It's not like I'm throwing out all my makeup and the entire contents of my wardrobe; I'm just going to be better prepared when I go to the coffee shop. And like the headlines say – it *is* cool to care, and I'm going to try my hardest to be a living example.

I just hope more people join me soon; between Randall's confession, the puzzling behaviour of the Bondi crew and the low take-up of *Use Your Own Mug*, I'm beginning to think this environmental activism business is impossible.

Eco-shopping excursion

Today I'm trying my hand at intentional eco-shopping. My yoga pants have become increasingly threadbare, and I fear I'm one downward dog away from disaster, so I'm dipping into my dwindling bank account to purchase new pants. Riding high on the success of finding bamboo undies I'm hopeful I'll find something eco-friendly in time for a one o'clock hatha class.

I'm only allowing myself one item today (believe it or not I'm a budget-conscious shopaholic), but I'm still totally excited about putting my shopping skills back into action.

Shopping and I go way back. I think the first sign that our relationship was serious was when I was three years old; my poor mother had to take me to every shoe store in three shopping centres before we found a pair I was happy to wear on my chubby toddler feet (red patent leather Mary Janes – I was making fashion statements even back then). Over the years we've been through thick and thin; shopping has kept me company on long lunch breaks and moving to a new country, consoled me after break-ups and provided countless après-work therapy sessions. Throughout our relationship I've amassed an impressive collection of shoes and clothing, and farewelled a bit of cash, but I wouldn't change one moment of it…not even those eight inch comic strip platform shoes that caused me to tumble across the university pavement one wet winter's day circa 1998.

I've also long prided myself on having the perfect outfit for any occasion.

Have a serious pitch at work? Put on a perfectly tailored suit, colourful blouse, statement necklace and serious stilettos.

Lunch with the ladies? Think Carrie Bradshaw for a thrown together, mismatched-but-harmonious skirt, top, heels and killer accessories.

Day at the art gallery? Channel Coco Chanel with timeless lines, black and white details, and a bold red lip.

Night at the Opera House? (I love Sydney!) Accept nothing less than perfect shoes, immaculate hair and a glamorous dress.

I could go on. Give me any situation and I'll figure out the perfect thing to wear, certain to turn heads and start conversations. I never tire of recreating myself, and despise wearing the same ensemble twice – it's inexcusable, really, what with all the options and accessorizing possibilities.

My favourite compliment? "You *have* to take me shopping!" Of course, what most of these compliment-givers don't realise is that one shopping excursion does not a perfect wardrobe make. Weekends and lunch breaks must be dedicated to the art of shopping. Holidays have to allow sufficient time to peruse the local shops. Market schedules must be memorised. And one must always keep her eyes open for that certain *something* that will complete an outfit that has been sitting in her closet for months. A true shopper is open to chance encounters every minute of every day, and the best finds are usually unplanned. I won't even attempt to calculate the hours I have committed to my favourite pastime because it goes beyond hours, beyond dollars, beyond consciousness – it's who I am.

I am so excited to go shopping today!

In spite of my excitement, I definitely want to make today's purchase as eco-friendly as possible. As I wander to Rebel Sport, home of all your sporting needs, I think about a recent greenie article that suggests asking the following questions before making any clothing purchase:

1. Do you need it or just want it?
2. Can you get it secondhand?
3. Is it made of natural fibres?
4. Did it travel far to get to you?
5. Is it sweatshop free?

1 and 2 are easy to answer – I don't want to flash my derriere to people in class, and I have a strict "No secondhand exercise gear" policy. So today I just need to scrutinise the tags for fabric, country of manufacture and Fairtrade/sweatshop-free labels. Should be simple enough.

I selected Rebel as my first port-of-call because it should have the greatest variety, but as I cross the threshold into the pumping, thriving organism of the store I fear I have played it all wrong. Pop-music booms like I'm in a giant aerobics class, then I'm hit with an artificial waft of neoprene and new running shoes, and nothing at all says 'eco-friendly'. I'm here now, though, so I start sifting through the sea of women's exercise gear.

Before I know it the smell of new clothes and the sound of hangers scratching along the rack lull me into a sense of calm familiarity – it's great to be on the hunt again!

There is so much to consider. First of all I need the right length - no ¾ length pant leg for me; why wear something that makes you look shorter and squatter than you really are? Next is texture – I prefer cotton for yoga since comfort is so important during meditation. Besides, as hot as those shiny nylon leggings are right now, I have terrible childhood memories of dance class and very shiny, very itchy, electric blue leggings. I rub all the pants between my fingers to assess the texture as I narrow down my selection. Of course I don't want anything too heavy; yoga demands a lightweight fabric. When it comes to colour I stick with basic black and dark charcoal – they are the most slimming and go with anything. Finally I consider the price. After about 15 minutes I find six pair that meet my criteria and make my way toward the change room.

Oh look! They have yoga blocks and straps! I should buy some so I can practice more yoga at home. But these are blue and my mat is purple, so they wouldn't really match. They have a blue mat, too! I can get the whole matching set!

Lisa! Stay focused. You don't NEED a block and a strap, and you definitely don't need a new yoga mat. How many times have you pulled your mat out at home, maybe four times in the past year? Get in there and try on these yoga pants!

The lighting is terrible (definitely not 'warm white' fluorescents, that's for sure) and the rooms are tiny, so I'm in and out of the fitting room with each pair to stand in front of the full-length mirror and evaluate how my bum looks. After about fifteen minutes I narrow down to two choices and do a final price comparison before heading to the cashier.

I'm forgetting something. . . colour, texture, length, price . . . of course! What is the eco-cred of these pants? I've been so distracted by the store and overwhelmed by choice that I totally forgot about my new eco-ethos.

I look at the tags and see that one pair is 95% cotton, 5% polyester – a high content of natural fibres, that's good. That pair was quite comfy and moveable, with just a hint of stretch to make my butt look fabulous. The other pair is a combination of cotton, polyester, Lycra and something called Coolmax®; come to think of it, I did feel some technology in those pants. But what is Coolmax®? It doesn't exactly scream 'natural' does it? I suppose the pair that's made of 95% cotton is the lesser of two evils.

Now to determine how far these pants have travelled to get to me. I first heard the 'country of origin' concept in terms of food miles – how far certain groceries had travelled from the farm to my plate. Greenhouse gases are emitted when shipping goods from one country to the other, so ideally I want to find an Australian-made product with low 'garment miles'. I have no such luck; one pair was made in China and the other in Indonesia. I suppose Indonesia is closer than China, but I don't think it's significant enough to sway me one way or the other, especially since I have no idea if they came by boat or plane, or where the fabric itself originated from.

Since neither tag has a Fairtrade symbol, the country of origin may also give me some insight into whether the product is sweatshop free, even though I know this method oversimplifies a very complex issue.

The devastating truth is that frequently our clothes are produced in places with cheap labour and little regulation on working conditions. Factory workers in these countries can be subjected to long hours and unsafe work environments; books like *To Die For*[1] and *Overdressed*[2] have highlighted a number of these issues. Then there were those horrific garment factory fires and the building collapse in Bangladesh in 2013, which has brought current inhumane standards into the limelight. I'm terrified of making a purchase that enables these atrocities, but it is so confusing to know what to do.

I do know that certain countries have worse track records than others in terms of worker rights, and generally speaking Australia and America have good standards (though even these countries are not exempt). Yet I don't want to encourage taking all manufacturing away from developing countries. Many individuals in these countries work in the garment trade to pull themselves out of poverty, and that is something I am more than happy to support – as long as they are treated well and paid a fair wage.

It's all getting so complicated! Definitely not in line with the *5 easy eco-shopping tips* article that inspired me to head out today.

Why am I even complicating things with sweatshop issues when I haven't yet mastered eco-shopping? I guess it's because everything I read about eco-shopping becomes a discussion on ethical shopping, and vice versa. I agree, there's no point in saving the environment if half the people on the planet are suffering as a result of my lifestyle. And for me, sustainability is about that magic combination of ecological and social responsibility.

One thing is for certain: it's not straightforward to know what I can buy with a clear conscience here at Rebel Sport. Since there is no Fairtrade certification mark on either garment I have to research the brands' social corporate responsibility policy, including whether they have worker-rights standards in place and publicly available performance reports. If either pair of pants in my hands were Nike

I'd feel reasonably comfortable making the purchase. The company faced major fallout years ago with the discovery that its shoes were predominantly produced in sweatshops. As a result of this debacle Nike now has strict standards for worker conditions – they are under constant scrutiny by consumer watchdogs to make sure they stay on the straight and narrow and have a publicly available policy that demonstrates how they are tracking. Nike was the first company to join the Apparel Industry Partnership, now called the Fair Labor Association, and is continually at the forefront of sustainability innovations[3]. How much more ethical would the world be if every company was required to do this?

I realise that in my excitement to go shopping this morning I totally missed the research step before I left the house. I don't know either brand's stance on social or environmental sustainability. Do they have solar panels or use other renewable energy sources? Do they recycle? Are the fabric dyes eco-friendly? Do they have a water conservation plan? There are a myriad of questions I simply can't answer, and the weight of these yoga pants just tripled in my arms as I start thinking about all the unknowns. I put them back on the rack, unconvinced either pair will satisfy the environmental goals for today. It's the first time I'm actively pursuing a green purchase and I don't want to make a mistake.

I leave the pulsating store, emerge into the relative silence of George Street and head toward yoga-wear heaven – Lululemon.

I'm quietly optimistic that Lululemon will be eco-friendly. I can recall seeing messages in their window about being kind to the planet by using stainless steel water bottles, and so many of the photos in the store show people doing yoga on a beach or in a forest. Besides, it's a Canadian company, and aren't all Canadians mountain climbing nature lovers? (Says the American with a friendly wink.)

Entering Lululemon is like stepping into a spa after the mayhem of Rebel Sport. Soothing jazz music and cinnamon-scented essential oils float around me as I drift among the racks of colourful yoga pants, tops, jackets and other goodies. I feel enveloped by the calming positivity that emanates from posters around the store, and happily sip on my complementary herbal tea as a North American

shop assistant warmly greets me then disappears. No pushy
salespeople here, just signs about goal setting, positive thinking, free
yoga classes and nutrition; I never want to leave.

My experience at Rebel has taught me not to try anything on
unless I'm happy with the fabric and country of origin. As I browse,
every pair of pants I examine includes luon®, fabric that *"wicks
moisture from your body and stretches in four ways"* (whatever that is
supposed to mean). I track down the friendly sales assistant to ask
what exactly luon® is and am advised:

"Luon is our signature fabric. It's very breathable, and feels like
cotton, but also has four-way stretch to provide support and allow
freedom of movement."

"Oh, um, great, but do you know what it is made of? Lycra?
Polyester? Something else?" I query further. Surely something that
allows 'four-way stretch' is synthetic.

"It's our trademarked fabric we created, but I don't know *exactly*
what it's made of."

I ask if there are any organic cotton pants and am directed to
some Wunder Under pants; I investigate the label and see they
consist of 89% organic cotton and 11% Lycra/spandex, and I am
thrilled at how incredibly soft they feel. The pants cost over $100,
though, so I leave them on the rack for now and linger just a bit
longer – it's such a gorgeous store. Lululemon has struck a beautiful
balance of active wear that is great for athletes and also looks really
fantastic outside of the gym; I want to buy one of everything. I
better go.

I didn't realise eco-friendly shopping would be so complicated; I
don't think I'll be making that one o'clock yoga class after all, I need
to head home and do more research. Before I cross into Hyde Park I
stop at a café to get a pick-me-up latte in my adorable green
reusable mug.

"Soy latte to takeaway, and can you please put it in here?" I ask
with a smile as I hand over my mug.

The barista looks a little confused, but she takes my money and my mug, and I wait with the other patrons for my coffee order to come up.

"Soy latte for Lisa!" calls the barista minutes later, and I look up and see – horror of horrors – she's pouring the coffee from a cardboard takeaway cup into my reusable mug and *throwing the cardboard cup into the bin!* I'm too shocked to say anything, and she looks extremely proud of herself as she drizzles the frothed soymilk into the top of my mug. I wonder how often this happens and I just don't see it? Didn't she realise that I was trying to avoid the waste of a cardboard cup?

I trudge through the park in a deep emotional fog. All I wanted to do was buy yoga pants that didn't harm the earth, but I've now spent a couple of hours and suffered a lot of frustration, and am coming home empty handed. Plus I've just added a cardboard coffee cup to the landfill – some environmentalist I'm turning out to be. I desperately want to do the right thing, but I'm so confused. Do I buy the pants that are mostly cotton but potentially sweatshop-made? Or do I buy pants with luon because Lululemon seems to have a positive corporate ethos? I used to get such a rush from shopping, but this all seems too hard and is definitely taking the fun out of my favourite pastime.

Then I feel the sun on my face and see a few buds of bright flowers sprouting out of the earth – this is what it's all about, isn't it? Protecting the beauty of nature? I shake off my blues and remind myself that it's only my first eco-shopping trip, and really, what else do I have to do today? It will pay to take my time and do more thorough research before I make a purchase.

At home I open my Mac with her familiar chime and decide to first understand eco-friendly fabrics a bit better. After reading many, many websites, blogs and online debates, I'm extremely disappointed to learn that bamboo is not the next eco wonder-fabric after all. It's true that bamboo is quickly renewable and requires no pesticides, but many countries have limited regulations around growing and harvesting bamboo, so it's hard to know for certain the eco-standards of the growing process. More damaging is the fact that in its natural state bamboo is a hard fibre, as opposed to cotton, which grows in fluffy little balls. To make bamboo pliable enough that it can be spun and used in fabric, it must be subjected to harsh chemical treatments, typically through a viscose process. This process includes dissolving the bamboo in a strong solvent and then pushing it into another chemical to turn it into fibre; the recovery rate of these solutions is roughly 50%, meaning the rest of the toxic chemicals are released into the environment. The US Federal Trade Commission has even gone so far to say that once bamboo is turned into fabric it is actually rayon, a synthetic material that pollutes the environment during production, and it warns shoppers to be wary of the eco-claims of bamboo fabrics[4].

As I read this I remember a phone call with my sister-in-law soon after I purchased my bamboo undies. She mentioned that she thought a lot of chemicals had to be used on bamboo, but I ignored her. I mean, who was the budding environmentalist in the family? The tag said they were better for the environment, why would it lie? Actually, the more relevant question is why did I, someone who previously wrote words on packaging using online thesauruses, dictionaries and word games, think that whatever was printed on the tag was gospel? I feel ridiculous.

On the other hand, organic cotton has a number of valid environmental benefits. Traditional cotton production uses 16% of the world's pesticides, more than any other single crop. Growing organic cotton without pesticides protects surface and groundwater quality and reduces the energy requirements and emissions from creating and transporting the pesticides. Organic farming also conserves biodiversity and reduces soil erosion when compared to non-organic cotton[5]. It also eliminates the concern regarding residual chemicals in traditional cotton that irritate some people's skin. Some sources claim it requires more water to grow than traditional cotton, but the general greenie-consensus is organic cotton is best.

So much for placing my hope in bamboo – thanks to my lingerie impulse-purchase I've experienced my first attack of greenwashing.

Green-wash (green'wash', -wôsh') – verb:

the act of misleading consumers regarding the environmental practices of a company or the environmental benefits of a product or service.[6]

In other words, exactly what I was asked to do at the design agency before I quit my job.

To be fair, it was a minor infraction. I don't think it was deliberate – or was it? Was the brand that made my bamboo undies capitalising on us new and aspiring greenies? Or had they intended to do the right thing but didn't do their homework? There is an overwhelming amount of conflicting information out there on bamboo; I can almost understand how a well-meaning fashion label could get confused. But don't they have people to research this sort of thing? Don't they have legal teams and fabric technicians? Whatever happened I feel horrible. Those undies used to be my eco-pride and joy, and now they make me feel shameful – not a *Playboy*, adults-only shop kind of shame, but shame nonetheless. It's now even more important that I find a great pair of eco-yoga pants to make up for this faux pas.

As I carry on I learn that the real environmental troublemakers are synthetic fabrics. I had no idea that polyester is made from petroleum. That's right, the same stuff that runs our cars and periodically stains our oceans is in our clothes. Lycra/spandex is also made from a by-product of petroleum; as I saw today, good luck finding exercise wear without it.

And despite some picky fashionistas (this one included) rejecting polyester, according to figures from the Technical Textile Markets, demand for man-made fibres, especially polyester, has nearly doubled in the last 15 years[7]. We can blame the cult of 'fast fashion' for the rise in its production. Fast fashion includes those $10 tops and skirts that you wear once or twice, and the slightly pricier, but still cheap, pieces from the likes of Zara, Mango and Top Shop. These are labels that pride themselves on always having the latest trends in shop and turning over their stock quicker than the competition – Zara's lead time can be as little as 13 days from design to store. They are also very reliant on polyester and other synthetic fabrics.

In addition to the use of petroleum in the fabric, the manufacturing of polyester and other synthetic fabrics is also very energy-intensive and polluting. The production process releases volatile organic compounds, particulate matter, and acid gases such as hydrogen chloride into the atmosphere, while nasty stuff like volatile monomers and solvents are released in the wastewater of manufacturing plants. I won't pretend to know exactly what all of those chemicals are, but the Environmental Protection Agency (EPA) in the US considers most synthetic textile-manufacturing facilities to be hazardous waste generators.

I'm beginning to see a very ugly vision of my beautiful world of fashion.

I move onto researching the brands I saw today for corporate social responsibility or environmental policies. Neither brand I tried on at Rebel has any relevant information on their websites, so I won't buy either pair. Lululemon, on the other hand, is fairly impressive. The organisation has a strong community focus, as well as a decent amount of charitable giving and a continually improving sustainability policy[8], not to mention all the positive energy that radiates from every page on the website about achieving your goals. Whether it's a marketing ploy or a genuine corporate culture, I'm feeling very inspired to become a Lululemonite, purchase one of everything, and float through life on a cloud of positivity.

Reality check! I'm not working right now; I don't think I should spend over $100 on yoga pants. I guess I'll keep looking for pants to satisfy the magical trifecta of environment, style and price.

My friend Sarah told me ages ago that American Apparel was sweatshop free, so I decide to check the website to see if it is also eco-friendly. I am pleased to find out it's definitely sweatshop free and there are some great environmental sustainability measures in place as well. Finally I feel like I'm getting somewhere!

Production (including knitting, dying and sewing), distribution, sales and marketing are all are done from American Apparel's downtown LA offices; this helps keep low garment miles (except for the part of shipping the finished product across the globe, that is). The label also produces a range of organic cotton products, and has a habit of reusing scraps to make underwear, bikinis, belts and hair accessories – now that's what I call clever material re-use. Other sustainability credentials include solar panels on factory roofs, subsidised bus tickets and bicycle rental for employees – about 150 bikes are rented out at any one time. The factories don't have any green building certification, but they are starting to take steps in the green direction.

In addition to its sweatshop-free status American Apparel also employs a large number of immigrant workers, providing them with valid work permits in a city plagued with immigration issues. American Apparel even launched its Legalize LA campaign to support US Immigration reform[9]. In my opinion American Apparel provides a vivid example of how sustainability can help an organisation's financial bottom line as well as society and the environment – the elusive triple bottom line frequently discussed but infrequently implemented in organisations around the globe.

I shut down my computer and walk the three blocks from my apartment to American Apparel. The shop doesn't feel 'green' per se, and is not as overtly soothing as Lululemon, but its cool urban atmosphere is welcoming and I find a pair of yoga pants and an organic non-bleached cotton singlet (an impulse purchase – old habits die hard!) in no time. The yoga pants are 95% cotton/5% spandex, so a very high percentage of natural fabrics for athletic wear; they are also only $50. I do wish the pants were organic cotton, but they are the best I can do right now, and I feel really good about my choice considering the sustainability and social policies of the company.

Most importantly, I have been a conscious consumer for the first time in my life and feel incredibly empowered – even if it took me all day to purchase two items, I am confident that I really know where they come from, what they're made of, and that I've supported an ethical organisation.

I have also learned the importance of doing my homework before shopping. Once inside retail spaces it's easy to buy without reflection because the music, scents, visuals and customer service are all working together to make us forget about anything except buying goods from that store. I should know, I used to help plan the situations; I can't believe even I'm not immune to the tricks of the trade. Next time I venture out to buy something I'll remember to research first, shop second.

❤✐👗👔💄🎵💍👠💡♡

My quest for eco-yoga pants and being greenwashed by my bamboo underpants inspired me to continue researching the environmental statistics of fashion, and I've quickly learned that there is so much more to consider as a clothing purchaser than I had ever imagined – definitely more than just this season's trends and colours.

A study by the Australian Conservation Foundation (ACF), *Consuming Australia*, reports that on average, every dollar of consumption in Australia generates 720 grams of greenhouse gas emissions and uses 28 litres of water. Similarly, according to UK government statistics, the British clothing and textiles sector produces around 3.1 million tonnes of carbon dioxide, 2 million tonnes of waste and 70 million tonnes of wastewater per year. The ACF report concludes with a very straightforward, if painful, recommendation:

> "People can make a difference to their individual contribution to greenhouse pollution by buying less, wasting less and choosing products that last." [10]

Buying less. *Gulp.* Choosing products that last? How am I supposed to know that? And I also whipped out my calculator: according to these statistics, my yoga pants and singlet cost me $75 and the earth 54 kilograms of greenhouse gas emissions and 2100 litres of water! And those little bamboo undies cost 11 kilograms of greenhouse gas emissions and 420 litres of water, not to mention who-knows-how-many toxic chemicals. They are so small to be causing so much damage! I certainly won't be throwing them out anytime soon.

And I better not; the waste generated in the name of fashion is overwhelming:

- Americans throw away more than 31 kilograms (68 pounds) of clothing and textiles per person per year[11]
- The Brits are a little better at 22 kilograms (48 pounds) per person per year[12]
- The average person in Japan buys ten kilograms and throws away nine kilograms of clothing a year[13]
- In Australia we spend just under $2 billion each year on clothes we never use[14] (For those doing the maths it's about $100 per person per year in unused clothing).

And if you excuse your shopping habit because you're helping those less fortunate when you drop a bundle off at the Salvos or Vinnies a couple times a year, think again. Statistics from the US report that only one-fifth of the clothing donated to charities is directly used or sold in thrift shops – there are simply not enough people to inherit the piles of unwanted items. About 45% of these clothes are shipped overseas and sold at markets in developing countries (ironically sometimes back to the same country in which the garment was originally manufactured)[15]. According to the International Trade Commission, between 1989 and 2003 American exports of used clothing more than tripled to over 3 billion kilograms (7 billion pounds) per year.

All of this has been extremely hard to swallow for this self-confessed shopaholic. At the risk of appearing quite daft, I really hadn't made the connection that all the clothes (and shoes, and accessories) I bought had such an impact on the environment. I mean, I totally understood why I should recycle, take public transportation and use compact fluorescent light bulbs, but no one ever mentioned anything about my clothes. It seems to me that the amount of stuff we all buy could be the elephant in the climate change room, and I'm beginning to see the significant eco-footprint left by my shopping habits as I reach a nausea-inducing realisation:

My lifestyle isn't sustainable. The earth literally cannot sustain a lifestyle like mine.

Whoa.

All those years spent trying to achieve the perfect look (or looks, as it were), I've been sending mega tonnes of carbon into the atmosphere. Forget about driving or recycling for a moment, my fashion-driven existence has done nothing except use dirty coal-powered factories, send waste into the landfill, and consume the earth's resources all so I could enjoy feeling like the prettiest girl in the room. If I thought I felt guilty for misleading people into buying something they didn't really need, this guilt trumps that 10 fold. It's more personal. I can't blame anyone but myself for all those dresses, jeans, shoes and handbags. I can try and blame the advertisers, but at the end of the day I was one of them – I'm truly a product of my own making. It's disgusting.

I'm also coming face to face with an even scarier question: who will I become now? I've already given up my job (and my perfectly styled hair), who is left if I give up shopping? For years I've used fashion to give myself confidence and create the image of a perfect, fashionable woman; I can't exactly do that if I'm not constantly updating my style. As I slowly peel away these layers of trendsetting and image I'm not really sure who I'll find underneath, or if I'll like her. To say it's scary may be the understatement of the century.

Maybe it's not so easy being green and staying yourself after all. Maybe that's why so many greenies look like stereotypical hippies – they know what I've just learned about all this stuff we humans collect. As I continue down this eco-path it seems that more aspects of my life will have to change than I initially thought. My friends don't seem to be on the same page as I am, and it's clear that I need to learn to live with less – less clothes, less shoes, less convenience. The early changes I made seemed easy enough, but I'm beginning to see the big picture of the climate change problem, it's worse than I thought, and it just got personal.

(In)Activism

Between leaving the familiarity of my advertising career and coming face to face with the dilemma of "Who am I without shopping?" I'm not really up for any additional identity-impacting eco-changes at the moment. I've decided to focus my energy on something less confrontational – greening my food choices – while I look forward to a much-needed weekend away with my friends. I imagine green-eating will be a harmless activity. And really, my eco-training can't get any more painful than it's been already! At the very least there won't be any of those pesky image issues to deal with. Actually, thanks to Hollywood, eating organically is quite fashionable; I can just picture my skin taking on an ethereal glow, on par with Natalie Portman and Julia Roberts…

More importantly, I can make a huge eco-impact by eating greener. ACF's *Consuming Australia* report claims that nearly 45% of the average Australian household's eco-footprint comes from the food we consume, which shocks me when compared to the measly 7% that is attributed to our household electricity and transportation[1].

Globally the story is similar. In 2006 the Food and Agriculture Organization (FAO) of the UN reported that the food and agricultural sector is responsible for more than one third of global greenhouse emissions[2], and a 2009 report by Worldwatch increased this ratio to 51%[3]. In 2013 the FAO further reported that the livestock sector alone is responsible for 14.5% of all greenhouse gas emissions (compared with 13% of emissions associated with global transport); this latest report includes guidance on achieving sizeable reductions using technologies currently available[4].

I don't know about you, but I always imagined cars, planes and smokestacks spewing out billowing black clouds as the big climate enemies, not farms. It makes sense that processed and packaged foods have higher environmental footprints than whole foods because of the production process, I just didn't realise that so much of the footprint could be attributed to the actual growing process.

Eating an organic diet will be a great first step to improve my environmental impact. As I've already learned, organic farming increases biodiversity and the health of the soil. Avoiding synthetic fertilisers and pesticides also keeps our water and soil clean of toxic runoff and avoids nitrogen, a powerful greenhouse gas. On top of all of that, emissions related to the production and transportation of fertiliser are minimised, making organic farming the greenest option around.

Eating organically has wonderful health impacts, too. There is overwhelming evidence that organic produce contains higher nutrient levels compared to produce grown with today's increasingly industrial farming methods – meaning more vitamins per bite![5] In addition, when you eat organic foods you ingest fewer toxins because of the lack of synthetic fertilisers and pesticides, which may explain the desirable glowing skin of Hollywood's healthy-elite.

Tell me again why I didn't switch to whole and organic foods years ago?

The short answer to that question is the cost and availability of the products. While some items are priced similarly, many organics are priced at a premium, creating a barrier for many of us on non-Hollywood budgets. I also find it difficult to locate fresh, organic options in my local grocery store, and there's no farmers' market nearby, making the whole thing terribly inconvenient.

Thanks to my previous job I'm already extremely cynical of packaged foods and read labels religiously – there are so many 'hidden' ingredients it really pays to find out what may be lurking in your box of cereal (usually salt, sugar and preservatives). Now I'll make sure I look for environmental credentials as well as health credentials in any packaged foods I buy. For instance, I won't purchase food that claims to be 'Organic' unless it is accompanied by the official certification symbol[6]. I'll also continue to be wary of claims like 'Natural', 'Made with Real Fruit', or 'Better For You'; these are common, unregulated claims that are used when *part* of a product has been made with natural ingredients. I find the most heinous greenwashing in packaged foods. A healthy grocery-shopping tip I learned long ago (and my former clients would hate me sharing!) is to stick to the perimeter of your grocery store where they stock the produce and fresh foods. Avoiding unnecessary packaging is better for the planet, and more often than not, healthier for your body, too.

Many environmentalists tout going vegetarian for the planet, and as I learn more of the statistics I'm beginning to understand why. Our obsession with meat contributes heavily to food's large eco-footprint. As I just learned from the FAO, livestock is responsible for nearly 15% of greenhouse gas emissions. It explains the difficulty of determining livestock's exact impact on climate change, however, because of all the steps required to get food from farm to plate:

> "At virtually each step of the livestock production process substances contributing to climate change or air pollution are emitted into the atmosphere, or their sequestration in other reservoirs is hampered. Such changes are either the direct effect of livestock rearing, or indirect contributions from other steps on the long road that ends with the marketed animal product."

This may be why the Climate Action Program reports that meat and dairy represent 50% of all food-related environmental impacts[7]; livestock require a lot of water, a lot of land, and emit a lot of greenhouse gases. Interestingly, and contrary to what many "localvores" may suggest, the transportation of food is not responsible for the bulk of food-related emissions, only 11% of life cycle greenhouse gas emissions of our food can be attributed to transportation. In fact, final delivery from the producer to retail outlet equates to just 4% of foods' life cycle greenhouse gas emissions[8].

The production process has the highest impact on our food footprint because of activities like deforestation and cultivation. Consider these statistics:

- One 150 gram serve of meat takes 200 litres of water to produce[9]
- Deforestation caused by clearing land for food accounts for 18% of the food and agriculture sector's emissions[10]
- Livestock production uses 70% of all agricultural land on the planet (including land required to grow livestock feed)[11]
- Livestock grazing occupies 26% of all land surfaces on the planet[12]
- Meat requires up to 17 times more land than soy per unit of protein produced[13]
- The US alone could feed 800 million people from the grains and legumes it currently feeds to its livestock[14]

The cultivation of livestock also releases the extremely potent greenhouse gases of methane and nitrous oxide. We hear less about these greenhouse gases compared to carbon dioxide because they are released in smaller quantities, but they are much more damaging to the atmosphere.

Okay, some more numbers.

- Methane is 21 times more powerful at warming the atmosphere than carbon dioxide, and nitrous oxide is *300 times* more powerful[15]
- Livestock manure is responsible for around 65% of global nitrous oxide emissions
- The livestock sector emits 37% of total methane emissions, primarily from 'enteric fermentation by ruminants.' Translation: animal burps

- Beef and dairy cattle production is responsible for 60% of total livestock emissions[16]

Poor, sweet cows (a prominent member of the ruminant family), they really get the brunt of the blame for these emissions, particularly the methane. Their complex stomachs (containing four compartments) enable cows to digest tough foods like grass through various stages of chewing and regurgitation, during which they belch out methane. When cattle are fed corn and soy they get heftier, but since neither food is part of the natural diet of cows, these foods lead to more chewing and more belching. Lamb, sheep and goats have the same type of stomachs, but because cows are raised in greater numbers, they are responsible for the bulk of our food-related greenhouse gas emissions (over 60 million tonnes of beef are produced each year[17], not to mention all our dairy cows).

The picture isn't getting prettier anytime soon, either, as current trends indicate meat consumption will continue to rise. During the past 30 years Americans and Australians have increased their annual meat consumption by 8 kg (17 pounds) and 19 kg (42 pounds) respectively – this brings Americans up to 84 kg (185 lbs) and Australians to 91.4 kg (200 lbs) per person each year[18]. The FAO suggests the global demand for meat and dairy will double by 2050 due to population increases, rising incomes and urbanisation – particularly in developing nations that mimic American and Australian consumption trends.

It's time for to me seriously consider how much meat I consume, particularly beef.

All this information is swimming around my head when I come across a light-hearted article about hosting a green barbeque. It sounds like a great way to talk with our friends about sustainability, so I suggest to Ty that we organise a green barbie.

"We're all going to Bluey's soon, why don't we suggest to make it a green weekend away?" he offers up.

Of course! About fifteen of us are getting ready to descend on the picturesque Bluey's Beach on the New South Wales coast in a couple weeks. There's been much hype around this weekend away –

it was the location of Ty's infamous bachelor weekend, and now we ladies have been invited to enjoy the pleasures of Bluey's as well.

"Fabulous idea, Babe! The article says to encourage things like not using disposable plates and cutlery, selecting organic or natural foods, not using plastic bags and either going vegetarian or not having beef, cooking kangaroo or free-range chicken instead."

"Cool. We can easily request they carpool – we probably need to anyway, not everyone has a car."

"And of course using your own mug when you go to the café," I suggest with a smirk.

"Of course," he smiles back, "and we'll definitely be going to the café, I've already pre-ordered two dozen date scones." The date scones are one of the tamer memories of that infamous weekend.

"I really hope people will do the no beef thing – I had no idea it was so bad!"

"I think they will, it's not like we're asking them to not have any meat, that would be too much to ask."

"I agree. Well, do you want to send an email to everyone with our suggestions, since you're the official weekend organiser?" If Tyler didn't organise events, I doubt most of the crew would leave Bondi – he's not just the official Bluey's weekend organiser, he's the official social coordinator of the group.

"Sure, I'll do it from work tomorrow."

Yes! I'm so excited to have a green getaway!

This week I'm working as a temp in a very tall, very cold office building to earn some money while I figure out what I can do for a living that doesn't disgust me (the list of possibilities gets shorter with each eco-factoid I uncover). When I check my email on my lunchbreak I am surprised to see this very limited message from Ty to the group:

Since we're going to this magical place to enjoy the unspoilt beaches, clean water, and fresh country air, I'd like to suggest that we attempt to make this a sustainable beach weekend. Well, as sustainable as moving 14

people 600kms round trip, consuming slabs of beer and vats of champagne can possibly be.

What do you think?

We could start with minimising our car numbers as much as possible, diligently recycling, etc. Any other ideas?

I thought he was going share all our suggestions with the group, and I had specifically said I wanted to ask for no beef on the weekend! I immediately sent a follow-up email:

Hi All~

My personal goal is that we consume **no beef** on the weekend - this does not mean no meat, for us omnivores, just no beef, please. Did you know that one kg of beef causes more greenhouse gas and other pollution than driving for three hours while leaving all the lights on at home? This does not even include the impact of managing farm infrastructure and transporting the meat, so the cost is even greater that this particular figure suggests. Much of the cow's greenhouse gas emissions come from methane, released from the cow's digestive system (aka cow burps)!

I realise that to some people no beef on a barbie might sound sad, but there are plenty of other yummy meats we can cook!

I'm also happy to help coordinate the carpooling if everyone can email me what time they can leave on the Friday.

About 20 minutes later I receive a reply from Geoff to me – no one else was copied:

Nice to see that you are keen on sustainability. Looks like you are doing a little research as well?

As someone who has been on the sustainability bandwagon for a long time, I would suggest treading lightly where possible and trying to get buy in from people where possible.

For whatever reason people, even smart educated people such as our friends, get shitty when they feel they are being lectured.

Saying this, it is good to keep gently reminding people to think about this stuff. I found the reminder useful!

Oh, and I suggest Kangaroo on the BBQ.

Good luck

I reply, acknowledging that I had noticed people get a bit strange when the environment gets mentioned, but that if you can't ask your own friends to make environmental changes, who can you?

I ring Ty to get his opinion on my email, and he tells me I've come across as too pushy. Defensively, I tell him I think he and Geoff are too closed minded, and I'm sure that our friends will take my email in the spirit in which I wrote it – hopeful optimism that we could make a contribution to the environment by not eating beef for two days.

I was wrong.

About an hour later I receive this email from someone who will be referred to as Beefeater from here on in:

Whilst I completely understand your reasons for wishing all of us to boycott beef during our weekend away, I do feel a little pressured by your approach. We all have our ideals and issues that are important to us individually but these should not be forced upon the group due to one person's stance.

I work extremely hard and am looking forward to a weekend away to relax with friends and have some fun. I don't want to jeopardise this, hence sending this email to you personally and not to the group as a whole.

I am very interested in the work that you do and would definitely like to get some information and advice on how I can 'do my bit' for the environment at home and at work. Tyler's idea and your offering to help co-ordinate the car pooling is a great example of how we can make a contribution as a group without alienating others because of their dietary choices in life.

Personally, I rarely eat red meat anyway but a weekend away surfing and being active is exactly the time when I would like to indulge and enjoy the things that I love i.e. sausages and steak on the barbie!

Feel free to give me a call over the weekend, I just wanted to make it clear that I will more than likely be eating beef during this weekend and don't want to be made to feel guilty for it.

As I read this email blood drains from my face and my stomach drops. What?! How dare Beefeater send me this written slap on the wrist!

I reread my email, and I guess bolding **no beef** could have come across the wrong way, but that's how I speak and write in general. Or maybe it was too long and preachy? But I always talk excitedly, whether in person or via email, and I tried to lighten it up with the cow burps comment. I suppose I assumed everyone would trust me not to publicly chastise or embarrass anyone, and that I welcome debate on this (or any) subject. But my intentions certainly weren't translated over the internet. Bloody email.

I read the email again and forward it to Ty, hoping for solidarity from my fellow green champion. My heart is pounding as I bounce between embarrassment, disappointment and anger. Sure, the words Beefeater wrote were polite enough, but the length of the email and the fact that it was only sent to me makes me feel like I've been naughty and need a talking to. And what's with the condescending tone of "I am very interested in the work that you do..."? I don't even work for the environment except for promoting *Use Your Own Mug* and making changes in my own household. If Beefeater had simply replied that he/she didn't want to boycott beef because she/he couldn't imagine a beach getaway without it, or replied to everyone, I doubt it would feel like such a personal attack.

And I honestly don't know what's so hard about saying "no" to beef for two days, and I'm quite annoyed that Beefeater can't even consider it, if for no other reason than it is important to me. A few weeks ago I agreed to renting the more expensive beach houses at Beefeater's request (which coincidentally used the same 'I work hard' argument) even though I'm unemployed. There doesn't appear to be any give and take in this friendship.

I call for reinforcements – emailing Lillian and Maryanne to ask if I was too pushy in my previous email (I don't tell them why, no need to drag everyone into it). They agree that the tone sounded like me, excited but not too pushy. They are happy to forego beef for the weekend; at the same time, they don't let the entire group know they supported this suggestion, just me. In fact, everyone who replied to my beef suggestion replied to me only. All other responses were positive, saying it was a fun suggestion they had not heard about, but no one 'replied all' about anything but the carpooling schedule. Like Geoff said, people are funny about the environment and no one felt compelled to share with the whole group their support of a beef-free weekend.

I'm feeling quite emotional and trapped in an over-analysing loop, so I call Tyler again.

"Hi Babe, did you see the email I forwarded from Beefeater?"

"Yeah."

"Well?"

"Well what?"

"What should I do? I'm really irritated."

"Beefeater's probably irritated, too. You should send another email and apologise."

"Why?!" Where is my spousal support network today?

"I don't want to risk the whole weekend. Can't you try and keep the peace?" Typical.

"Why should I have to back down?! It's not that big a request. Beefeater can eat beef if she/he wants to. Besides, if you had included all our suggestions we discussed it wouldn't be an issue."

"I wanted to get people's buy-in first, I didn't want to be too pushy."

"Well you should have told me you thought it would be controversial. I didn't think it would be, and I really don't think I was that pushy. Besides, I'm passionate about it, why should I have to be quiet?"

"I can't talk now," he mumbles.

"Fine." And I hang up, tears welling and a lump forming in my throat.

I'm hurt that my friends and particularly my husband won't openly support my green goal and, as an extension, me. I thought he loved my being opinionated? And isn't he required to take my side? I'm sure that was in the vows somewhere. Instead of supporting me he's treating me like a petulant child who's having a tantrum over sharing her toys.

And, as much as it pains me to say it, this event makes me question my friendships; if someone can't even consider changing a certain behaviour for two days, are they the type of person I want to be around, environmental aspirations or not? I don't expect my friends to do everything I ask, but hope to surround myself with thoughtful and adaptable individuals who have the ability to see beyond themselves in the here and now. At the same time, I don't want to be forced out of our group because of my newfound commitment to the environment. I also don't want to risk Tyler's friendships – banishment by association – let alone our marriage.

I don't know if I have the strength to be an eco-warrior after all.

It's hard enough challenging my own lifestyle choices as I try to be greener, let alone trying to positively influence my friends. I'm exhausted! I'd been so excited to suggest a sustainable weekend, but after the emails from Geoff and Beefeater, and Tyler's complete lack of support, I feel utterly deflated and backed into a corner. Sending another email would be humiliating and go against both my belief in the environmental movement and my conviction that everyone should be able to speak his or her mind among friends.

Am I really going to have to choose between my friends and the environment?

Somehow I make it through the workday. When I get home my head is pounding and I'm sick to my stomach. Tonight Ty and I are meeting David and Maryanne at the outdoor cinema at Mrs. Macquarie's Chair – normally a very pleasant summer activity – so I take some painkillers and have a lie down before heading out.

"I hope you're going to perk up for Dave and Maryanne," Ty says as we walk through Darlinghurst toward the Domain.

"What do you mean?" I hiss miserably.

"You're going to have to get over this, you're making it a bigger deal than it is," he says, dismissing my afternoon-long emotional struggle.

Oh no. *Hold it in, pull yourself together*, I will myself, but it's too late. Within seconds I collapse into a sobbing, convulsing, spluttering nightmare, unable to walk or speak, right here on a dark, stained corner of Crown Street. Tears are streaming down my face, my nose is running like a spout and I'm gasping for breath. Every pain, insecurity and challenge from the past few months is pouring out of me onto the dirty Darlinghurst pavement.

Ty is startled and pulls me to him, begging me to tell him what's going on, asking me what's happened.

"I don't know," I gasp, through a hiccup, "I'm so confused. I think everything today has made me start to question a lot of things, and (sniff) I wonder if we're really friends with the best people. And I'm upset that you didn't take my side. And I'm afraid people won't like me anymore. I used to be fun. (Hiccup!) I used to have beautiful clothes and pretty hair, and I had a cool job and I was funny (sniff), and now what if people don't like me? What if you don't like me?

What if I don't want to be friends with people who won't change their behaviour? (Sniff.) I really believe in saving the environment and no one seems to want to help me. It's totally doomed. And you won't even stand up for me! Your friends are more important to you,

and I'm in trouble. Why am I the one who has to give in? I'm trying to do a good thing, and everyone else is just being selfish!"

Phew! It feels good to get all that out in the open.

"That's not really fair," Ty releases me, deflating me once again.

"God! You just don't understand!" I push away and storm off ahead of him.

"Wait! You can't just walk away from me!" Ty rushes to catch up.

"I don't know what else to say to you. I'm exhausted, and trying to explain myself and you just think I'm being selfish and mean. I didn't realise becoming a greenie would require so much of me. Do you know I haven't even picked up my camera in months? I've been so consumed with the environment! I can't go shopping; I don't even want to look at stores or magazines anymore, all I see is greed. And waste. And things that don't matter. But that's who I was, and I spent years doing it! It's all I used to talk with people about, so now I don't know what to talk about with our friends anymore, they don't know what to talk to me about, and now I'm making them uncomfortable. I think my old life was so frivolous and stupid, and so I think of them as being frivolous. I know it's not true and it's not fair, but it's how I'm feeling. It was so much easier when I didn't know about this stuff. I knew where I belonged and I wasn't alone. Now I don't really fit in anywhere."

Tyler looks shell-shocked, probably wondering what happened to his confident, carefree wife, and is speechless.

I manage to pull myself together and we make it to the movie. Luckily the screening is *Marley and Me* so I'm allowed to continue crying for the next two hours.

Once we're back home I begrudgingly send the following email to the entire group:

> I've been advised that perhaps I came across too strong - I will not chastise anyone for eating whatever they like, was just making a fun 'sustainable' suggestion because I was so surprised when I learned about beef's emissions. Suggestion only, I will not be a beef policewoman on the weekend.

No one replied.

This has been the hardest day of my green existence to date – today I realised just how hard my quest for environmental change is going to be, because I am doing it alone.

⌣ ∅ 🜊 ⚱ ⚷ ⚸ ⚹ ♀ ◓ ◑ ♀ ♡

I'm sitting inside an incredibly glamorous home on Bluey's Beach, solo. I am pouting, but enjoying my solitude in this glass-walled modern masterpiece as I watch a storm roll over the ocean. Don't you love it when the weather matches your mood?

Ty and I had another big fight last night. I wanted to pull out of coming on the weekend. He told me I was being selfish, I told him he was choosing his friends over me; it was ugly. I rode up with Kate instead of him, and tried to get him to sleep in the other house – since there are fifteen of us we booked two houses next door to each other. I honestly can't remember ever being angrier with him than I am today.

Adding insult to injury, I saw Sam coming back from his second coffee run of the morning with four takeaway cups. He's a repeat offender! I'm still feeling wounded. I didn't intend to put him on the spot, but I was so frustrated when I saw him that the words just flew out of my mouth:

"Why didn't you bring a mug?!"

He didn't even respond, the look he shot me said that I had crossed the line.

58

So I've stayed back while everyone else has gone to Boomerang Beach for the afternoon, feigning a migraine. They all piled into cars to drive the 500 metres, "You don't expect us to carry our surfboards that far, do you?"

Between these events and the copious amounts of mince beef and steak that have been purchased for tonight's barbeque (apparently it's more than just Beefeater who can't live without beef), I am in desperate need for some alone time.

I had hoped to be a positive influence, introducing environmental awareness into the collective identity of our group. But for most people this doesn't come without a price, as it means giving up the pleasure of carefree spending and consumption as a reward for hard work that is inherent in our lifestyle. I'm fighting a losing battle.

There have been a few green victories. Barry supplied a case of carbon neutral beer, and Emma bought a very cute beach bag made from reused city banners. David was on the grocery run and made sure not to take any plastic bags – putting things right in the boot of the car because he forgot to bring reusable bags with him. He also toasted Ty and me last night for suggesting the green-themed weekend, but I felt it was an empty victory. I feel terrible about myself, I'm pissed off at Tyler, and I feel like I don't belong in my Sydney family anymore.

It's about six months into my green transformation and I'm learning (the hard way) that in order to create social change the right balance of emotional and social courtesy must be found – I certainly have not struck the right balance with most of my friends. As a result, I'm not having much luck influencing their eco-behaviour. I'm also not very popular because instead of focusing on uninhibited fun, I'm asking people to consider their personal impact on the environment. I don't feel like I fit in with this group any longer, and right now I don't know if I even want to.

I'm ready to give up hope. I still believe wholeheartedly in the environmental cause, but my emotions and eco-ego have taken a brutal beating. If my friends won't change their behaviour, what hope does the planet have? I feel we're in the best place to make a change – we're young, educated, and have expendable income – but there are definite hurdles we haven't yet overcome. I want so badly to encourage people to embrace environmentalism, but I am really struggling emotionally against the pitfalls. Sure, Lillian is helping

promote *Use Your Own Mug*, but besides a few token gestures over the weekend I don't see that anyone else even cares.

I'm tired, I'm sad and I'm a bit lonely. I feel that the environmental cause is lost because people are too selfish to change their lifestyle of convenience and consumption. Everywhere I look I see waste, ignorance and greed, and feel I may be wasting my time, emotions and energy.

Part Two

How to live sustainably, with style

Natural beauty

♡

GREEN BEAUTY DIARY DAY 1

Green beauty products purchased: 2
Green beauty home remedies: 2
I feel: Amazing.

Ahhhhh, there's nothing like a bath: the uplifting serenity of lavender and citrus-scented water, the gentle flicker of candlelight, the tranquil lapping of water blending with the hypnotic sounds of José González and his enchanting guitar. Heaven. I've been so stressed lately, this is exactly what I need to forget all my –

"HELLO?!"

"Oh!" I ungracefully slip and slide and slosh water out of the tub as I lift myself upright at the sound of Tyler's voice and knocking on the bathroom door, "come in!"

"I've been calling your name since I got home," he says as he opens the door, "what did you make for dinner? There is food all over the counter. . ." he trails off into a chuckle.

"I've been trying some home beauty treatments!" I explain as a few mushy oats fall off my chin, plopping into the bath. "Did you know that oats are naturally cleansing *and* moisturising? So I'm clearing my pores without over-drying my skin!"

I'm hoping my enthusism and new green knowledge will impress him enough to overlook the fact that I'm lying in the tub with what looks like this morning's breakfast rubbed all over my face.

"Nope, never knew that," still smirking, "um, what's going on with your hair?" he asks, looking quizzically at my head.

Oh yeah, forgot about that.

"Avocado, banana and olive oil. It's like a natural deep conditioning treatment. Isn't that fascinating?!" I say, with a little too much excitement.

"You obviously did some research today."

"What are you doing here, anyway?" I ask defensively; I had intended to wash all this off long before he returned from the Bondi house.

"Oh you know, I missed my beautiful wife. But since she's not here, I'll leave you alone with your oats and avocado," he backs out of the room.

"No no no, I'll get out, just give me a minute to wash this off...You know Babe, it's all edible..." trying to flirt my way out of this embarrassment.

"Ummm, as tempting as that is, I'll just wait for you out here," he says as he backs out of the room.

Ty and I have made peace. We've also come to an understanding that I'll be limiting my time with the Bondi crew while I think through what's happened and what it means for my relationships as a result of what I've come to think of as the Beefgate scandal. I don't want to be so harsh as to say, "you ate beef and ignored my eco-requests so we can't be friends," but I also don't want to feel pressured to put my values on the backburner. I still believe that among friends I should be able to express myself honestly, and I don't feel like everyone in the group encourages that behaviour. I'm feeling slightly embarrassed, too, so I'm taking time out from group activities for awhile. Besides, I have enough to work on (like finding a job, saving the planet – you know, the basics) without having to deal with the horrible emotions I'm currently associating with the group.

So while I hide, licking my wounds from my failed activism attempt, I'm continuing to make personal green changes. After the stress of the past couple of months – quitting my job, learning the real damage caused by my shopping habit, and alienating myself from my Sydney family – greening my beauty routine seemed like a great place to start.

I had braced myself for the worst, assuming it was going to be as tricky as eco-fashion, but I've been pleasantly surprised to find an abundance of eco-beauty and body products in the stores. Sure, there's a decent amount of greenwashing in this area, but once you know what to look for it's surprisingly easy to find really lovely natural products. Take tonight's luxurious bath: I was able to find exactly what I was looking for at my favourite department store David Jones, no specialty shop required. (My bath really was a luxury, too, since it used almost 4 times more water than a shower would have.)

When I left my house this morning it was with the intention to find some eco-friendly bath salts to create a beautiful home-spa experience, so when I arrived at DJs I went straight to the Burt's Bees counter. I was pretty sure it was an eco-aware company and I quickly found 100% natural citrus-scented bath salts that came packaged in a recyclable tin. The ingredients are sea salt, baking soda, various plant-based essential oils and vitamin E – I love a short ingredients list.

All Burt's Bees products have the percentage of natural ingredients printed right on the front of the packaging – I love it! The products on the shelves today varied between 98% and 100% natural, and I was impressed to find such high values of natural ingredients in an industry rife with scientific wonder ingredients like 'super-concentrated amino-peptide with B3 complex' or 'life re-newing molecules'.

Burt's Bees embraces sustainability from a variety of angles. They use high levels of post-consumer recycled content in their packaging, all packaging is recyclable (with a goal for all packaging to be compostable or biodegradable by 2020), a portion of sales and employee time is spent on environmental and social not-for-profit organisations, and they have a transparent reporting system regarding every aspect of the company. They also have a zero-waste policy, and anything that cannot be recycled or composted is turned into biomass fuel. Impressive. Even though it's not the sexiest brand around, this home grown American company seems to be ticking all the right sustainability boxes.

With the bath salts sorted out I turned my attention to body moisturiser. As any bath aficionado will tell you, there's no point in soaking yourself in a gorgeous bath if you don't follow it with equally gorgeous moisturiser. Burt's Bees sells this, too, (98.3% natural, in case you were wondering) but I thought it would be more fun to spread my eco-dollars around and extend my time in DJs – I was savouring my shopping time. I looked at a couple brands that appeared 'green' from the name or natural-looking graphics on their packaging, but a closer look uncovered many unfamiliar chemicals lurking within the ingredients or packaging with a huge eco-footprint.

Before I knew what happened I found myself wandering amongst intricate glass containers and artfully etched metal canisters in the more luxurious end of the department. I don't know what happened, I couldn't help myself. I like pretty things! I was drawn to a display of black tin tubes of moisturiser with delicious names like 'Vanilla and Orange Peel', 'Mandarin and Rosemary Leaf' and 'Rose, Acai and Pomegranate' printed down the face of the tube in stark white typography. Surely this company wouldn't meet my eco-standards. Would it?

Grown – a modern-day apothecary, it would seem – created these beautiful products and packaged them in cool raw-paper boxes made of 100% uncoated, recycled cardboard[1.] The boxes were printed with a black and white photograph of a partially squeezed tube of moisturiser with the trendy typography continuing on the other sides of the box; the styling spoke to me and I couldn't help but try the tester. While rubbing the moisturiser into my hands I read the box:

Grown is a lover of nature. Be Climate-Neutral. Recycle this packaging and anything else you can. Stop Animal Testing.

With my eco-hopes raised by this sustainability declaration, and the fact that it's an Australian product so has low 'beauty miles' (although I now know miles don't account for a huge percentage of a product's footprint), I took a peek at the ingredients.

Yes! These are natural products! No greenwashing by Grown! All ingredients are sourced from natural plant sources. Now *this* is a company I can relate to – one combining beautiful aesthetics with earth-friendly principles. I can't help but think of my old client Luke, and his (un)natural body products - everything about Grown puts that entire hoax to shame. I bought a tube of the Mandarin and Rosemary Leaf body lotion; at $26 for 120mL I can't afford to make this my everyday body moisturiser, but the glamour girl inside me just *had* to take it home to complete my green home-spa experience.

Actually, to *really* complete the experience I needed a facial and a hair treatment, and *The Daily Green*[2] told me how to do both using items already in my kitchen. I found a few facial 'recipes' for various skin types and ended up combining oats, baking soda, honey and a bit of water into a sort of chunky paste for a mask that was meant to purify and moisturise my skin. It was unlike any mask I had used before and took a bit of effort to stick on my face. I wasn't spreading it around so much as I was pressing it onto my skin – too much rubbing caused the bulky concoction to fall off. I eventually got it to stay on long enough to coat my hair in the avocado-olive oil mask and slide gently into the tub where I could lay back and let gravity do the work.

Which brings me to the abrupt end to my home-spa just a few minutes ago.

Even though Tyler caught me in a less-than-glamorous moment, my initial dabbling at green beauty was smooth sailing. I found natural beauty products in my usual stomping grounds and learned how to make my own facial and hair mask with ingredients already in my kitchen. I'm totally loving green beauty!

GREEN BEAUTY DIARY DAY 4

Green beauty products purchased: 1
I feel: Still glowing from my home 'spa' treatment. Slightly frustrated at the makeup counter's lack of green cosmetics. Ecstatic with my new best friend, Gorgeously Green.

When Lillian texted a few days ago to line up today's yoga and shopping session I admit, I hesitated. It's so ridiculous – my good friend has asked me to participate in two of my favourite pastimes and I have to talk myself into it? I'm feeling fragile from Beefgate but I can't hide forever. And truthfully, I'm relieved my behaviour at Bluey's hasn't caused permanent banishment. Besides, I'm running dangerously low on mascara and toner. Clinique trained me years ago on the importance of the 3-step face cleansing system, so I actually need this après-yoga shopping session to maintain my complexion.

I have a really good feeling about today's foray into eco-shopping because I'd recently discovered every green girl's must-have reference, *Gorgeously Green* by Sophie Uliano. I saw the charming Sophie with Julia Roberts on Oprah the other day – apparently they're great friends – and once I heard her talking about how easy it was to be gorgeous and green at the same time I felt I'd found my saviour. I rushed to the bookstore, bought a copy and read most of it in one sitting, absorbing as much as I could from her tips for shopping, eating, cleaning and eco-beauty. Sophie provides a list of toxic ingredients to avoid in cosmetics and body products, even categorising them by level of danger, making it really easy to green my beauty routine.

When I arrive at the yoga studio Lillian bounds toward me, full of her usual energy, red hair coolly pulled back, and proudly shows me the thermos that has replaced takeaway cups.

"Hey Lise, isn't this just gorgeous? I bought it in a vintage shop ages ago and am so excited to have an excuse to use it! This is the one I wrote about on Facebook!" she exclaims in her uniquely-Lillian Swiss-Australian drawl.

Now that I think about it, I shouldn't have even thought twice when Lillian asked to catch up today; she's been one of my greatest eco-partners so far. Besides her immediate uptake of *Use Your Own*

Mug, Lillian has shown great enthusiasm for the concept outside of Facebook. Initially I was quite surprised, as she's someone I wouldn't have thought to have a green streak lurking inside, but soon after I started talking about the environment she began sharing ideas to promote reusable mugs, like designing little *Use Your Own Mug* cards with catchy messages to hand out to people with takeaway cups.

The reason I hadn't expected Lillian to join the cause so easily was because we had so much in common before my green transformation began. We met at the height of my 'poster-child for consumerism' phase and I felt that Lillian understood me. She had worked in fashion and design and we quickly bonded over shopping and trips to galleries; we love chatting about all the gorgeous things this world has to offer, and can effortlessly while away an afternoon discussing the pros and cons of red patent leather ankle boots, this season's shades of lip colour and the latest shows at Blender Gallery and the MCA.

Having faced the harsh reality of what my lifestyle was doing to the planet and making some difficult changes to my habits – shopping taking the hardest hit – I assumed Lillian would be a tough convert because she would have to make similar changes. Instead she seems to be turning her passion for vintage shopping into real environmental action and wants to use her design skills to further promote the cause. It's inspiring to see these changes in my friend and also to witness there are many ways to join the environmental movement, it's not just for hippies anymore. (Maybe I should make a bumper sticker with that phrase. Or a bike sticker, that's even greener…)

After 90 blissful, hatha yoga-filled minutes I feel refreshed and peaceful and ready to brave the stores. After the ease with which I located natural bath products the other day and reading Sophie's list of ingredients to avoid I am looking forward to showing Lillian how easy it is to be green.

"You still up for some shopping?" Lillian asks while we change after class – just because I'm starting to embrace a more natural lifestyle does not mean I will wear my yoga gear shopping on a Saturday afternoon.

I pull on a rainbow-coloured, Indian-inspired sundress I bought from Bondi markets a few years ago and last year's silver gladiator sandals. Lucky for me the footwear style has not changed dramatically since last summer so I can get away with another season in these sandals.

Wow. I never imagined I'd utter such a phrase: another season in the same sandals.

"Absolutely," I reply to Lillian, "I'm literally scraping the sides of my mascara tube, the situation can now be classed *Emergency* status. Hey, do you know who does natural or Australian-made mascara?" I timidly ask, putting my eco-hope in her fashion and beauty skills.

"Oh, um, let's see," do I sense a bit of environmental fatigue? "Let's try Kit. I need new nail polish anyway and they have really great colours.

"Why do you want Australian-made?" she inquires (phew, no eco-fatigue after all).

"Oh, if it's made in Australia, it means there's no travel footprint – sort of like beauty miles instead of food miles."

"Huh, I never really thought about that."

"I didn't use to, either," I sigh, then smile – I'm all about the cause now! "I'd normally just go to Clinique and buy a couple tubes of Long Pretty Lashes, but not anymore."

We make our way to Myer at Pitt Street Mall and when we reach the playful Kit counter Lillian immediately locates a bottle of flame orange nail polish that will look fab on her.

"Excuse me, where is this nail polish made?" she asks the very 'Kit' saleswoman channelling '1960s sex-kitten' with a flawless complexion, the perfect updo, cat-eyes and on-trend bubble gum pink lipstick that is somehow matte, pastel and vibrant all at the same time. She looks gorgeous, and I am suddenly very aware of having just come from yoga wearing very little makeup and my hair jumbled in a nest on top of my head.

"It's made in Australia," she brightly replies, and Lillian beamed with pride as she completes her first eco-purchase.

"Do you have any natural or Australian-made mascara?" I asked, hoping to be as lucky.

"Hmmm, let me think," she ponders, looking around at the shelves, "well I'm loving this one, I'm wearing it now" she pulls out Too Faced Lash Injection and I admire her long lush lashes (do I detect some fakes in there?).

"Is it made here, though?"

"No, it's made overseas," she looks confused – I suspect my American accent may have caused her to think it was a tourist request.

"It's not so much that I want an Australian brand," I attempt to explain, feeling a bit self-conscious about my eco-request, "I'm trying to get the most natural, eco-friendly mascara, so I don't really want one that's been shipped from overseas."

"Well, the Korres mascara is the most natural, it's really lovely and makes your lashes so healthy. But it's not made here, it's made in Greece."

She leads me to a corner of the shop that entices me to throw my credit card at her and shout, "I'll take one of everything!" The boxes are artfully displayed on glass shelves resting on crates and feature an array of vibrant macro photography. I see various fruits, plants and segments of makeup products overlain with Greek letters that appeared to have been written with a mascara-covered finger. It is a breathtaking sight, and I am excited even at the prospect of taking home one of the beautiful products.

Before I purchase on looks alone, I remember to take a look at the ingredients. I like that the mascara includes Rice Bran, but there are still a lot of ingredients that sounded quite chemical. Why didn't I remember to bring the 'Ingredients to Avoid' list with me today? Typical. Anyway, I hold out hope for a natural product made in Australia, reluctantly put the beautiful mascara down and step away from the rest of the beautiful products.

This environmentalism business isn't always that fun…

I test my luck and ask if they have any toners made of natural ingredients, and specifically that don't include alcohol or salicylic acid; I remember these being on my eco-cheat sheet because I was so surprised to see these two very common ingredients on the list. Alcohol gets added to many products because it's a drying agent and is frequently found in toner. Depending on the type of alcohol it can promote aging and cause dermatitis (Isopropryl Alcohol), be an irritant to your eyes and respiratory system (Benzyl Alcohol), or release toxins that are readily absorbed by the skin (Denatured Alcohol). Salicylic acid is an exfoliant that strips away the outer layers of your skin, but it's very harsh – not that I'm surprised, what with the word 'acid' in the title. Not only does its use frequently result in over-drying your skin, causing you to require a heavier moisturiser than you may actually need, it's also absorbed easily by the skin and linked to toxins that can accumulate in your body[3].

The saleswoman directs me toward the Mario Badescu range, and carries on about how it's the most beautiful product and used by all the celebs (I remember reading once that Jennifer Aniston uses the stuff). She says it really changed her life when she started using it earlier this year. I look at the bottle of this life-changing toner and am delighted to see only natural ingredients:

> *Deionized Water, Aloe Gel, Seaweed Extract, Lemon Extract, Grapefruit Extract.*

That's it, that's all the ingredients. I don't even need to worry about forgetting my 'Ingredients to Avoid' list. If it weren't for the celeb endorsement I wouldn't trust that it worked, but I'm willing to give it a go and so purchase a bottle. (It's not made in Australia, but I want skin like Jennifer Aniston!)

Lillian and I trawl through the entire Myer cosmetics department, and after thirty minutes and half a dozen sales assistants (some friendly, some rude, most of them perplexed by my request), I go home without mascara. This is so depressing. In a few days time my eyelashes may just disappear altogether.

On my stroll home I reflect on the positives from the day: besides being so excited about my new all-natural toner, I'm really impressed with Lillian's support. She bought herself some Aussie-made nail polish, and stuck with me as I tried counter after counter for natural, Australian-made mascara.

I am a bit disappointed that she drove into town, though. She lives in Bondi, and there's a bus into town every 10 minutes. But she had things to do after meeting me, and it was going to be too inconvenient to take public transport. I'm now (painfully) aware of how important it is to find the right balance of activism and avoid seeming too judgemental so I didn't say anything, but the disappointment must have shown on my face because she said:

"Lise, it's not like my one less car on the road is really going to make a difference; everyone else is still driving, so I may as well."

She wasn't being harsh or cynical, just stating the facts as she sees them. I guess she doesn't subscribe to my 'every small step adds up' philosophy. Or more likely, there are eco-requests that are non-negotiable to her, including her car. She's able to make environmental choices and maintain her image and lifestyle by using vintage clothes and thermoses and Australian-made cosmetics, but can't maintain her carefree, independent lifestyle without her car.

But one thing at a time. I'm really happy the shopping trip went so smoothly. Knowing that at least one friend is not totally repulsed by the changes in my life helps me feel better about everything I'm going through.

GREEN BEAUTY DIARY DAY 8

Green beauty products purchased: 0
Products I need to discard immediately: 12
Products I need to replace when they run out: 8
I feel: A bit dirty; my face is quite oily despite using the fabulous toner-of-the-stars. Overwhelmed by information.

As with issues of ethical fashion, Fairtrade and child labour, I have learnt that the stakes of eco-friendly beauty go beyond climate change. The biggest issue in the books, blogs and websites about green beauty products is the amount of toxins we inadvertently slather on ourselves (hence the 'Ingredients to Avoid' list) [4].

The skin is the body's largest organ, and anything we put on it eventually gets absorbed; with the average adult woman wearing 12 (and teenage girls 17) products each day consisting of 126 unique ingredients[5], it's frightening to learn that nearly 90% of the 10,500 ingredients found in beauty products have never been safety-tested[6].

Many ingredients are known carcinogens, and others become carcinogenic when mixed with other chemicals – apparently any of us could unwittingly apply two different products that interact negatively and cause unthinkable harm to our health. I've definitely thought about making sure my blush and lip colour go together, and that my foundation matches my skin tone, but never once have I considered the underlying chemicals and their properties; it's never even been on my radar.

I try to read green-living resources with a healthy dose of scepticism. I am wary of resources with panic-inducing tones; the scare strategy certainly isn't working regarding climate change action, and I doubt it will work here, either. Like my education about global warming, I want the facts about these ingredients – information that has been researched and peer-reviewed – before I change all my habits.

It turns out that a lot of research has been done in this area, and it's been reviewed and collected by the Environmental Working Group (EWG). The EWG is a non-profit organisation with a mission to use the power of public information to protect public health and the environment. They maintain a 'Safe Cosmetics Database'[7] containing information on over 9,200 ingredients found in body products, as well as a system that provides safety ratings on 74,000 body products in the marketplace. Rigorous reviews of all research and information available provide a thorough overview and recommendation on each ingredient and product listed in its database. Once you start clicking the data can be overwhelming. It's difficult not to freak out when you read the various diseases and disorders that have been linked to ingredients in our body products. I know 'linked to' doesn't always means 'leads to', but just as I avoid smoking and excessive alcohol consumption for the sake of my health, I'm beginning to understand the importance of protecting myself from harmful chemicals in beauty products.

The EWG has recently conducted a study of teen girls to test for specific hormone-disrupting chemicals from cosmetics in their bodies; the results are overwhelming, with between 10 and 15 chemicals found in each girl's body[8]. This particular study focused on teen girls because they use more products on average than adult women, and at a time when their hormone systems are undergoing accelerated development. This study references many scientific research findings about skin absorption of chemicals and their various effects (including breast cancer and premature development), and the researcher in me is satisfied that this information is not merely a scare tactic, even if the results are terrifying.

Of the chemicals in the study, parabens concern me most. Parabens are common preservatives in cosmetics, and have been linked to oestrogen and hormone disruption; this disruption has been shown to increase the risk of breast cancer[9]. Two types of parabens were found in each test subject, and two out of the twenty participants tested positively for all six parabens of concern. After reading about the dangers of parabens I threw out all the products I owned that contained any trace, and there were plenty. Why are these dangerous chemicals still allowed in our products now that we know how dangerous they are?

I am also on alert about anything petroleum-based. Mineral oil, petrolatum and paraffin are all by-products of the crude oil refining process used to obtain gasoline. There's a lot of conflicting research on the safety of these products – the FDA regards them as safe in cosmetics but natural body care experts claim that they prevent the body from naturally releasing toxins by creating a barrier on top of your skin. Once the products do get absorbed, they cause damage to our internal organs because they are unnatural for humans to consume. Regardless of the health concerns, I'm committed to working towards a future free from non-renewable polluting resources like oil and don't want to use by-products in my daily beauty routine. Besides, the idea of coating myself with living plant derivatives is so much more appealing than anything derived from crude oil.

In addition to personal health concerns, products we use eventually get washed down the drain (in however small quantities) and contaminate our waterways. Is it just me, or does the news just get worse and worse the more you know about these chemicals?

At any rate, until there is mandatory eco-labelling or harsher restrictions on personal care ingredients, I plan on avoiding parabens and petroleum-based products in particular, and keeping my 'Ingredients to Avoid' list on me at all times to make sure I don't buy something dangerous.

GREEN BEAUTY DIARY DAY 10

Green beauty products purchased: 1
I feel: Clear about my goals when buying new products, but straying from a climate change focus.

I need new shampoo and as I head to the shops I (finally) remember to bring my 'Ingredients to Avoid' list with me. I'm also hoping to find something that:

- Is not tested on animals
- Uses recyclable packaging made from recycled content
- Avoids excessive packaging
- Required low beauty miles

Normally I would visit my sensational hair salon and pick up a bottle of MOP C-system shampoo for colour-treated hair. When she first introduced MOP my stylist told me that it was good for the environment because it didn't contain Sodium Lauryl Sulfate (SLS); even as a pre-environmentalist I felt good about this choice, even if I didn't know *exactly* what it meant besides having fewer bubbles. Now I know SLS is a foaming agent with links to dermatitis and other skin irritations – so it's a health concern but not necessarily an eco-claim. However MOP products are also made with some organic ingredients: MOP = Modern Organic Products.

Whatever's in MOP, it smells DIVINE – like a citrusy mango concoction – and I love the bright yellow and orange square containers. I've recently checked the shampoo and conditioner against my 'Ingredients to Avoid' list and other green requirements, and happily they pass the eco-test. I really can't bare the thought of going into my salon and not sitting down for the works, so I'm heading to the drugstore instead in hopes of finding something that satisfies my eco and beauty requirements (and possibly softer on my pocketbook, too).

Priceline is as bright and friendly as ever as I waltz into the shampoo aisle to confront the wall of bottles I must scour in my quest. The bright fuchsia 'value' signs are shouting for my attention, but I take a moment to allow my senses to adjust before I get to work – since my initial eco-shopping excursion I've been training myself to tune out bright colours and loud music inside stores so that I can focus on the eco-task at hand; listening to my iPod is a big help.

I let my insider marketing knowledge guide me through the various colour cues in the aisle toward the likely candidates. While premium products like MOP and Grown can write their own rules, in the world of fast moving consumer goods shoppers spend just seconds making purchase decisions, so the more visual clues that help identify your product the better. I dodge the aquamarine and lime coloured bottles that scream, "I'm hip and trendy (and synthetic)". I bypass bottles with huge images of flowers or fruit; large pictures often equal heavily scented with synthetic fragrance. I'm looking for bottles that are off-white with earth tones, like tan or green, the colours typically used for eco-friendly products.

Jackpot.

I find a few options that appear promising, and they are even shelved next to each other. I spend a few minutes reading labels, comparing, referencing my list, and finally make a selection. I take a quick peek at some of the brighter bottles that claim to include plant and herbal extracts to make sure that my instincts were correct, and sure enough those crayon coloured containers are filled with many damaging ingredients (including SLS, parabens, fragrance and alcohol – both isopropyl and benzyl). Many shampoos claim to be better for the environment because they don't include SLS, but that's just one ingredient to avoid, and is really better for your health rather than the environment; another reason why I can't emphasise enough getting in the habit of reading labels.

I settle on a bottle of Sukin shampoo. Sukin is an Australian company, and in addition to avoiding all the ingredients on my list and incorporating natural ingredients like aloe vera, lavender and tangerine, it's also a carbon neutral company. It's exceeded even *my* eco-expectations. Sukin nearly didn't make the cut, though, because it uses my pet-peeve font, Papyrus. (Please companies, I'm sorry to sound so harsh, but I beg you to stop using this font; it doesn't make you look new age or natural, it just makes you look like you designed your logo in Microsoft Word). However, since the shampoo meets my strict eco-requirements – ingredients, recyclable packaging, made locally, not tested on animals, plus the added bonus of being carbon neutral – and only costs $20 for an entire litre, I suppress my style instincts in this instance.

Sukin has an entire range of hair, face and body products, so I'll definitely keep it in mind for future purchases.

As I ponder Sukin's carbon neutrality in the very long cashier's line, I start feeling like I've gotten sidetracked. I joined the environmental movement so I could help combat climate change, but I've now spent days learning about the dangers lurking in my bathroom. Is this really the best use of my time? It's not like I want to be rubbing a known carcinogen or hormone disrupter into my body, but it's too much information. Why can't I just shrink my carbon footprint and stay ignorant to all the other 'green' lifestyle changes until climate change is sorted out? I'm trying to stay in that 'neo-green' piece of the eco-pie the editor described to me, but now the 'toxics' are starting to pull me into their slice as well – what's next? Will I be chaining myself to trees with the 'nature lovers'? I'm starting to feel like the hard-core greenies are infiltrating all the resources and forcing us newbies into deep water before we're ready. Have I veered too far off course? Well, at least Sukin is carbon neutral in addition to avoiding the nasty chemicals.

GREEN BEAUTY DIARY DAY 20

Green beauty products purchased: 6
I feel: Like a teenager. A hormonal, greasy-faced teenager. I have major breakouts and my skin feels oily all day – not impressed. To top it off, my hair doesn't feel super clean after using the Sukin shampoo. On the plus side, I'm excited to have found eco-friendly mascara!

My face has broken out like crazy, including around my hairline, and I have not felt so unattractive in ages. This is not doing good things to my mood. Good thing Tyler took vows 'for better or worse,' as this is definitely one of those 'worse' moments they warn you about.

I've been looking at blogs and other online resources seeking information (and support!) to help me cope. The majority of information suggests that I should stay the course, that my body has become used to overproducing oils to counteract the drying properties of my previous chemically laden products. I merely need to wait it out for an average of six weeks while my body re-balances itself.

Six weeks?! I have to look like this for six weeks?! I may not leave the house. If I do you can bet I'll be wearing a hat and very large sunglasses. I have a reputation to uphold. One that is dangling by a thread at the moment, I admit, but I'm not willing to throw it all in without a fight.

The funny thing is, I'm not even that hardcore. Others out there practice the abhorrently named "No 'poo method". (There were clearly no clever advertisers behind this name – a name not associated with faeces is required if you want more people to join your non-shampooing brigade). I'll admit to losing a couple hours to the internet watching video diaries and looking at photos of the no 'pooers' hair transitions, trying to determine if I'm courageous enough to do it. The answer is a definitive no; I'll stick with my natural ingredients shampoo for the time being. Even if I didn't detest the name of the movement I don't think I could handle that big of a change right now.

On a brighter note, a few very serendipitous things have occurred that have eased my transition to green beauty.

First, I spotted a *Marie Claire* issue that was themed 'Fashion with Heart' and it was filled with articles and references to eco and ethical fashion and makeup (green going mainstream, I love it!). I hadn't purchased a fashion magazine for months, so I bought it immediately and ran home to get my fashion-fix, devouring the magazine in one sitting. Among the many interesting and helpful articles was one about natural makeup, pointing me to my new mascara.

Musq is an Australian luxury makeup brand that is all natural – they occasionally do makeup at Fashion Week so you know the stuff is good. Musq produces everything this glamour girl could hope for and more: mascara, mineral powder, bronzer, eyeliner, eye shadows, lip gloss and lipstick. Musq's website also includes a few other brands of natural skincare products, which is where I found my new paw paw ointment.

Every Aussie gal is familiar with Lucas Paw Paw – the red tube or jar of ointment that we rub on our lips and cuticles for moisture, on cuts and stings, and even on our eyelids for a natural shimmer. Unfortunately it turns out our red tubes-of-wonder are actually petroleum-based. Ew. Musq has kindly uncovered a substitute that has no hidden ingredients, and now Suvana brand Paw Paw Salve is my new bestie – it smells much more tropical and heavenly, has the added sweetness of honey, and works just as well as the other stuff. Well, better, really, because it's all natural; so avoid those red tubes, ladies, and look for the yellow ones instead.

Then, perhaps the biggest breakthrough: I wandered into a health food store on the hunt for steel cut oats and was delighted to discover that *this* was where all the natural beauty and body products were hiding. Forget the department store and pharmacies, make your way to your local health food store and you'll be amazed at the options they have in terms of body care, hair care, make up, soaps, deodorants – you name it. Even the tiny one near my apartment is filled to the brim with divine natural beauty products. So far I have tried AloeDent natural toothpaste (very good), Ere Perez rosehip oil lip gloss (loving it) and Dr. Hauschka's miracle-working concealer /

blemish corrector. I'm also pleased to report the entire range of Sukin is stocked at my shop, so I feel reassured I made the right decision with that purchase. I have a feeling I'm going to become a very frequent shopper. Actually, I've been quite jealous of North Americans and their access to Whole Foods and its Premium Body Care Quality Standards that apply to all products, ensuring the products are safe, environmentally sound, and still do their job[10]. Thankfully now I know where I can go to find equally eco-healthy products for myself Down Under.

I also bought some natural tea tree oil deodorant from the health food store. Aluminium is the active ingredient in most antiperspirants, which regularly contain parabens as well. Scientific studies have linked these chemicals to breast cancer and other tumours from oestrogen increases in breast tissue[11]. The FDA has yet to rule these ingredients unsafe[12], but the studies I've read are scary enough to make me try aluminium- and paraben-free deodorants for now. I'm a little nervous about this change, though. I'm even starting to sweat just thinking about not being protected by strong antiperspirant! I'm willing to experiment, but I exercise a fair bit and wonder how well the natural deodorant will work.

But really, with oily skin and greasy hair, can it really get much worse? Sorry Tyler!

GREEN BEAUTY DIARY DAY 22

Green beauty products purchased: 1
I feel: Unattractive. My hair seems to be getting greasier and greasier, I'm not sure I can last the recommended 6 weeks that it will take for my body to rebalance. My face is still breaking out like crazy; I don't really want to apply for any jobs right now because I'm feeling too self-conscious. And a bit moist thanks to the natural deodorant.
On the up side, I'm thrilled with my mascara purchases. Musq's mascara glides on silky smooth, and layers beautifully. Best of all it's SO easy to wash off, just requires water! I bought a tube of Korres as my beach-day waterproof option.

A happy side effect of researching safe and green beauty products has been extra bonding opportunities with my girlfriends. Maryanne and I have previously swapped favourite products (I gave her Lucas Paw Paw ointment years ago, and now Suvana, and she gave me a gorgeous natural body moisturiser), so I've emailed her the most troublesome ingredients to avoid. Do you know what? She was really happy to receive that email, and requested I share information as I learn – a small victory for the environment but a large victory for me!

Similarly, Kate asked my opinion on her shampoo – she'd picked it up at her chemist and it was one I hadn't seen at Priceline – and it fared pretty well. It was made in Australia, included organic ingredients, and didn't include SLS or mineral oils. I think it had fragrance, but overall it was a good option. I am so excited she's starting to join the movement, too.

I'm toying with the idea of blogging my research for my friends – I'm not sure if I can be that committed, but I feel like a lot of this information should be shared. Between Lillian, Kate and Maryanne's reactions so far, I am beginning to think that most of my girlfriends will appreciate this type of advice. And if what I'm learning is true, don't I owe it to all my loved ones to tell them about the dangers lurking in our beauty routines? I decide to take the risk and send a quick email about parabens:

> Hi Lovely Ladies,
>
> I try not to get up on my greenie-horse and preach too often, but the stuff I've been reading today is super scary and so I wanted to pass on a quick tip.
>
> When you are buying any cosmetics or body products (including shampoo, body lotion, bubble bath, etc) PLEASE avoid anything with Parabens. They can be labelled as Paraben or methyl-, ethyl-, propyl-, isopropyl- and butylparaben.
>
> We absorb these through our skin when we use the products, and there are a number of studies linking parabens to disrupting oestrogen and other hormones, even a couple studies that have linked them directly to breast cancer.

So please, keep yourselves safe and healthy, and avoid buying anything with parabens.

There are some other things we should avoid, but this is the area with the most scientific research to back it up, so I wanted to pass it on.

Okay, that's all, I hope you're all doing really great!

Xo Lisa

In response to my email I receive a number of emails back thanking me for the information, and one in particular saying I wasn't preachy at all (phew!). I also get an amazing phone call from Lillian:

"Hey Lise – have you heard of this book called *Gorgeously Green*? It's got this beautiful illustration of a pin-up girl on the cover," she asks excitedly.

"Yes! I love that book! That's where I get a lot of my information on green beauty products."

"I like the idea of the 'Green Goddess' club, I think we should do it, what do you think?"

The book suggests that women gather friends together on a regular basis and tackle one issue at each meeting – like trying eco-friendly makeup or shampoo, or learning about composting – and then use this network of 'Green Goddesses' to promote sustainability within their social networks.

"Well yeah, if you think others would be into it then I think we should totally do it. I already have lots of tips I can share," I say, as impressed as ever at Lillian's enthusiasm.

After a bit more chatting Lillian opens up even more, "You know Lise, I can see this as something I can really get passionate about. I don't know, maybe it was always inside me and now you've helped it come out. Growing up in Switzerland the environment was something that everyone took care of, so it wasn't seen as a 'movement'. Then I moved here and they don't seem to have it built into the culture the same way, so I forgot about it. Now I think I'm really ready to get right into it again."

I feel my insides glowing green with love, pride and happiness.

GREEN BEAUTY DIARY DAY 25

Green beauty products purchased: -1
I feel: Guilty, but almost back to my previously-gorgeous self after running back to Clinique for industrial strength toner to clear up my skin.
I'm getting the hang of using Sukin shampoo. I'm using Musq as my everyday mascara and continue to love it! I'm definitely a convert.
I'm still feeling a bit sweaty as I get used to using the deodorant as opposed to antiperspirant. I may have to try a few more brands; I think I'm smelly and it doesn't come 'naturally' to me to feel moist under my arms.
Happy that all the responses I received from my parabens email were grateful or inquisitive; excited to be finding the right voice to share my environmental tips with people.

In addition to the factual lessons about ingredients to avoid I'm beginning to understand that my patterns and habits must adjust to enable green living. Looking for makeup may no longer be as glamorous and carefree as walking up to the Napoleon Perdis or Kit counter and asking for a free makeover; gone are the days of buying hair care products from the salon, and I can kiss impulse purchases goodbye. I learned from my initial attempts at eco-shopping to "research first, buy second"; now it seems I need to add, "don't go to mainstream stores for your environmental purchases" to my eco-shopping mantra. (For now, anyway. I like to encourage mainstream stores to stock eco-products, and recently sent Coles a thank you note for stocking organic Fairtrade teas and organic cotton balls in hopes they start stocking more eco-goods.)

It also hasn't escaped me that if I were to adopt a completely green beauty routine I would forego most of these products altogether. I wouldn't need to find the most sustainable mascara or eco-friendly lip gloss because I'd stop wearing makeup and embrace my natural beauty. I'd reject shampoo and conditioner because my scalp's oils would naturally clean and moisturise my hair. And forget about toner, a natural vegetable soap would be all I needed to clean all of my skin, including my face. So instead of my current three-step facial routine I'd be down to one step for my whole body (imagine all the water I'd save!).

But let's come back to my reality, shall we? I've been wearing makeup for more than half my life. And risk my gorgeous hair by rejecting shampoo? You'd have to be joking. Ever since I got my first highlights and 'Rachel' haircut back in tenth grade I've loved experimenting with different colours and styles, all perfected with the latest rage in shampoo, conditioner and styling products. As far as I'm concerned, I've given up my highlights and luxurious shampoo, and that's as far as I go. For now, anyway.

I'm not sure if it's a self-esteem thing, because I do feel noticeably better when I make the effort to glam it up a bit, but it's definitely image-related. I don't feel like myself if I don't wear makeup and style my hair. And it's a lifestyle thing, too, because I find it fun to create different looks with my beauty tools. Makeup and hair have been key to my identity and so, for now at least, I feel good that I've been able to find green beauty substitutions.

I'm also very aware that, thanks to the media, we're surrounded by thousands of images of perfection every day and have been conditioned to strive for that look to achieve happiness, love and success. The academic in me knows that these beauty standards are unrealistic and harmful, and the advertiser in me knows they are fictional (I myself am guilty of directing a designer to Photoshop 'wrinkles' off an 18 year old model – shameful but true). Yet I still buy into this beauty myth[13]. Even if I wanted to, I doubt I could turn off my desire to look beautiful overnight. And I don't want to pretend that I don't value beauty because, for better or worse, I do, and my journey into environmentalism wouldn't be the same if it wasn't important to me.

Who knows if I'll ever overcome my obsession with beauty. I'm not really sure I want to. What's so wrong with wanting to look beautiful? (Insert frustrated feminist arguments here.) I want it all –

stunning looks and a healthy planet. So, armed with the help of my local health food store, *Gorgeously Green*, and the internet, I'll continue to tackle this challenge and prove you *can* have it both ways, sustainability and style, and keep sharing my tips with my friends so they can have it both ways, too.

Green groceries

"Um, are you sure you want to purchase this?" the beautiful Brazilian boy asks me from behind his unbelievably long eye lashes.

I'm smiling and nodding even before I see what he's pointing at.

$78.57 for olive oil!?

"Wow! Well, I can't exactly put it back, can I?"

The beautiful Brazilian blushes and chuckles in agreement. I'm at my local food Co-op and the beautiful Brazilian has just helped me fill up a two-litre tin canister I brought from home with local Hunter Valley organic olive oil; I'm sure the manager would frown upon me trying to pour it back into the barrel, something about health codes. Who knew my desire to make package-free hummus would be so expensive?

The beautiful Brazilian continues punching in prices for the rest of my items, carefully weighing each plastic takeaway container and glass jar I've set before him, as I nervously wait for the grand total. Tyler is not going to be impressed. When he came here last week he returned home bragging about how much money he had saved on bulk-bin rice, oats and coffee – I'm already up to eighty bucks with only olive oil! In my defence, it's two litres of really divine organic olive oil; maybe if I make something delicious for dinner with it Ty will overlook the fact that I spent so much money …

Now that I've settled into a (mostly) green beauty routine I'm ready to tackle my next set of eco-changes – greening my groceries. Food is an increasingly industrialised sector due to increased factory farming, packaged goods and convenience foods. In fact, groceries are responsible for 2/3 of all packaging waste[1] and food production ranks as one of the top five fuel consuming industries in the US[2]. Of course, it's also my personal archenemy after five years working for FMCG companies.

Like the other changes I'm adopting, greening my groceries involves more than just worrying about climate change. Films like *Food Inc.* and *Supersize Me* and books like *Fast Food Nation* and *The Omnivore's Dilemma*[3] highlight the complexities surrounding sustainable and ethical food as it relates to health, economics and animal and human rights. Despite the complexities, for now just one question guides my food choices:

Is this the lowest-carbon option on the menu?

It's a slightly different take on the question that guided my food choices during the low-carbohydrate craze of the early 2000's (around the same time I also stuck photos of Victoria's Secret models on the fridge for *thinspiration* – which sounds really horrible now that I see it in print). I find that seeking the lowest-carbon option typically leads to food choices that are also healthy and ethical, and I'm thankful the simplicity of my criteria makes it easy to adhere to while achieving great results.

So what is a low carbon diet? It's a diet with increased organic and local foods and decreased meat, dairy and packaged foods. It's such a simple formula, and I'm finding it quite easy to adjust.

I've already made significant changes to my meat consumption since having my eco-consciousness raised. These days I only eat meat about once a week and favour free-range chicken or pork over those gassy ruminants when I do partake. For a while I allowed myself beef once a month, but the last time I ate it (an organic, pasture-raised, gourmet beef burger) all I could think as I chewed was, *Eww, this is really meaty*. I couldn't finish it and I've had no beef since. I won't go so far as to say I'll never have it – there is something special about a perfect steak – but I will commit to only eating super eco-friendly beef (grass-fed, hormone-free, local) and only on very special occasions.

Similarly, I don't feel comfortable saying that I'm a vegetarian, and I'm not considering becoming a vegan. Instead of denying myself any foods altogether, they've become treats, and something I enjoy every now and then. I'm afraid if I say I can *never* have those foods, that one day I'll cave in and binge on them, and then fall back into my old habits. I'm much more comfortable with this reduction tactic, which feels very achievable and like something I can maintain for the long haul.

I've also made an attempt to lower my dairy consumption since recognising that dairy cows have the same biological eco-shortcomings as meat cows. I've switched to soymilk for my cereal, tea and coffee, and my latest 'guilty' pleasure is soy ice cream. Okay, it's no Ben & Jerry's, but it really is delicious in it's own way, especially when covered in fresh blueberries and pineapple and Fairtrade dark chocolate pieces. I admit I'm having a harder time giving up cheese, though; soy cheese just can't replace the gooey deliciousness of a bouche d'affinois or the punch of a true, sharp reggiano. I try and limit my cheese intake and keep to organic and local when I do succumb to my dairy desires.

I continually incorporate more and more organics into my diet, too. Organic products can be more expensive and difficult to find than their non-organic counterparts, but they also make a huge difference in achieving a low-carbon diet. If everyone converted just 10% of their diet to organic, it would be the equivalent of taking two million cars off the road each year[4] – surely I can achieve a 10% change, right?

It helps that I've discovered Lettuce Deliver – an online organic food store with an extremely lovable name that delivers direct to my door. Some items cost more but overall it's very affordable. Easy and convenient – such a refreshing occurrence in sustainable living!

Even better all the produce from Lettuce Deliver is packaging-free. I don't know if there's anything more wasteful than vegetables covered in plastic wrap and stuck on a Styrofoam plate. And what exactly is the point of shrink-wrapping avocados, anyway? Is it just so that I'm forced to buy two of them? I stopped using those flimsy produce bags in the grocery store long ago – it's really okay if my peaches and apples touch my tomatoes and cucumbers. If I need a bag, like for green beans or spinach leaves, I reuse a bag from home, always keeping a few produce bags tucked inside my reusable grocery bags so I am never without.

Herbs are another prime example of unnecessary packaging, not to mention waste. I never seem to use the entire bunch before they go off, so in addition to the excessive plastic I've wasted herbs and money, too. I hate throwing away wasted food. Conservatively estimated, Australians throw away more than $5.2 billion worth of food a year; it's estimated that household food waste is responsible for 5.25 mega tonnes of carbon annually, similar emissions to the manufacture of all iron and steel in Australia[5]. This means that when combined with emissions from food production, total pollution from our food is much higher than the seemingly 'dirty' iron mining industry. Statistics like these really call our food practices into question and make me glad I'm focusing on greening my groceries now. I am also getting some fabulous tips from the 'Love Food, Hate Waste' campaign like planning my meals, remembering to eat my leftovers and using vegetable scraps to make my own (free range) chicken stock.

Actually, I've been having a lot of fun with food these days. Take last night for example:

CHOP CHOP CHOP CHOP

"Hello….."

CHOP CHOP CHOP CHOP

"Lisa!"

CHOP.

"Hi babe, busy making salsa. I didn't hear you come in!"

It seems not a day goes by lately that Ty doesn't find me working on a new culinary creation; I was chopping with a vengeance and making the most out of my coriander before it bolts (that means 'going to seed' for us herb farmers, I recently started growing my own coriander, basil and chives). So far I've made several batches of salsa and flavoured many other dishes with the coriander, so even though I'm sad we're nearing the end of our time together I feel I definitely got my money's worth of that $5 starter plant I purchased a couple months ago.

"That seems like angry chopping, if that's possible."

"Ha ha, you're right, it is angry chopping. I'm frustrated with my job search," I admit with a small smile.

"And taking it out on the onions," he joked, "What's going on?"

"The only jobs recruiters are calling me about are design agencies or client-side roles in FMCG land. None of the places I really want to work are calling me back. I've been rejected by Greenpeace, World Vision and the World Wildlife Fund. I finally got in touch with a recruiter for one of the other non-profit jobs today, but they already have a shortlist of candidates with '*more appropriate qualifications*.'"

"I'm sorry…"

"Doesn't a burning passion count for anything these days?!"

"It will, somewhere, don't worry," he tried to console me.

"Anyway, tomorrow I have an interview at a design agency," I quietly added.

"What?! Why are you even going?" Ty asked me incredulously.

"I know, but the recruiter told me they do more than just FMCG, they have a couple banks and even a non-profit client, so I figure it's worth investigating. I'm tired of casual work; it's nearly been a year since I left the agency and I want a permanent job again. Plus, maybe

I'll be able to infiltrate the enemy and create environmental change from the inside."

"I think that may be *too* optimistic," Ty sighed, "but it's your choice, just please don't take something just for the sake of having a job, okay? We'll be fine as long as you do a bit of casual work here and there. It's more important that you're happy."

Could he be any lovelier?

"So, what else have you made today?"

At least that's what I *think* he said; it was a bit muffled through a bite of salsa fresca on an organic tortilla chip.

Prior to quitting my job I didn't take much of an interest in cooking so Ty was our family chef. Now that I'm home frequently between temp gigs and not bringing in much income I figure the least I can do is make dinner. It's all been made even easier by the fact that I'm really enjoying the creativity that planning low-carbon meals affords.

I've been making a number of things from scratch that I normally would've purchased pre-made, in packaging, and probably full of preservatives. A couple of my favourites are homemade salsa and hummus, and I can't imagine going back to store bought now that I've tasted the difference of fresh, natural products. I've also dabbled in making my own pasta sauce, using homegrown basil of course. And – ready for it? – dill pickles! I'm happy to report that my pickles now only contain cucumbers, salt, vinegar, garlic and dill – no nasty artificial preservatives in sight.

If I can't find a job soon I may become the greenies' answer to Martha Stewart (without that whole insider trading debacle).

After proof reading as many food labels as I have it's hard not to be sceptical of packaged foods and their hard-to-pronounce chemicals, including inside so-called 'natural' muesli bars and yoghurts. Now I have added motivation to reduce my packaged foods since, compared to whole foods like fruits, vegetables and grains, they require additional energy to process. On average it takes seven to ten times more energy to produce our food than we actually gain from eating it[6]; I'm happy to forgo packaged foods where I can to help reduce that particular energy requirement.

When I do have to buy something in packaging, like my soymilk, I'm strict about making sure the packaging is recyclable and not excessive. Even more important is that I do recycle it, and recycle it properly. Australia produces 4.2 million tonnes of packaging each year, and only about half of it gets recycled[7] – this is partly because some is made from non-recyclable products and partly because people aren't recycling or trying to recycle soiled packaging. It can be really confusing to know what can and cannot be recycled, especially since each town council has slightly different rules – I've stuck my council's guidelines on my fridge so they're always close at hand.

So, between the energy requirements of packaged foods, the chemicals and preservatives added to many products, and the waste generated from packaging, I was delighted to discover my local food Co-op, which has greatly reduced my need for packaged foods.

And now here I am, facing an $80 olive oil bill. I glance around the shop and think to myself that it doesn't *look* like the type of place where one could spend $80 on olive oil. If I were in foodie-heaven, more commonly known as David Jones Food Hall, I might expect these sorts of prices, but not here. Don't get me wrong, I love the Food Hall with its brightly lit wide aisles filled with gourmet delights from around Australia and the world, counters of prepared salads, sandwiches and sushi, and the drool-worthy cheese counter. I can picture the queue of busy suited-up office workers and socialites pushing to get their triple cream Brie and gourmet quince paste before the next person. And don't even get me started on the brilliant frenzy of the holiday season in the Food Hall – it's heaven! (Well, in an overconsumption sort of way.)

The Co-op is the antithesis of DJ's Food Hall. It's quite small, only two short aisles, and rather dim. There are a couple dozen large opaque plastic barrels stacked in roughly-constructed wooden shelves, hundreds of glass jars filled with a variety of dry goods and baskets holding a small selection of organic produce, some tenderly swaddled in sheets and blankets to protect against bruising. I have cautiously walked passed by the shop before, peeking in every time, unsure if I could enter. What was this place? Some sort of club? There are no bags, no carts, and the people inside don't look like my type of people (not that there is just one type of person inside – today it's a mix of long-skirted Birkenstock-footed mums, sporty-spices in their running shoes and Lululemon cropped leggings, and backpackers). One day I thought, who are my people these days anyway? I'm in limbo. So I decided to just go inside and I discovered that the food Co-op[8] is nothing short of an eco-foodie's wonderland.

This tiny shop enables a nearly package-free food existence. In this magical place the bins runneth over with local organic oats, dried beans, pasta, dried fruit, olive oil, spices, organic produce, eco-friendly soaps and artisan breads. Shopping here supports local and organic farmers while also greatly reducing packaging and preservatives. Volunteers, like the beautiful Brazilian boy, run the shop to ensure prices are kept as low as possible. It's also a great place to stay up to date on community eco-news and encounter like-minded individuals. Some are here for the (usually) low prices, others for sustainability or health reasons, and overall there is a strong sense of positive community within the store.

My relationship with the Co-op is not all love hearts and romantic poetry, though; it's a bit more complicated. Here's a quick run-down:

I love the access to organic, local, unprocessed, unpackaged foods – I feel my eco-footprint shrinking just by walking through the door.

I love learning about eco-friendly options I've never previously considered (like bringing your own egg carton to collect free-range eggs).

I love thinking with every scoop of organic package free oats or almonds "Take that Nestle! Take that Unilever and Kraft and all other giant food conglomerates! I can bypass you and eat a healthy, well-balanced and low-carbon diet!"

I hate the amount of organisation required to shop at the Co-op. For example, today's visit required me to consider the following:

What time is it? The Co-op has very limited hours, generally 10am to 3pm, but that's only if they are able to find volunteers

to staff the shop. It's best to arrive sometime between noon and 1pm just to be safe.

Do I have containers with me? I have plenty of containers to use at the Co-op; the problem is they are kept at home, so I can't decide while I'm out and about to pop into the Co-op. There are a few donated containers there, and some small brown sacks you can purchase, but it's definitely best to go prepared.

What am I wearing? No, there's no dress code, but shopping at the Co-op requires bending low to scoop oats and beans, reaching up high to grab spices and taking a very hands-on approach to filling olive oil containers and collecting honey, so it's best to avoid short skirts or dresses. Also, by the time all my containers are filled my bags are quite heavy, so flats are required to negotiate the walk home.

Do I have at least an hour to spare? The Co-op always takes longer than I think it's going to. Upon arrival you must wash your hands and dry them with the supplied cloth towels because you'll be handling food. Then you have to pre-weigh and label all your containers, because everything is charged by weight. The large opaque bins are not labelled with photos, only words, so I have to read my way around to locate the oats, lentils and chickpeas. Then of course each item must be entered manually at the cash register, discounting for the weight of the empty container; it's definitely slower than those nifty self-scanners at Coles or Woolies.

How are my math skills today? Because everything is sold by weight, and there are three different prices on everything (non-member, member, and volunteer), it's harder to keep track of how much I'm spending than when I'm at the grocery store. Hence the $80 olive oil.

Having said all that …

I love the feeling of empowerment that comes with supporting independent farmers and growers instead of global food corporations, while simultaneously supporting the environment. So even though it takes me awhile to get myself ready and then actually shop, I really do feel part of the environmental movement, and it makes the effort worthwhile.

I love and hate a few items available at the Co-op that I haven't yet embraced, like toothpaste made of clay (seriously, clay?), and reusable cloth sanitary napkins or moon cups, the waste-free tampon replacement. I just can't. I know it's hypocritical, after I've been talking about how great it is to forego wasteful packaging and disposable items, but the thought of it is too much for me to bear. I'm more likely to embrace the no 'poo hair care method before I start using moon cups. I'll stick with organic cotton feminine supplies for the time being – which thankfully the Co-op also stocks. In a way, I enjoy these reminders of how far I've yet to go if I'm to embrace a truly package- and waste-free existence.

I especially enjoy the package-free breakfast that the Co-op enables. Tyler deserves all the credit for this one – he bought a large glass canister to keep the finished product in, and he's the one who goes to the Co-op every fortnight with all the necessary containers to collect the various ingredients that go into my favourite muesli. It's always my favourite because we change which dried fruits and nuts go into each batch depending on our mood – muesli on demand and it's all organic and package-free. My favourite muesli at the moment includes:

- 9 C oats
- 2 C bran
- ¼ C linseed (So healthy for us ladies)
- ½ C chopped almonds
- 1 C cranberries
- 1 C chopped dried pear
- ½ C coconut shreds
- ¼ C sunflower seeds

Is it wrong to want a bowl of this at 4.45 in the afternoon?

⚬⧷𝆑🦷🕯🜂🜊𝆑💍👁👄💡♡

"Hello my dear," I answer with a smile when Maryanne's name pops up on my phone.

"Oh-my-gosh-Lisa-you-will-never-guess-what-I'm-about-to-tell-you-about-Brisbane-airport!" she rushes.

"What?!" panicked that there is some crazy security breach happening right now.

"I've been walking around for at least thirty minutes and cannot locate a single recycling bin anywhere!" Phew – only an eco-emergency, "I was already annoyed with myself for buying a plastic bottle of water tonight, and now I can't even find a place to recycle it! This is totally irresponsible behaviour from an airport in an Australian capital city. Think about *all the food* they sell here," I can just picture her gesturing with her hands, squinting her eyes and bobbing her head as she highlights her point, "I mean, there are so many people just sitting here, waiting for a flight, buying food, and there is no place to recycle *anything*. I am just livid!"

"That is really horrible – like it would be so hard for them to put some recycle bins around the food areas at the very least," I commiserate.

"The airline industry really could do so much more! I mean, on my way up here yesterday I asked the flight attendant if the mini water bottle they gave me got recycled at the end of the flight, and do you know what she said?"

"Ummm…"

"She said she didn't think so! Can you believe it?! She told me that everything – the bottles, the food containers, the foil, the utensils – all went into the same bin. It's just disgusting. I mean, it's the *airline industry*," she emphasises, "they already do enough damage with the pollution from flights, the least they can do is *recycle*. I mean, it must be millions of bottles *every single day*[9]," her tone is hushed, frustrated.

"Oh!" I've caught her agitation, dragged myself off the sofa and am now pacing the floor of my apartment, "I just realised. So many of the bottles are probably making their way to Plastic Island!"

"What? What's that?"

"It's this place in the Pacific, like in the middle of nowhere, a thousand miles north of Hawaii or something, where there's a *huge* collection of bits of plastic floating in the water because of the way the ocean currents work – our garbage gets stuck there. It's called the North Pacific Gyre."

"There's a whole island made out of plastic? That's disgusting!"

"Well, it's not technically an island. It's worse – it's more like a soup than an island. Apparently you occasionally see larger pieces of plastic floating around, but most of the plastic is breaking down into tiny pieces, sometimes even microscopic, and polluting the ocean. Then birds and fish are eating these colourful little pieces of plastic thinking it's food-"

"And then we eat the fish!" she finishes my sentence.

"Yep – it's horrible. I watched this documentary[10] on the scientist who discovered it – it was really sickening – and sad. So many of the fish and sea birds are dying from eating the plastic."

After another ten minutes of lively discussion Maryanne convinces me we need to draft letters and petitions to airports and airlines expressing our environmental concerns and suggesting small actions they can take. It is one of those optimistic and passionate conversations when, despite all the odds, you believe anything is possible.

And then Maryanne says, "I know! We can try and get onto *Sunrise*! I bet they would love to talk to us about this!"

"You're right! We can send them copies of all the letters we draft and keep them informed if we get any responses – they would *love* a story about two everyday Aussies taking on big corporations."

(Hmmm, what exactly am I agreeing to? I may have gotten carried away in the moment. . .)

After a bit more ranting and scheming we say goodnight, determined to take on big polluting businesses and bring the environment out of the closet.

Maryanne's phone call is another stark reminder that food packaging is everywhere – it's not just in our groceries, it's strewn throughout our culture in convenience and takeaway foods, too. I try to get around this by toting around my treasured stainless steel water bottle and reusable coffee cup. I even have my own containers for takeaway food – the restaurant owners tend to look at me like I'm crazy but usually agree to put my food in them (though on occasion I've been told that health code requires them to put food in their own containers).

The lack of recycling bins in public places is also a disgrace. I can't tell you the number of times I've carried home a juice bottle or plastic container because I can't find the appropriate recycling bin, but waiting in an airport you'd be hard pressed to find anyone who's willing to bring their food packaging on the flight with them in hopes of recycling it at the other end. I find it inexcusable in this day and age that our cities aren't capable of taking our recyclable products when we're anywhere but at home.

Our society certainly has a long way to go to make green-living easy and mainstream. And while it's not hard to blame governments and councils, I feel like it's up to us citizens to demand changes through our personal behaviour and beyond – like letter writing and other community campaigns – in order to transform our convenience-based society. I'm thankful that Maryanne is paying more attention, and that she's reminded me to keep pushing for these changes, because while I am making great strides in my personal life I don't want to forget the bigger picture: change at a societal level.

"Dominic Flash," my peppy recruiter answers his phone.

"Oh hi Dominic, it's Lisa Heinze, you asked me to ring you after my interview today?"

"Yes, Lisa! Tell me, how do you think it went?" Dominic booms in my ear with his radio announcer-like voice.

"Well, um, okay I guess," I hesitate.

I'm sure as far as a non-environmentalist goes it was good. It was my second interview with one of the city's up and coming agencies. Last week I saw the beautiful studio filled with vibrant artwork and felt the lively energy throughout, and I couldn't help but sell myself like the good little marketer that I am. It didn't even occur to me at the time to question whether I liked the job, like a moth to a flame I was wooed by the agency lifestyle once again. I just wanted to hang out in that space as long as possible, be surrounded by cool people in a cool atmosphere and have people think I was cool just because I worked there. Today the director talked about various clients, dangling a lot of impressive brand names in front of me, and introduced me to a couple of designers and the creative director. I read the signs – the job was mine if I wanted it.

But I didn't.

Although the agency had some slightly altruistic clients on their roster, they wanted me to do what they believe I do best and sell junk food to innocent consumers. When I asked about the non-profit clients I was told that they belonged to an employee who had recently been promoted, and that all the 'best' clients, the 'fun' clients, were saved for this role; she seemed surprised when I told her I was passionate about the environment, and at a loss for what to say in response.

I played along and finished the interview, and I walked home feeling a bit dirty because I'd come so close to walking straight back into my old world. There's been a fundamental shift inside me – besides just feeling that many FMCG products deceive consumers and waste resources and packaging, I'm completely convinced that the process is just so wrong. It's healthier for us, for the environment, for our waistline and our wallets to take things back to basics, back to a way of life that involves whole foods and fewer chemicals, and I can't work somewhere that enables the opposite. After everything I've learned, and all the salsa, hummus and muesli (and pickles!) I've made, I can't even consider changing that world from the inside, I loathe it too much. And after having that phone call with Maryanne the other night I'm all the more convinced I must focus my energies on the environment. I can only hope that some other eco-warriors will be helping to change that system from the inside, because we definitely can use help from all angles.

"Well, I just got off the phone with the client, and they loved you! They are willing to offer you the role at $80K plus super, and put you on a plan to achieve $95K by the end of the year," Dominic Flash booms.

"Oh…" that's a lot of money…

"I know, I know, you want more money. Leave it with me, I'm sure I can get them up to $90K and then six figures by the end of the year."

"No, wait!" Deep breath, "I don't want the job."

"What do you mean, it sounds like it all went so well, you'll be a perfect fit," he sounds so confused.

"It's a great agency, the manager is fantastic, they do beautiful work, but I can't do FMCG anymore. My passion's not there. I thought that if I could work on the non-profit or even bank clients it would be a good fit, but they told me today that's not available."

"That's not what you do; you have such strong FMCG experience."

"I'm sorry. Thank you for your help on this one, but it's not the role for me," thinking I've let him down easily.

"To be honest Lisa, I don't think I have any roles that will suit you. I suggest you look elsewhere and not apply to any more of my listings."

"Oh, I. . ."

"Good luck," *click*.

Farewell Dominic Flash, and farewell FMCG, for good. I guess I've finally done it, haven't I? I have definitely passed the point of no return into full-fledged environmentalism. In honour of my renewed commitment to a world free of packaged, processed, preservative-filled goods, I grab some containers and head to the Co-op to find inspiration for dinner.

☙ ⌀ ☖ ♀ ⚷ ♫ ♀ ☼ ☕ ♀ ♡

"Hi doll!" Eve says. She gives me a hug when I arrive at the coffee shop she co-owns with her sisters, "how did it go?"

Eve used to be my client at the agency, and she left around the same time I did to open the shop. They've been going for a little over a year and have already won awards for their coffee roasting – I am so proud of them! I've come by for some lunch after my first interview with an amazing green organisation, the Green Building Council of Australia.

I hadn't heard of the company before I saw the job ad, but a review of their website told me everything I needed to know, including that it was the perfect workplace for me. It's a non-profit organisation that operates an environmental rating system for buildings; since buildings account for 23% of global greenhouse gas emissions[11] it's a very important industry to make sustainable. They encourage a mix of innovation and passive design to create greener buildings, a blending of modern design and technology with basic environmental principles to get the most impact. In other words, they encourage buildings to incorporate sustainability with style.

Once I stepped off the elevator for my interview I was even more convinced I belonged there. The office, known as the GreenHouse, overlooks Hyde Park and Sydney Harbour, not exactly what I'd expected when I answered an ad for a non-profit environmental organisation. More importantly, the interior design of the place is fantastic, using a mix of refurbished furniture with modern pieces and an abundance of plants, and I felt it was the ideal location for a recovering style-addict to continue to green her life.

"I think it went well – I'm definitely keen to work there," I tell Eve, "They've created these rating tools for buildings to make sure they get designed and built to really high environmental standards, it's pretty amazing stuff."

"I'm sure they loved you, don't worry."

"I hope so!" I'm still on a bit of a nervous high, "anyway, we'll see how it goes. How are you?"

"Great, so busy, and here, I have a present for you – a Vella Nero Keep Cup!"

"Oh you got them!"

Keep Cups are the most amazing invention – quirky reusable coffee cups that come in a variety of colours (you can even design your own on their website). They fit under the heads of espresso machines, so baristas don't actually mind using them – no more paper cups being used to brew the coffee and then tossed into the bin! Companies can get them branded, too, which is what Eve has done. They are made of safe food grade plastic so they are lightweight, and can be recycled if you ever need to discard one. Even better, their independent Life Cycle Assessment demonstrates that in one year of substituting a Keep Cup for disposable cups you use only half the carbon, one third the water, and half the energy; the numbers improve even more over the expected four-year lifespan of the cups. There is enough plastic in 28 plastic disposable lids to create one Keep Cup – what else do you need to know?

"They are flying off the shelf. The other morning I looked up and saw about eight of them all lined up from a group of our usual customers – you would have loved it!"

It was Lillian who first told me about Keep Cups; she forwarded me an email from a trend-watching newsletter, and I forwarded it onto Eve. I'll have to make sure I tell Lillian, she'll be so pleased. I love being a witness to these eco-connections being made around me and seeing more of my friends learn how to embrace environmentalism in their lives.

I sit back with my soy latte and tell Eve all the details of my interview, butterflies still flying around my body as I think about the possibility of working at such an amazing organisation... fingers crossed I get the job!

Sustainable fashion

This dress looked amazing on the hanger, but now that I've tried it on it's just not doing it for me. I hate when that happens. The dress is ivory with a feminine fuchsia and lavender floral pattern running across the bottom hem, which lands just at my knee, and, in quintessential vintage style, is cinched at the waist and very flattering to a feminine figure. But the neckline is a tad too high and the fabric across my chest is a tiny bit too snug so it looks like I have a uni-breast. It's very obvious the dress is not "now" and I definitely don't feel like myself wearing it. It's a shame, it's a great quality frock from Grandma Takes a Trip – one of the best vintage shops in Sydney. At $80, the price may be high compared to other vintage dresses, but when I think about the $400 designer dresses I'd crave elsewhere, it's a steal.

I've never really been a vintage lover – admirer, yes; purchaser, no. I could never get over the patience required, the potential tailoring or the smell (you know it, that distinctive musty mothball scent). None of it appeals to my very modern sensibilities; I'm used to seeing what I want in a magazine and buying it (or an affordable version of it) immediately. Plus my personal style tends more edgy and contemporary than overtly feminine, and I haven't been able to find much of my style in secondhand shops in the past. However, I start work on Monday, and I can't imagine starting a new job without a new outfit, so I've come vintage shopping in hopes of finding a 'reused' new outfit for my first day in the office.

That's right – I got the job!

Shortly after my second interview the HR manager rang with an offer, which I promptly accepted. I am now the newest member of the marketing team at the Green Building Council of Australia (GBCA), and couldn't be more thrilled. I am so glad I came to my senses and rejected the agency job last month; I'm exactly where I'm meant to be right now.

I decided to begin my secondhand shopping day in vintage-shopping Mecca (more commonly known as Crown Street, Surry Hills) at Grandma Takes a Trip because it almost makes me forget I'm in a secondhand shop. Natural daylight streams into the airy showroom (which also means there's little chance of bad lighting hiding an old stain), they tend to play modern, current music and the mannequins are always dressed in timeless gowns so immaculate that it's hard to imagine they are pre-loved. Everything in the store is colour-coded, which I find very visually appealing, and it also helps me shop because I know what colours look best on me. I've been in a number of times but have never made a purchase – I'm hoping today I will!

It didn't take long for me to collect a few items to try on (from the white, yellow and pink sections) and hit the changing area tucked into a sunlit corner of the shop's upper level. Now as I stare at my unfamiliar reflection I am filled with mixed emotions. I'm excited to be shopping again; it's been way too long since I've purchased clothing for myself besides yoga pants, and even that was many, many months ago. But I'm also a little anxious – will I be able to find something that suits my style and helps me fit in at my new workplace? I want to be taken seriously as an environmentalist and not seen as a conspicuous consumer, but I still want to represent myself as a woman of style. I think a cool vintage dress or blouse could be just the thing to create this sustainably stylish image, but this dress is not going to cut it. I take advantage of the natural light to examine my face and am happy to see my eco-makeup holding up quite well – this morning I kept it simple with just a little Dr Hauschka's concealer, Musq mascara and mineral powder, and Ere Perez lipbar – you'd never guess it wasn't the department store stuff.

I wiggle out of the dress and try on a pretty mustard silk top with ruffles running down the front; the tag says it's from the 1970s. I can picture it looking great with skinny black pants or a pencil skirt, and it's definitely closer to my personal style than the dress. Damn, the sleeves are too short. They don't quite meet my wrists and I don't think the shirt is long enough to tuck into my pants. Something else I hate about vintage shopping – nothing comes in another size. Well, on to the next item.

This one's a vibrant carnation pink day dress dotted with small red flowers. The v-neck really suits my body shape, unfortunately it's definitely too short for me to wear to work. What a shame.

Oh well, it's only the first shop. There's half a dozen more for me to check out in this neighbourhood. On my way out, I spy a really great scarf. Very 'Hermes' with a bold orange and white geometrical pattern. It's only $15 – things are looking up! I make my purchase and wander next door.

Ugh. This store represents everything I dislike about vintage shopping. It's dark, the clothes are really squished together and the sales kids seem completely detached from the activity in the store. Is it really that difficult to say "hello" to a customer? I poke around for a few minutes, but the vibe of this place encourages me to walk out the door before I've even pulled anything off the racks.

I pop in and out of three more shops without having any luck – the clothes are either too dated, too short or too crammed together to look at properly – and I'm nearing vintage shopping fatigue, a common ailment among vintage novices I'm sure.

I find myself in C's Flashback, my final destination today, and put all my faith into these two rooms of pre-loved clothes. It's no Grandma Takes a Trip, but seems to have items more in line with what I'm looking for – things that can be worn into a corporate office, not just hanging out a tea house or working in a creative space in Surry Hills or Newtown. After a couple more "not quite" dresses

I come across a really unique jumper. It's short-sleeved and has a wide cowl neck and features a zigzagging line pattern, alternating black and multicolour, woven from a combination of autumnal shades. It is so comfortable and so distinctive and so, well, *me*. Who'd have thought? If I didn't know it was circa 1970s I would've thought it came from The Corner Shop or perhaps a cutting-edge Melbourne boutique. It's only $50, which I gladly pay for this timeless funky piece. It will go with so many things in my wardrobe and its perfect for my first day on the job.

After a few hours, lots of patience and too many tiny fitting rooms to count, I'm still not in love with vintage shopping, but it's growing on me.

☞ ∅ ⛏ ℘ ⚖ ⚚ ♀ ☼ ⚭ ♀ ♡

"Do you read *Peppermint*?" Piper asks me with a smile, blue eyes sparkling with a hint of mischief.

"No, what is it?" I ask, leaning over the lunch table for a look.

"You'll love it!" she exclaims, "it's a fashion magazine that has only sustainable fashion and makeup. It's really hard to find in the newsagent so I have a subscription. You can take it home tonight if you want!"

"Are you serious?" I ask with glee, "thank you so much!"

A few minutes later Piper heads back to her desk, sliding me her *Peppermint* as she goes. Printed just above the title are the words "fresh green fashion" – I love it already! A fashion magazine with all the beauty and none of the guilt, who would've thought? Inside this issue is a feature on a super role model – meaning she's beautiful for what she does as opposed to solely what she looks like – Lisa Shannon, an American activist fighting for the rights and dignity of women of the Congo. So inspirational. The pages are filled with eco and ethical options of everything from clothing and makeup to books and movies and even a little something for the fellas and the kiddies, and I can't wait to devour the content on my way home tonight.

It's printed on 100% FSC (Forest Stewardship Council) certified recycled paper using eco-friendly inks and no additional processes, and 35 cents of the issue price is donated to a charity, this issue it was East Timor Women Australia, so this magazine is sustainable from every perspective.

I've only been at my job for a couple of weeks but I've already learned the significance of FSC certification; it's internationally recognised as the most rigorous environmental and social standard for responsible forest management for timber and paper resourcing, protecting against deforestation and working with local forestry communities to protect workers and respect cultures. When something is 'FSC recycled' like *Peppermint* it means the product was manufactured with 100 percent recycled fibre of which at least 85 percent is post-consumer recycled material.[1] FSC is becoming more and more popular, which is fantastic, and a number of book publishers and greeting card manufacturers are also ensuring their products are FSC certified, so I always look for the symbol to be assured I have selected a truly sustainable option.

Flicking through *Peppermint,* even for these few minutes, has further fuelled the shopping urge that originated after just one week of working at GBCA. I hate feeling like I'm not fashionable anymore, and I don't like wearing clothes I've owned for so long. It's terribly boring. Now that I have a stable workplace I'm totally craving more clothing options. I know I shouldn't over-consume and I doubt my colleagues are judging my clothing, but I can't help it, I feel dowdy and out of date. I sense a shopping spree coming on! I am a dedicated greenie, but I was a style addict first and I want my image back. I didn't realise that being unemployed had helped me ease into environmentalism from a shopping perspective – a forced hiatus if you will. Hopefully *Peppermint* can feed my fashion fix without me blowing this whole sustainable-living thing in one decadent afternoon in Paddington.

The fantastic eco-tips from people at work are just the start; the past couple weeks at my new job have been a total whirlwind – and I'm loving every minute of it! If I thought I understood sustainability before it's now clear I was only scratching the surface. I now find myself at the eco-epicentre and my knowledge is expanding exponentially as I live out my dream of being a full time environmentalist. And if I thought things couldn't get any better than working for this amazing organisation, on my first day my boss nominated me to be the Marketing department's representative on the internal sustainability team. A member of the internal sustainability committee of a sustainable organisation – can it get any greener than that?! To top it all off, one of the hard-core greenies paid me the greatest compliment by expressing his excitement that, "finally we have a Marketing person who understands sustainability." I'm ecstatic!

I love being surrounded by other greenies all day, too; I feel like I've come home to the fold. It's so wonderful to not have to explain why I don't eat beef or why I use my own mug – we don't all follow the same eco-practices, but we get each other, so I'm not constantly explaining my choices. My preconception that all greenies are hippies is completely shattered, too. There are about 40 people in the Sydney office, and they're all varying shades of green, and express themselves in nearly as many ways. We're here working together on innovative projects to green the built environment, yet we still have unique identities. My desire to find the perfect vintage outfit to wear on my first day now seems so naïve.

To top it all off, everyone here is so *nice*. I've never worked someplace where all the employees are so friendly and kind and treat each other with such respect. Compared to the sometimes-catty world of advertising and design this is like an alternate universe. Is everyone really this nice? I suppose most of us are here because we want to make a difference to the environment, so maybe that means there's no need for petty office politics? I hope so. I'm such a happy little greenie right now.

☞ ∅ ⚱ ♕ ⚖ ⚘ ♀ ☉ ☕ ☙ ♡

I wrap up another inspiring day at work and head to The Rocks to catch up with Ty and some of the gang after the boys' basketball game. They have played in a Thursday night competition for years now, and beers at the pub after the game are nearly as important as the game itself.

I feel a bit nervous, I haven't hung out with our group as a whole very much since Beefgate, nor have I seen many friends since I started my new job. In the past I'd seriously consider buying a new outfit to boost my self-esteem, but since that's not exactly a green choice I stayed with an old fave from my wardrobe. Actually, work was so busy today I didn't have the time to obsess about it – I did touch up my eco-makeup before heading out, but that's standard practice when going out after work.

"Hey Lisa," Randall mock-sighs comically as he sits next to me outside the Australian Hotel, "how's it going?"

"Good, mate. You?" I am happy to see him and I relax immediately.

"Oh, you know, great, busy, blah-blah," he rattles off, gesturing in his very New-Yorker way.

"I've started my new job – I work just around the corner from you!" In a funny twist of fate my office of hard-working greenies is on the same block as Randall's tower of fashion, gossip and shopping magazines.

"Cool. Oh, I, uh, started using my own coffee mug," he adds, very nonchalantly.

"*You have?!*" I shriek, elated.

"Yeah. I finally said to myself, *forget about what your co-workers think, you really want to do something, so do it.* So, I just started doing it."

"I love it! How's it going?"

"Really well. No one at the office has even said anything, and the first time I handed my mug to my barista he didn't even blink. Actually, it's been easier than I thought it was going to be."

"Randall, it makes me so happy to hear this!" I feel like hugging him, but no one likes a desperate greenie.

"You know, it makes me feel really good, to know I'm contributing a little bit to the environment," he continues, "It makes me wonder if I should try to do something more?"

"Well, you came to right woman," I say cheekily, "have you switched to compact fluorescent light globes? That's a pretty painless change that has a big impact – something like using 20% of the power and lasting ten times longer."

"Oh I don't know. Aren't they really dark?" he asks suspiciously.

"Well, not anymore," I laugh. I can totally appreciate where he is coming from, especially remembering some of the early bulbs, "and now they have a *warm white* option that's pretty similar to regular light bulbs so you don't feel like you're inside a dingy convenience store."

"Thank God."

Hearing Randall openly talking about using his own mug and wanting to do more is exactly what I need to set me at ease, and I settle into the comfort of spending time with good friends.

I'm still floating as I try to fall asleep, imagining Randall bringing his own mug into the sparkling core of consumerism of his magazine's offices, influencing the glam-girls he works with, just as I dreamed all those months ago. Did he just need to get used to the idea and build up some extra self-esteem at work? Or is he identifying more with me and less with his co-workers? Perhaps a bit of both.

Maybe he realised he could maintain his image, fit in with his work colleagues and still do this one thing for the environment. Just like my colleagues, who spend the majority of their day working toward environmental sustainability but may not use their own mug or worry about eco-fashion, 'Green' isn't their entire identity, only part of it. I'm really proud of Randall for overcoming his fear of rejection, and a bit chuffed with myself for giving him the idea to do it in the first place. Maybe I'm not such a hopeless activist after all.

Ring a ding a ding a ding!

Sophie is ringing the bell at the reception desk in the GreenHouse, "Time to clothes swap everyone!"

A couple weeks ago Sophie organized a clothes swap in the office, and today at least a dozen of us brought in gently used clothes, shoes and accessories. I brought in a beautiful knit Witchery skirt that I've only worn twice and a handbag I haven't used for years, but nothing else fit my giveaway criteria: unworn in over a year; in good condition; not a timeless wardrobe piece.

We have no strict rules at the swap, it's a free for all, and even if you didn't contribute anything you can peruse the collection. Any items left at the end of the day get donated to St Vincent's. Since I know the stats on yearly clothing donations from my initial study of fashion figures, I hope we're able to swap the lot.

"Oh my God it looks just like a real op shop!" someone exclaims.

"Look at all this stuff! This will take ages to look through!"

We've filled the entire boardroom with items in various sizes, styles and colours – it really is amazing to see such an array of clothing spread across eight tables. Someone has lovingly separated the items into shoes, accessories, tops, dresses, skirts, pants and casual wear. Where to begin?!

I find a few items with potential and take them into the ladies room to try on.

Fuchsia sleeveless top with ruffles down the front: perfect fit, perfect colour, perfectly playful. I'll take it!

Long kelly green skirt with pink and white flowers: doesn't quite fit around my hips, but if I hoist it up and wear a belt . . . yep, a great strapless sundress.

Black button up shirt: nope, a bit too snug and the sleeves are too short.

Black cotton harem pants: a bit big, but they're so comfy and will be perfect for lounging at home so I'm taking them.

Can I take three items? I only brought in two. I feel a bit greedy. The girls encourage me to take them all home, though, finders keepers.

Okay, twist my arm.

As I return to my desk with my goodies I feel something strange and familiar welling up inside…

Ah! That's it!

The unbridled joy that comes from shopping for pleasure!

I didn't have to read labels or think about where anything came from because everything is secondhand. It is even better than vintage shopping, because nothing is that old and plenty of pieces are still entirely in fashion. Really, I am saving things from the landfill, giving them a second life, and performing a good eco-deed. It's delightful to simply find clothing items that I like without the eco-guilt or (even better) spending money. I think it may have even halted my urge to go on a shopping spree – for now, anyway.

Clothes swaps are a great way to maintain personal style sustainably. The Clothing Exchange is an Australian organization that kick-started the trend in 2004, organising swaps for budget and eco-savvy fashionistas, and these days plenty of work, social and community groups are arranging their own clothes swaps. The Clothing Exchange has strict quality control, meaning only wearable items are allowed. At each event every garment you donate earns you a button to swap for another item – there are no prices attributed to anything, it's a one for one exchange. So whether you attend an event arranged by groups like the The Clothing Exchange or hold a swap in your office or neighbourhood, it's a fantastic way to get some new items in your wardrobe without succumbing to fast fashion or parting with your hard-earned cash. I have a feeling swapping will play a prominent role in my future style.

⌒∅♈♊⚏♫♀☼⌒♀♡

Gaia has recently returned to work after being on maternity leave, and to me she embodies her name perfectly, a real earth mother. On her first day back I overhear her comment on her dress, "This was my first attempt at sewing my own clothes using eco-fabrics"; I knew immediately I could learn a lot from her.

And today she shouts across the office:

"Lisa, you are totally pulling off that look like no one else could!"

I have arrived.

I feel like my old, stylish self again and I'm especially excited to be able tell her I am wearing an eco-ensemble.

I'm wearing a new (used) dress from Zoo Emporium's bargain basement – literally in their basement – that only cost $35. It's a mauve long-sleeve number, with wide shoulders, a cinched waist and hits just below the knee. I had it tailored to remove shoulder pads that made the shoulders a bit too wide – this brought the total price of the dress up to $65, still a bargain for something so unique. I picked it up yesterday and couldn't wait one more day to wear it. How lucky are we eco-fashionistas that styles come back around? I mean, honestly, who ever would've thought the wide shoulders trend of the 80s would make a comeback? And yet here they are. I also bought a mustard yellow shoulder-padded jumper on my latest vintage excursion.

Today I've paired the dress with grey tights, grey suede ankle boots from two seasons ago (I've recently had them resoled and the heel tips replaced to lengthen their life), a neutral belt and a chunky loop scarf from American Apparel that's black, white and grey tie-dye cotton.

I share with Gaia where I got my new/used dress and sweatshop-free scarf, and we talk about how fun it is to be able to score these finds. She tells me about all the toys she bought her little girl for under $5 at the Salvos last weekend. There is a real culture of celebrating reuse at work (another woman admitted to finding her child's new bicycle in the neighbourhood clean up piles on her street) and I feel so fortunate to work somewhere I am surrounded by like-minded people to share my eco-shopping success stories.

I'm definitely coming into my own when it comes to vintage shopping, too. I'm learning to be patient and not expect to find exactly what I'm looking for on any given trip. I'm also trying to be open-minded about what will fit my personal style and accept that I won't necessarily buy something every time I go shopping. Learning to love vintage shopping allows me to participate in my favourite hobby, just with slightly different rules. Lillian has been shopping with me, too, and over the weekend we had a blast browsing shops and drinking tea – just like the good old days.

~∅🗣🗣⚖🗝⚘🕯👁👁💡♡

I haven't seen Beefeater since Beefgate, but tonight the entire crowd has come together for Lance's graduation celebration. I haven't been avoiding Beefeater, but so much has been happening in both our lives that it's been easy to miss each other. As we attempt to talk I sense our mutual discomfort and our small talk quickly stalls.

Thankfully Lance's American fiancé (who was not part of that fateful weekend) breaks the silence, "Oooohh, I'm going to have kangaroo – is it good?" she asks.

"When it's cooked well," I say, purposely avoiding the eco-answer while sitting so close to Beefeater.

"And it's really sustainable, too," adds Tyler. My heart sort of skips a beat.

I see out of the corner of my eye that Beefeater glances at Ty, surprised, then just as quickly looks back at the menu.

"Because of food miles?" asks the fiancé.

"Yes, but mostly because kangaroos don't emit methane like cows and sheep, and they're commonly harvested from the wild," I nervously say, and leave it at that – tonight is not about me, or the environment. Still, no one orders the beef.

A little while later the fiancé says to me, "You look gorgeous, by the way. I love that dress!"

"This ole' thing?" I tease, thankful for an eco-free conversation, "Thank you – I got it for my bachelorette party and still just love it!"

It may be the perfect little black dress, at least for me. It's a black matte silk Sass & Bide number, with ruching on top, delicate floating cap sleeves, and a flattering mini skirt. I've paired it with my favourite glittering platinum-gold shoes (actually, my wedding shoes!) and am feeling more glam than I have in a long while.

Now that I think about it, my dress is an eco-topic. Even though I'd have loved to buy a new dress for today's special occasion, I chose something I already own. My how times have changed!

If anything good came from my rampant fashion overconsumption in previous years it's that I'm able to ease my way into eco-fashion. Thanks to the massive size of my pre-greenie wardrobe and the fact that I tended to buy quality items, I have plenty of pieces that enable me to mix and match to create 'new' outfits all the time.

Though my bank account suffered at the time, I'm glad I have expensive taste. 'Quality not quantity' is an eco-fashionista concept that I didn't even realise I was practicing long before Al Gore and coffee cups rocked my world. Okay, maybe I was practicing quantity AND quality there for awhile, but for now I'll simply be grateful I have the pieces to help me coast into eco-fashion. (I'm also thankful to be equipped to purchase new green fashion thanks the stack of dog-eared *Peppermints* on my desk!)

Knock knock knock at my front door – quick! Light the soy candle!

"Hi, you must be Susie," I say as I welcome the adorable, petite blonde into my apartment, along with her cousin.

"Come on in. I have the dress in the bedroom for you to try it on, there's a huge mirror in there."

I guide the two girls into my bedroom where I've tried to set a luxurious and pampering scene with a candle and fresh flowers. This is potentially one of the biggest clothing purchases of her life, and I want to make it as special for her as it was for me when I first tried on this dress – my wedding dress.

Yes, you read that correctly, I'm selling my wedding gown.

I show her the easiest way to get into the gown, then tell her to take her time and snap as many photos as she likes before I shut the door.

Tyler and I got married pre-greenie days so I have no idea of the eco-credentials of the gown, and I have no desire to check now. All I know is that I thought it was the most beautiful dress in the whole world, and I still do. It's a fitted ivory lace gown from Spain with lovely, light chiffon straps and a delicate ribbon detail around the empire waist, accentuated with a flower constructed of roughly-cut chiffon and silver beading. Even just thinking of it makes me smile.

The dress was the focal point of my wedding plans. I was a somewhat reluctant bride, and very tempted to elope and avoid having a big wedding, but as a fashion lover the dress was something I could definitely get excited about. Everything else we organised – location, food, flowers, invitations – all had to match the dress. I figured it may be the only time in my life I could buy exactly what I wanted without limitations and I took full advantage of the opportunity, searching high and low for the perfect dress for me. When I put on that gown I felt like the most beautiful woman in the world.

But despite my love affair with the dress I never intended to keep it forever. I knew I'd never wear it again, and I'm not overly sentimental or traditional. The last thing I'd want is for my possible future daughter to feel pressured to wear this dress simply because I'd saved it. Mostly I didn't want any of the 'stuff' from the wedding to have more importance than the marriage itself. Besides, we'd always have the photos and the memories.

But what to do with such a gown?

I'd heard of brides who trashed their dresses in amazing photo shoots in the sea, waterfalls, mud or even paint, and I admit I was intrigued. But the gown is too beautiful to be destroyed and I couldn't bear the thought.

I considered taking it to a charity shop; bestowing a designer gown on a low budget bride sounded terribly altruistic. But I couldn't help but think of all the old wedding gowns I'd seen over the years at costume parties splattered with fake blood and torn to shreds. No, this dress deserves something better.

I realized that the best future for my beautiful gown was to find a new owner – someone who would wear the dress with the excitement and reverence it deserved. And what an exquisite form of reuse. I really adore the whole concept of selling pre-loved goods; someone saves money, we all save the environment, and in this instance, we extend the life of a beautiful piece of wearable art.

So, voila, after posting images and measurements of the dress on the Easy Weddings website and responding to a few inquiries, I find myself here today, with a future bride in my bedroom trying on what may be her wedding gown, and another bride booked for tomorrow.

The sound of giggles interrupt my reverie and I see the flash of a camera burst around the bedroom door – the dress is obviously working its charm on Susie just as it did with me.

A few minutes later Susie emerges, visibly flushed with excitement.

"What did you think?" I ask.

"It really is beautiful," she gushes, "it's the most amazing gown I have ever seen."

I smile, remembering how I felt the first time I tried it on.

"I'm looking at two more gowns today, so is it okay if I let you know tomorrow?"

"Of course," I say as I show them out, "I have another girl coming tomorrow to try it on, so I'll let you know if she decides to buy it."

A couple hours later my phone buzzes with a text, the longest I have ever received:

> HI LISA IT'S SUSIE, I'M WRITING ABOUT THE DRESS. I REALLY LOVE IT, IT'S SO BEAUTIFUL. I'VE BEEN LOOKING AT IT FOR MONTHS ON THE WEBSITE BUT IT'S SLIGHTLY OUT OF MY BUDGET. THAT'S WHY IT TOOK ME SO LONG TO CALL AND TRY IT ON. I'D HOPED I WOULDN'T LIKE IT WHEN I TRIED IT ON, BUT NOW I LOVE IT EVEN MORE! I DON'T WANT TO OFFEND YOU, BUT WOULD YOU CONSIDER ACCEPTING $1500 FOR THE DRESS? I'LL HAVE TO GET THAT BACK BUTTON REPAIRED AND THE BOTTOM IS KIND OF DIRTY. IF YOU CAN'T ACCEPT IT I TOTALLY UNDERSTAND BUT I JUST THOUGHT I'D ASK BECAUSE I LOVE IT SO MUCH!

I was asking $2400, so it would be quite a discount. But, it had been for sale for a while, and Easy Weddings suggests you drop the price over time to account for the age and style of the dress. And though it will come in handy, I really wasn't doing it for the money.

I text back:

> HI SUSIE, I'M THRILLED YOU LOVE THE DRESS AS MUCH AS I DO, IT REALLY IS A SPECIAL ONE! WOULD YOU BE ABLE TO SWING $2000?

To which she counter offered:

> THE HIGHEST I CAN GO IS $1700, CAN YOU CONSIDER THAT?

And I replied:

> DEAL! WHEN DO YOU WANT TO PICK IT UP?

Any hesitations I had about farewelling the gown (which were minimal and only reared their heads as I zipped my dress into its carrying bag for the final time) are erased when I see the joy in the bride-to-be's face as we hug goodbye.

"Babe, it was such a beautiful moment!" I gush as I show Tyler the cash from the dress purchase. He was surfing when Susie came to pick up the dress and missed our magical moment.

He looks a bit perplexed but doesn't say anything.

"I mean, she was a stranger until yesterday, and we were pulled together in this totally unique experience because we loved the same wedding gown. Isn't that just so special?!" I say as tears well in my eyes – not from the sadness of saying goodbye to the dress, but from the joy of this unexpected feeling of sisterhood.

"I'm glad you're happy with your decision," he says and pecks me on the forehead as he heads for the shower.

I know Susie felt the same. I could see it in her eyes and feel it in her hug. She promised to email me photos from her wedding in a few months – I can't wait!

⌣ ✐ 👗 🚶 ⚖ ♫ 🖊 💡 ♡

This morning at work Gaia sent around an email:

> Hi Everyone. I'm about to order 'Alpargatas' shoes from Etiko and they give free shipping on orders over $200, so if anyone wants to buy anything let me know and I'll do a group order.

If Gaia's recommending Etiko it *must* be a great eco-brand.

I followed the link and learned it's a Fairtrade certified sustainable label; they create footwear, clothing and some sporting goods guaranteed to have not been made by children or exploited workers. It was the first non-food brand in the Australasian region to achieve Fairtrade certification, and as an added bonus they've helped create more than 300 micro-businesses in Pakistan. Well, now I *had* to buy a pair of shoes.

Lucky for my wardrobe the Alpargatas are really cute, a slip-on canvas shoe that will definitely go with jeans or even a skirt or dress in summer. They look similar to TOMS, which I've had my eye on ever since learning about their "One for One" policy (you buy a pair of shoes, and a pair of shoes gets given to a child in need in a developing country). Slip-on canvas shoes seem to be the sustainable style this year. I settled on a black and white pattern and placed my order with Gaia.

When I got home from work I showed Ty the shoes online.

"Look at these fabulous shoes from Etiko that I ordered today; it's a Fairtrade ethical company."

"Do you need new shoes?" he asked.

"They're so cute, and will be perfect little flats for me. And it's such a great cause!"

"What's wrong with your Vans? Aren't they pretty much the same style?"

Ugh. He was right. I knew there was reason I hadn't purchased any TOMS yet.

"Well, I already ordered them, it's probably too late to cancel." Besides, I really, really wanted them! Didn't he understand that I needed them to create my eco-fashionista image?

But now it's 2.27 am and I'm tossing and turning, sleep evading me because of my impulse purchase. Sure they are Fairtrade and support a really great cause, but at the end of the day it's a pair of shoes I don't really need. I wanted them. I wanted them to help build my green image. I wanted them because they were cute. And I wanted them because (apparently) I'm still addicted to the thrill of shopping for pleasure.

Damn.

I guess I'm not as enlightened as I'd hoped.

Eco-stuff and Fairtrade-stuff is still stuff, after all. Still something I'm buying that I didn't necessarily need. Sure, it's better than non eco-stuff, but it's stuff[2] nonetheless. Stuff that needed energy to create, transport and sell. Stuff that used resources. Stuff that will probably end up in the landfill.

Geez. Just when I thought I'd learned all my lessons, it turns out there's still more for me to understand.

∼⌀🧿👚👳‍♀️⚱🔔💍🍶💡♡

Payday!

Plus an upcoming board presentation at work as we plan for the upcoming Green Cities conference. Eco-shopping, here I come!

This is totally not an Alpargatas scenario, though. I've recently been given a promotion at work and feel the need to amp up my corporate wardrobe. I wear as much secondhand and faves-from-my-wardobe as possible, but this is one of those times when a few new pieces will go a long way.

I've got this sustainable shopping thing down, though. I've done my research (research first, buy second!) and head over to Veronika Maine on my lunchbreak. This label, as well as its parent company, Cue, has been accredited by Ethical Clothing Australia. The fabrics and materials are not necessarily sustainable, but at least I can shop with confidence that the 'Made in Australia' garments have been made in a safe factory where employees are paid a living wage. As an added bonus, my personal style won't be compromised with this gorgeous, modern label.

Oh, the lunchtime shopping excursion. It's been too long! This used to be my routine a few times a week. I certainly don't want to become an excessive shopper again, but I am thoroughly enjoying the nostalgia of the moment. After trying on a number of items at Veronika Maine, and then following up with some time in Cue, I purchase a few items that will really help me stretch my wardrobe.

- Slim fitting black tuxedo pants with a lovely satin detail around the waistband and down the legs
- Pencil skirt with an eye-catching black and white diamond contrast panel
- Sharp and crisp white blazer

These are definitely pieces that will stand the test of time. Both labels are quality-made, and black and white are so easy to wear with everything.

When I get home from work I spread my goodies out on the bed – it is so exciting to have brand new clothes! From a regular store! I'm totally going to rock that board meeting next week.

But I do loathe the idea of a completely monochrome wardrobe. Corporate attire does not have to mean 'boring'. And as one of the lawyers at work said to me recently, "You're in Marketing, you can wear all sorts of creative clothing and no one will bat an eye!"

So I turn on my computer and partake in some online shopping. I'm a little hesitant – I'm a big believer in trying clothes on before purchasing, you just never know how something will look on your body. As it turns out, many sustainable labels are hard to find in bricks and mortar stores, so in order to be a sustainable fashion shopper, I need to get comfortable with online shopping. I'll just make sure there are great return policies.

Thanks to regularly reading *Peppermint* and a few blogs, I know some labels to look up that should add some colour to my work wardrobe.

I recently came across a lovely, small label called Sara C. The designer is based in the UK, and the draping tops and dresses are handmade in Britain using sustainable fabric like Cupro (a cotton waste byproduct, an impressive textile technology!), and feature really unique and colourful prints inspired by nature. Thankfully I don't have to order all the way from the UK, the Australian online shop GreenHorse stocks a few of her pieces. I order a sleeveless 'Swirl Midnight' top, which features a gorgeous print of black, white, red, blue, yellow and even a dash of purple. Definitely an eye-catching number!

Next I head over to the Sosume website. I love this great basics label, they are completely committed to sustainability, too. Everything is made from eco-friendly fabrics from environmentally-sound mills all around the world. I order a bright blue scoop neck shirt made from a modal-silk blend; modal is a sustainable, man-made fibre created from the wood pulp of beech trees. It also uses just one-tenth the amount of water as cotton, and holds its shape and colour twice as long as cotton. It's also very silky soft – not unlike my bamboo undies. Unlike most bamboo fabric manufacturing, the modal used by Sosume is processed in a closed-loop chemical cycle, meaning no nasty chemical runoffs into waterways.

Finally I spend some time lingering on the Indigo Bazaar website. This is a really special online store dedicated to style with story – trousers hand-woven in India, skirts created in Africa from Khanga fabric – and all made ethically. I order a pair of grey and tangerine Ikat slouch trousers, certain to make 'Casual Friday' much more fun.

Well, I'd say the credit card has had enough of a workout today. I've probably also filled my 'new item' quota for the year! At least the things I purchased are not super-trendy fast fashion purchases. I'm confident the style of the pieces will last and the quality manufacturing will uphold the garments for years to come.

Oooh, I have that old familiar post-shopping euphoria feeling! I'm excited because I know I'm going to look stylish and professional at work, and feel like myself in these contemporary designs. The amazing ethics and environmental sustainability practices of my new purchases are just icing on the cake.

Here's hoping more labels keep putting more icing on more cakes!

Home green home

"Kate, lean your head over here," I say.

"Why, chick?" she leans over with a laugh and her big, gorgeous smile.

"There!" I scrape a long, thin stripe of dried paint out of her hair and we collapse in a fit of giggles.

Kate and I are at the Manly Wharf Hotel with Ty, Lillian and Zoe; I roped the girls into helping us paint our new apartment today. Tyler and I picked up the keys last night, and are moving furniture tomorrow, so we only have today to get the job done. We picked everyone up this morning at 7am and worked a hard six hours before this well-deserved pub lunch, feeling like a proper troupe of painters.

"I think it'll take hours to get all the paint out of your hair, Lise," Lillian says, "there are little flecks of paint all over!"

"I guess that's the hazard of holding the ladder. You were so clever to wear that scarf around your hair," I say, admiring her Rosie the Riveter look.

"I didn't realise it'd be so functional, I just thought it looked good. If it makes you feel any better the soles of my feet are completely white."

"You mean *Royal Beige Quarter*," I joke in my most pretentious tone, reminiscing about the myriads of 'white' interior paint options I scoured through on the hunt for just the right neutral shade.

"Of course," she replies, "Ty's got a nice swipe of *Royal Beige Quarter* across his cheekbone."

"What?" he whines, rubbing at his face with the back of his hand, "I didn't realise I had it on my face – I think that means I've earned another beer!"

We all explode into laughter again – it's been a hysterical day for us five painting novices. Kate's been climbing on top of counters and underneath cabinets to access all the tricky areas in the kitchen. Ty and I have tackled the edges with a makeshift ladder consisting of a couple milk crates and a chair (an OH&S disaster in the making). And Lillian and Zoe have been a very professional pair – quickly covering the walls using paint rollers with expert precision. They also made sure there was extra 'love' in the house by suggesting we draw hearts and smiley faces on the walls beforehand. And of course there are drips, spills and white footprints decorating the drop cloths strewn across the floors; we've created our very own Jackson Pollock-like installation.

Our giggles are definitely not the result of nasty paint fumes, though. While I'd been feverishly studying the tonal differences between Taubman's *Big White* and Wattyl's *Bohemian White,* Tyler had taken the reins on the environmental concerns of household paint. We selected a low VOC (volatile organic compound) option – 'fume free' in layman's terms – from Dulux's eco-range.

Simply stated, VOCs are chemicals that evaporate at room temperature, 'off-gassing' into the atmosphere where we breathe them in. You can assume VOCs are present when you catch a whiff of fresh paint, new cars, or freshly laid carpet – unfortunately those familiar smells could be causing you more harm than you realise. Some research suggests that VOCs emit ozone-depleting emissions, but of greater concern are the negative health effects[1]; the Green Star rating tools created by my company, the Green Building Council of Australia, encourage buildings to use low-VOC paints, carpets and upholsteries for the sake of the building occupants' health, and I'm glad I know to avoid these as I paint the walls of my home.

Exposure to VOCs can cause irritation of the eyes, nose and skin, headaches, nausea, loss of coordination and even damage to internal organs including your liver, kidney and central nervous system; these symptoms are sometimes referred to as 'sick building syndrome'. Extended exposure to VOCs increases the likelihood and severity of these effects, but even limited exposure can have a negative impact on your health. Paints have been known to off-gas for weeks after application, making it all the more important to use low VOC paints in your indoor spaces.

Another eco-friendly trait of our low VOC paint is that it's water based, and very easy to clean off our bodies – no paint thinner required. And I'm extra thankful since these are frequently crude-oil based and can also be hazardous to your health.

We wrap up around 7pm, scrub ourselves and the paintbrushes with soap and water, and follow the instructions for disposing of extra paint the eco-friendly way – pouring it onto newspaper to dry then discard instead of running it down the drain and into the water supply. We planned well and bought only the quantity of paint we'd need, so thankfully we aren't throwing much away. We're also keeping a small amount reserved to cover any marks in coming years.

Today's painting adventure came about because Ty and I recently purchased our first apartment in beachside heaven, Manly. And what else do you do when you move from being a renter to owning your place? Paint the walls whatever colour you like, of course!

Before we signed our life away on the mortgage dotted line, there were a few choices we made specifically with the environment in mind (some of which can also be made by people who are renting, I don't want to give the impression that greening your home is just for owners). First, the apartment is close to public transportation, with buses and ferries only two blocks away. Second, the apartment block has a large clothesline in the back garden to negate the need for a dryer – the place we're moving out of wouldn't even let us dry clothes on our balcony because it 'doesn't look presentable' from the street. I confess, I used to sympathise with that rationale – now I see that was completely short-sighted. Third, there is an abundance of natural light in the apartment, reducing the energy requirements of our home, not to mention being a lovely aesthetic feature. Fourth, we selected a place that was the right size for two people, so we won't be wasting electricity with extra rooms. And that mortgage I mentioned? We selected it based not just on rates, but also on the sustainability practices of the bank; we went with Westpac, a real standout in terms of environmental and social sustainability in the Australian market[2].

With all those choices made, low VOC paint on the walls and signing up to 100% green power, I'm well on my way to creating my very own eco-chic dream palace.

Moving into a new apartment has also triggered an urge to fill it with lots of beautiful new things. This desire stems from the fact that my home is as much a part of my image as my clothing and hairstyle – it provides me another opportunity to express myself by creating a space that represents who I am. It wouldn't be sustainable for me to buy all new things for my apartment, of course, but there are a few green details I can add that will represent the environmentalist in me.

The apartment was built in the 1950s, is quintessential Aussie red brick with white trim, beautiful high ceilings, and external doors with quirky bubbled glass inside rounded frames to let the light in (and keep nosey neighbours out). An idea has manifested in my little green head to find antique doorknobs to add a bit more character to the bedroom and bathroom doors. Antiquing can't be any harder than vintage clothes shopping, and it's still a fabulous exercise in reuse!

I enlist Lillian and Zoe to help hunt for the perfect antique doorknobs. These two style queens will certainly be able to point me in the direction of beautiful home accessories, you should see the masterpiece of interior design they've created in Zoe's new flat; it should be featured in *Vogue Living*. Every detail, from the collection of mini green Dinosaur Design bottles (an eco-aware company) to the Missoni duvet cover, vertical book tower and framed vintage prints, has been meticulously thought out and flawlessly executed.

I'm hoping some of their collecting prowess will lead me to my new (used) doorknobs.

I meet the designing duo at Café Sopra inside Fratelli Fresh in Potts Point for a bit of sustenance before we hit the antique trail. We catch up over a fabulous low carbon (read: vegetarian) lunch of stuffed zucchini flowers and pasta tossed with chilli, garlic, broccolini and anchovies (an acquired taste, but these small salty fish are incredibly sustainable). As I'm swooning over a little pocket of cheesy zucchini flower-heaven Zoe shares, "Hey Lise, I've started turning my TV off at the power point so it's not on standby when I'm not using it."

"Oh, that's fantastic!"

It may sound like a small thing to do, but in fact over 10 per cent of Australian households' energy consumption is attributed to appliances on standby[3]. If you aren't already in the habit, turn off your appliances when not in use and you'll save money whilst shrinking your eco-footprint.

"Yep, and I've made sure my flatmate does the same thing – we're trying to do the green thing," she smiles, clearly proud of their efforts, "I even make her put on more layers instead of turning the heat on now that it's getting a bit cooler."

"Nice work! All these things really add up you know."

I really enjoy being the resident environmentalist. As corny as it may sound, it's so rewarding when friends share their eco-victories with me; in a way it gives me momentum to keep going when I'm feeling frustrated with certain environmental actions (or lack thereof) in the wider community.

With our bellies full we mosey down Macleay Street and Zoe says, "Do you mind if we stop in Becker Minty to buy my sister a housewarming gift while we're in the area?"

Becker Minty is *heaven*. I'll gladly shop vicariously through Zoe.

We turn onto Manning Street and approach the shop entrance, and I feel unexpected pangs of nostalgia for carefree shopping days even before we enter the huge glass doors – I thought I'd cured my shopping addiction?

Becker Minty's ethos is 'The Best of Everything' and it certainly has achieved that *you know you want to buy it all* vibe. The walls are covered in intricate mirrors, some large enough to cover an entire wall of my new home, and the tables and shelves are expertly merchandised to help us shoppers feel that we're not really in a store, but in our very stylish friend's place, complete with instrumental music and inviting fragrances. I absorb the scene with all my senses: see chairs made with large animal horns, run my fingers across satchels made of the softest leather and whisper-thin cashmere tops, and admire bowls and vases of every shape, size and texture. I follow my nose to an array of candles and body products vast enough to keep me entertained for at least an hour. While Zoe and Lillian examine a number of frames I busy myself reading some labels on the body lotions. To my delight I find some that are luxurious *and* natural, and I try a tester of Be Genki's *Sensuality* body cream, packed with oils of Sweet Almond, Sunflower and Macadamia, and scented naturally with essences of Ylang Ylang, Jasmine and Rose. Divine.

I take my chances to see if they carry earth-friendly candles – surely a new home warrants a new candle, right?

Like many of life's little luxuries which I've enjoyed over the years, candles have a chequered environmental record. Candles were traditionally made with lead wicks until it was discovered that burning them put those who inhaled the smoke at risk of lead poisoning[4]. Although lead wicks have been banned in Australia and the USA, the ban only came in place in the early 2000s and some imported candles still contain lead in the wicks.

In addition to the potential toxins from lead wicks, most candles are made from paraffin, a petroleum by-product, which emits horribly dangerous fumes when lit including toluene and benzene, a known carcinogen[5]. Scented candles are even worse, as synthetic fragrances (frequently based in mineral oil, another petroleum by-product) also contain pthalates, known hormone disrupters, and can emit even higher levels of benzene[6]. While the extent of the health risks is not certain, a recent study linking paraffin candles to indoor pollution and benzene emissions advises against frequent paraffin candle use, particularly in enclosed areas[7].

We don't have to live without candles, though; we can seek out beeswax or soy candles with cotton or hemp wicks to enjoy a clean-burning candle. These candles do not emit any toxic fumes, and have the added benefit of not being related to petroleum extraction. If you still crave a scented candle, opt for natural essential oils instead of synthetic fragrance.

Unfortunately it's not always easy to know what you're buying. Labelling is not mandatory on candles. There are also no regulations that require companies to advise what percent of the candle is soy wax or beeswax or naturally fragranced, so unless you want to be a casualty of greenwashing, look for labels that say '100%' of these ingredients to make sure your wax hasn't been blended with paraffin or your fragrance blended with synthetics.

The candles in Becker Minty claim to be made of vegetable oil and use pure cotton wicks but there is no indication of percentage. Also, the only comment about the scent is that the blend of vegetable oils 'allows the addition of the perfect perfumes'; the word 'perfume' makes me think the scent may be artificial. I ask a salesperson if he knows whether the candle is scented with essential oils, but he doesn't, so if I really want this candle I'll have to do my research.

There's my shopping motto again: research first, buy second.

Hmmm. These candles are $99 each – Becker Minty really *does* fill its store with the best of everything – I don't think I'll bother researching these candles after all.

This fun pit stop has not only been a great reminder of my shopping motto, but also highlights a trend I've noticed for eco-luxury products – those that blend beauty and aesthetics with the environmental mindset. Whether it's the beautiful Korres and Grown make up and body products, Ginger & Smart's ethical fashion line, Five-Star eco-resorts, The Hanging Space's immaculate selection of vintage clothes available online, or the growing availability of organic cotton linens and reclaimed timber furniture – there's a lot of eco-luxury out there for those with the bank account to back it up.

I leave Becker Minty empty-handed and we poke in a couple antique shops in Potts Point before we hop on the 389 bus to Woollahra. Three cheers for public transportation! I'm happy to see that Zoe loves her weekly travelpass as much as I do, one flat fee for unlimited public transportation around town, and no stress with traffic or parking – it's fabulous.

We spend another couple hours in and out of gorgeous antique, refurbishment and home stores in Woollahra and Paddington. Antiquing is hard work! Some stores are beautifully merchandised while others are dusty, musty and more disorganised than my makeup drawer (well, before I threw away half the contents for being toxic). I don't find any doorknobs and the entire afternoon is yet another reminder that eco-shopping is not like traditional shopping – I can't expect to find exactly what I want exactly when I want it.

Even though I come home empty-handed I had an amazing day cherishing my friendships with Zoe and Lillian. The girls were totally on board with my hunt for reused doorknobs and patiently waited as I asked shop after shop if they had any, and even though our discussions frequently centred around creating my eco-chic dream home they didn't seem exasperated, but supportive. I've learned that even though I'm taking the 'shopping-spree' out of our friendship equation there's enough strength to survive my tumble down the green-living rabbit hole. And reflecting back on the laughs we all shared the day we painted my flat I know we'll grow beyond where I had pigeonholed us. Why had I presumed we were so shallow that our friendships survived on frivolity alone? Did I really think so little of myself that I thought all I could offer was my sense of style? And why did I let that aspect of our friendship mask the other amazing traits of Lillian and Zoe? I'm appalled that I've been selling all of us so short.

⌒𝄞🜊🜍🜎🜏♀👁️🜔💡♡

Geoff and I are sitting at my local, the Manly Wharf Hotel, on a sunny afternoon; he has come to surf with Ty and see our new place. I look at the sparkling water as the sun prepares to set behind the hills of the national park and feel the light is beaming upon us lucky folks as a reminder to enjoy the idyllic moment and appreciate the natural beauty of our home. We're guarding our prime spot on the edge of the dock as Ty gets our drinks, and Geoff asks with his usual cheeky grin:

"How's things, Lise? Still enjoying work?"

"So busy, but loving it," in a funny twist of fate, we're now in the same industry; his engineering company is a member of GBCA. "It's inspiring to see the building industry making such big strides for the environment, it gives me a wider perspective on the change that's needed, that's for sure."

"You know, sometimes I think people are too selfish to change their behaviour. I used to have so many arguments with my family; it was such a waste of time. Now I put my faith in industry and the big changes."

"So what, you're giving up hope on people?" I ask, saddened that one of the people who inspired me to fight for the cause is so disenchanted. But I can understand, after Beefgate I, too, felt like I may be wasting my time with activism.

"Sort of. Even if individuals started to change, it wouldn't be enough. We need industry and infrastructure to change, because individual changes won't really make much difference."

I hear this opinion a lot – and not just from my friends or sceptics, but from other environmentalists as well.

"I just can't agree with that. I think if people start making individual changes, it will make them more likely to pay attention to the larger issues and demand the changes from the government and business. Even if all our 'small' changes won't make the difference, the power of people to influence change is huge."

"I don't know, Lise, I think we have to focus on technology instead of people to get the big change we need."

"Who do you think is going to demand the technology or insist governments and cities implement the innovative changes? Citizens need to demonstrate they really care if they want government to act in a green way."

Ty comes around with drinks so we agree to disagree for now, but I'm left feeling so confused – is this the same person who advised me at the start of my journey that what was needed was to understand human behaviour better in order to get the change we wanted? It sounds like maybe Geoff is in his own rollercoaster relationship with the environmental movement. I'm determined not to let his opinion sway mine; even if change is happening slower than I want, I can still feel the tide turning and I'm not about to give up hope.

✑∅ℜℚ⚖ℐℙℴℴℙℑ♡

We've been in our new apartment for a few months and I've learned to appreciate reuse in a way I'd never imagined.

Thanks to my new favourite shopping buddy, eBay, I'm now the proud owner of three sets of antique doorknobs. Prior to these purchases I'd only used eBay for buying concert tickets (before it was illegal, of course) – I'd filed it next to vintage shopping under 'too hard' because it takes time, patience, and the things you buy aren't perfectly shiny and new. Now that I've learned to embrace the beauty of reuse in other areas of my life I've realised eBay is an eco-shoppers dream world! You can find nearly anything second-hand, reusing someone else's unwanted goods and saving them from going to the landfill, or selling your own to keep them from the same fate. After learning how easy it was to buy things on eBay I sold a wardrobe and a bar table setting that didn't fit in our new apartment; I was incredibly pleased when they went within a week and I had that extra cash in my wallet.

In addition to eBay I've been tackling some fun eco-DIY refurbishments of used furniture. The first piece I completed was a second hand hardwood bookshelf given to me by a colleague. It was in excellent condition, all I needed to do was stain it to match the rest of my dark furniture.

Instead of going back to Bunnings for wood stain, I investigated greener options. I recently read in *Green Living* magazine that most paints are based on synthetics derived from petroleum (even my low VOC wall paint) and that manufacturing them is very energy intensive, with each tonne of paint produced resulting in up to 30 tonnes of toxic waste, most of which is non-biodegradable[8]. It seems Ty and I only did half our homework when selecting our beautiful *Royal Beige Quarter* wall cover, falling prey to that habitual tendency to go straight to the shops we knew.

People usually joke about becoming a new homeowner and spending every weekend at Bunnings or Home Depot, but I've been spending mine at Eco at Home, the environmentalist's dream home store. I first came across this shop while investigating organic cotton towels and sheets, and I've quickly become a regular – I knew I'd find eco-friendly wood stain here. In addition to paints and linens, they also stock cleaning supplies, organic cotton balls, stainless steel water bottles, loads of books, compostable-nappies, and every other gadget this eco-geek could ever hope for. A personal favourite is my toothbrush with a replaceable head, so you're only throwing away one part when the bristles have lived their life, not the whole thing – genius! To top it off, the owners of the store are the most delightful couple. I suspect they've been 'inner-circle greenies' since the 1970s; they ooze comfort in their eco-skin with their long grey hair, natural fibre clothing and footwear, and warm faces full of beautiful smile lines. They are calm, friendly and incredibly helpful; I've started to think of the woman as my own personal Earth Mother. She was so patient while helping me select eco-wood stain, even encouraging me to take a small sample home last weekend to make sure I was happy with the colour.

My Earth Mother told me I'd probably need two coats to achieve my desired results, which *seemed* completely reasonable. Unfortunately, the actual timeline looked more like this:

3.00pm – start first coat, confident that I will be done around 7pm to connect with Ty and some mates for dinner.

5.00pm – the first coat is dry. There is NO WAY one coat will be enough.

6.45pm – the second coat is dry, and it's definitely going to require more, the colour is still quite translucent. I tell Ty to head to dinner without me; I'll catch up with them for drinks later.

8.00pm – I'm getting quicker at painting, but still not achieving much density of colour. Maybe I'm thinning it out too much? I worry I won't have enough stain to complete the whole bookcase so I stop painting the back. I wanted to stain the entire thing in case one day it's not against a wall, but it's more important to conserve my resources.

9.15pm – it's completely dark outside. Thanks to my eco-friendly (read: dim) compact fluorescent lights, I can't tell how well the last coat went. I retrieve my reading lamp and I'm sad to see I'm still not done.

11.00pm – five coats done, I'm exhausted and text Ty that I'm going to bed – not my most exciting Saturday night.

8.00am (Day 2) – I investigate my handiwork. There are definitely a few patchy spots, and I psyche myself up for coat six. I'm nearly out of stain, so the final coat requires a very strategic use of materials.

8.45am (Day 2) – Done.

So, for only $50, two trips to Eco at Home, nine hours of labour and one litre of eco-friendly stain, I have a beautiful sustainably refurbished second-hand bookcase.

Thankfully the second piece of furniture I refinish is much easier. I found a dresser on the street (yes you read that correctly, little Miss Recovering Shopaholic now takes free items off the street) and I am going to repaint it a fresh aquamarine.

My beachside neighbourhood is transient in nature thanks to the large number of travellers who make it their base, which means a lot of unwanted furniture and household items find their way onto the streets around town. Technically it's illegal to dump unwanted goods, but there are so many other travellers and students (and environmentalists?) looking for cheap furniture that anything remotely clean and presentable is quickly scooped up. I used to loathe this aspect of my neighbourhood, thinking it was the tackiest thing possible, leaving your unwanted items on the footpath. Now I've become one of the vultures.

For the dresser, I work with the lovely folks at Eco At Home to mix the perfect shade of clay-based paint. It takes about a week to get it the correct aquamarine hue; they use only natural pigments to create the colour and it can take a bit of trial and error to get it right. Due to the nature of natural pigments there is a smaller range than the multitude of colours you see on the paint wall at Bunnings, but thankfully there are options beyond just earth tones.

The painting process itself is much easier, too, with only the expected two coats. The paint has an interesting viscosity; its thickness covers up flaws quite well, and you can create a 'textured' look with the bristles of your paintbrush if you wish. It finishes a beautiful flat matte, which is exactly what I wanted, and gives much-needed vibrancy to the dresser, especially once I add the antique Mexican ceramic knobs I bought on eBay.

Next I tackle a really fun eco-chic DIY project – re-covering my kitchen chairs. I bought a dining set from a work colleague a couple years ago and have wanted to re-cover the chairs since that day. The current off-white fabric shows every stain imaginable, and since the tabletop is made of glass they are always on display. I've been keeping my eye out for eco-fabrics for awhile, even taking a few swatches and making some inquiries at the Finders Keepers sustainability markets a few months ago, but I couldn't find anything I liked in my budget. I was *thisclose* to buying some hemp fabric printed with a gorgeous teal bird pattern from Thea & Sami last week when I heard Gaia mention a store called Reverse Garbage; I loved the name and needed to learn more.

Reverse Garbage is a wonderland for artists and environmentalists alike, a non-profit organisation that's been around since the 1970's arranging what they call 'resource reuse'. As an organisation they:

> Make available industrial and commercial discards, off-cuts and over-runs to creative and practical people, reducing the amount of waste going to landfill[9].

Essentially the shops contain random, reasonably priced bits and pieces that would otherwise be thrown out, which many people use in art, DIY and other creative projects.

Because of the nature of Reverse Garbage you never know what's going to be in stock, so I tried to manage my own expectations even as I excitedly approached the Taylor Square shop (with mannequin legs appropriately sprawled in the arched window of the old T2 building). My initial impression after stepping into the shop was not good, and I felt it was more 'garage sale' than 'art store' (just when I thought I was getting comfortable with green living). The ground floor was dimly lit, smelled a bit musty and was filled with disparate piles of crayons, mannequin pieces, beads, mounting board off-cuts and even promotional notepads and toys. My senses quickly adjusted, though, and after a few minutes I saw a method to the apparent madness and understood why this place has been so popular with creative folks for decades. There are affordable and unexpected goodies stashed in every square inch of the shop.

As I wandered into the fabric room my heart dropped again - they certainly weren't making it easy for me. The huge pile of fabric rolls was problematic, I lost my grip on one and it thudded quite loudly on the ground. The pile contained a lot of white and off-white cotton, jersey and polyester blends, but nothing suitable for covering chairs, and the few rolls of upholstery material weren't really my taste (the best were pale green, blue and golden corduroy, not exactly the look I was going for). There were also hundreds of swatches hanging on a rack, but nothing large enough to cover chairs. Although I tried not to expect much, I was disappointed after all the hype.

Since I was there anyway I headed up the stairs into the lofty second floor just to have a peek, and the lovely light streaming through the windows lifted my mood immediately. There were leftover Mardi Gras costumes, dresses and belts, containers and art boards of all shapes and sizes, and cute wooden stencils with Aussie animals - the potential was amazing! If I were an artist or kindergarten teacher, I'd hang out there all the time.

I spotted some hessian coffee sacks and my creative wheels started spinning - could these fun pieces of fabric be used to cover my chairs? The material was not as scratchy to the touch as I thought it'd be, though it needed a wash and might shed. At $3 a piece it was a very low-risk investment, so I purchased two and hoped for the best. Now, after thoroughly washing the smelly sacks and hanging them in the fresh air and sun for a few days, they come out fresh and clean and chair-ready.

I borrow a staple gun from my friend Drake to complete the job. Borrowing is kind to my budget and, more importantly, I'm not buying something I may only use once. I'm lucky enough to have a great friend who owns every tool imaginable, but if you don't have a Drake, don't despair, try a website like Open Shed or Friends with Things[10] and borrow the tool from a new friend, instead.

It only takes me an hour to cut the sacks into the shape and size to cover the chairs, convince Tyler to do the stapling because I'm afraid of anything with the word 'gun' in it, and have two chairs completed. By chair #3 I decide I am brave enough to wield the staple gun and promptly break it, so the project is on hold. Typical.

I buy a new staple gun and have Ty finish off the job he started (so I don't end up having to buy *another* new staple gun – totally unsustainable); I couldn't be more pleased with my 'new' kitchen chairs! They each have a slightly different print but fit together quite nicely. I blog about my experience and Reverse Garbage is kind enough to share the blog post with their Facebook fans. I love social media!

I don't always refurbish things myself; sometimes it's best left to the experts. I've invested in a beautiful 1950s-era armchair and ottoman, lovingly restored using modern fabrics by the clever designer at the Armchair Collective. I also bought a number of reclaimed timber photo frames – some even built to order to my size specifications –from Mulbury Gallery in Victoria.

Looking around my home there are only a few pieces of furniture that were purchased new and I love the way I'm creating a space that is reflective of my sustainability aspirations and my personal style.

⚬🖌🐈🐇🍴🎶🕯☕💡♡

I'm typing out the latest edition of the sustainability newsletter for work and include an invitation for employees to take home worm juice to fertilise their gardens, which reminds me of the growing pains I've been experiencing with my new Bokashi Bin at home.

Ty and I bought the Bokashi Bin a few weeks ago because it seemed the most reasonable composting option for our lifestyle. It's small and easily fits in our kitchen, smaller than the other compost bin options we researched, and (theoretically) easy to use. Every time you put food scraps in you add a layer of 'Bokashi', which looks like flakes of fish food but is actually a specially designed microorganism that assists the composting and prevents bad smells. You can put most food waste into the bin, including fruits, vegetables, eggs, coffee grinds, tea bags and even meat, fish and cheese (meat and dairy are not recommended in other compost bins until you are a compost expert). Once you fill the bucket and let it ferment for a couple weeks, there is 'juice' you can drain from the bottom, to dilute and use as fertilizer or a natural drain cleaner, and solid compost that you bury in soil, where it will breakdown completely after a few weeks, fertilising along the way.

Our first problem is that we filled it too quickly; Ty and I cook a lot and eat plenty of veggies (especially now that we're eating much less meat), and the scraps nearly filled the bin in just one week. We also read, too late, that you should cut food scraps into small pieces; by the time I read that I'd already put whole cauliflower leaves and broccoli stems in. And, despite what Earth Mother at Eco at Home told us about the benefits of Bokashi, it smells like rotting food – I literally gagged last time I opened the lid. I'm really not sure how we went wrong.

And now that the bin is full and has been fermenting for a couple weeks as per the instructions, we're not actually sure what to do with the compost. There's a lot more of it than I realized – I thought that it would get smaller in size as it 'cooked' in the bin, but it doesn't. The juice is great, and easy to make into liquid fertiliser for my potted plants and herbs, but the solid compost is another story all together. There is some garden space around our block of units, but we don't own a shovel to dig the recommended 20-25 cm deep trench to bury the compost. Even if we did, there doesn't seem to be a clear area of dirt without roots; it's suggested that you don't allow any roots to touch the compost as the high acidity can burn them.

Was this particular eco-gadget worth it? Or have we wasted money, not to mention the plastic that the bin is made of, since it appears we may dump it into the rubbish after all? We were trying to avoid the methane and other greenhouse gases that are emitted from food breaking down in the landfill, and I'm not sure if we're accomplishing that goal or not. I'm beginning to think that the most sustainable thing would've been to get a proper compost bin for our whole apartment block. I have heard there are people who will collect compost for their own gardens, so I'll research that to see if anyone wants our fermented Bokashi. Otherwise I'll have to throw the compost into the garbage bin and rethink the entire situation.

Other eco-operations have been running much smoother around my home, though. One of the most successful changes I've made is greening my cleaning habits.

When I took stock under my sink I had no fewer than a dozen varieties of cleaning supplies. I found dish soaps, laundry detergents, glass cleaner, all-purpose cleaner, shower cleaner, carpet cleaner and other specialty products that I don't even remember buying, let alone using. It was quite the collection. And nearly every bottle warned about the dangers lurking within – including one that insists rubber gloves be worn at all times and to not let the product sit for too long after spraying lest it corrode sink fixtures and bath tiles. I'd previously never thought beyond the fact that I must need strong chemicals to clean grease and soap scum, but now I know I must also consider what happens once I inhale those chemicals or they run down the drain.

In addition to those chemicals emitting VOCs and contaminating our land and water, cleaning supplies contribute to the environmental problem of toxic algal bloom. Blue-green algae (cyanobacteria) are naturally present in fresh water, and have been around much longer than we have – fossils have been found that date them to at least 2.5 billion years ago (to put this in perspective, the earth is 4.5 billion years old and humans are less than 200,000 years old). The problem today is that human activity causes particular algae-feeding chemicals (phosphorous and nitrogen) to enter waterways and grow so quickly that the bloom takes over the aquatic environment, sucking oxygen out of the water and causing the death of other oxygen-dependent life such as fish; some species of blue-green algae are even poisonous to humans and animals[11].

Nitrogen from fertilisers is one food source of the algae, so increasing organic farming reduces those. Another food source is phosphorus from 'phosphates', found in laundry and dish detergents. Switching to phosphate-free cleaning products will remove more of the algae's food supply and help keep our waterways healthy.

The good news is there are already a number of products that have axed phosphates, and some states in the US have banned phosphate use altogether[12]. While it is not mandatory for cleaning supplies to list their ingredients, green products tend to be transparent about the ingredients and promote the fact that they are phosphate-free.

To avoid being greenwashed while I'm green cleaning, I've committed to a combination of Co-op, eco-brands and self-made cleaning supplies.

The Co-op supplies our liquid dish soap and dishwasher powder, as well as castile soap, all packaging-free. The laundry detergent from the Co-op left my clothes with a lingering vinegar smell, so I've happily made the switch to certified organic soapnuts. These little wonders have been used for centuries as a natural, versatile cleaning agent in India, and also have a history with indigenous people of Asia and the Americas. The shells contain saponin, which when mixed with water is a natural surfactant (detergent), and you just need to toss a few into the wash inside a small bag to get naturally clean clothes – the only difference is the lack of artificial fragrance from store-bought detergents. I'm a complete convert. I add a couple drops of lavender essential oil to the bag and my clothes come out naturally clean and fresh. I've also given up fabric softener altogether – I suspect it's a bit of a marketing scam (and so does Choice[13], Australia's consumer watchdog).

While we're on the subject, I love the clothesline at my apartment. This fashionista has long known that avoiding the dryer helps my clothes last longer and keeps them in great shape, and now I realise I'm saving energy as well. Besides, it really is like those cheesy commercials depict, there is nothing like the scent of laundry that's been naturally dried outside.

To ensure my laundry is completely green I only wash with cold water, reducing my energy requirements. Also, my clothes last longer and colours won't fade as quickly as if they were washed in hot water. Hot water as a cleaning necessity is mostly an urban myth; even hospitals have stopped washing their sheets in hot water because evidence shows that cold water removes the germs and bacteria just as effectively[14]. Hot water can make a difference on heavily soiled clothes, though, because it more effectively removes grease from fabric, so I just use my best discretion.

The rest of our cleaning supplies are homemade. I'm reducing my plastic consumption by reusing spray bottles and I'm constantly amazed at how much you can do with a few simple ingredients. For example, "Lisa's All-Purpose Spray" consists of:

- Water
- Vinegar
- Castile soap (vegetable based liquid soap)
- Essential oils – I mix and match depending on my mood
- Tea tree and eucalyptus oils (we Aussies have the benefit of having these miracle working, naturally disinfecting, oils readily available)

Thanks *Gorgeously Green* for the inspiration. I tweaked the book's recipe slightly because hydrogen peroxide is not as readily available in Australia as the US. I use this spray on bathroom and kitchen counters, sinks, the toilet and the shower. Okay, so you do have to scrub harder than if you were using Bam! to clean your tile grout, but you don't have to worry about what you're inhaling, what's touching your skin, or what's going down the drain. And like my colleague says – it's a better workout when you have to scrub harder.

Other homemade solutions include: olive oil to polish my wooden furniture; lemon juice and baking soda to spot clean the carpets; lemon juice instead of bleach as a natural disinfectant; vinegar as a replacement to Windex (unlike with the laundry the smell quickly dissipates). The list goes on and on, and thanks to all the eco and budget-wise folks in the world, there are numerous websites and books with varying recipes and tips for cleaning with non-toxic, readily available ingredients[15].

Add to all of this the fact that I reuse old t-shirts and yoga pants as rags, and cleaning my home has easily become one of my greenest activities. I just toss the rags in with my laundry – I'm sure the neighbours wonder about the little scraps of fabric flapping on the clothesline, but I love being a green cleaner.

In general, I've found it's been really easy to green the running of our home. Of course we recycle, though we've stopped using the Bokashi bin for now, and because we've greened our groceries we have very little food packaging to dispose of each week. We turn things off at the power point. We turn lights off if they're not needed. We take short showers (it helps that our water heater is small so there's really no time to linger). We use recycled toilet paper (I've even opted for the hard core brown paper – surprisingly soft – because I want people to know it's recycled), organic cotton balls and biodegradable bin liners. We installed ceiling fans instead of air conditioning and use cloth serviettes instead of single use paper options – just like my cleaning rags, I find there is always enough space in any load of laundry to accommodate the week's serviettes.

There is always room for improvement, however, and the next thing on my green home wish list is an insulating cover to fit around our hot water heater. The US Department of Energy states that unless your hot water system has a high "R-value" a water heater blanket can reduce standby heat losses by 25%-45%, and save you around 4%-9% in hot water heating energy[16]. If you don't know your tank's R-value (I sure don't, I don't even know what that means), you can determine if you need to insulate it by touching the outside – if it's warm to the touch you should insulate it. Not as sexy a purchase as my recovered armchair, but more impactful and my next priority.

～∅🛆🜍⚱🜏🜊♀☼🜍♀♡

As an apartment dweller there are a number of green home improvements that are out of my reach. I don't have space to grow my own veggie patch, and have to rely on what I can reasonably grow in pots on my small balcony. I can't put in a rainwater tank or a large compost bin. I don't have my own plot of land to build a home of hay bales or the next eco-wonder material.

I also have to accept the possibility that I may always be an apartment dweller, and not just because Sydney's real estate prices are astronomical. More than half the world's population now lives in urban areas. Experts predict we'll continue to move up, not out, and acre plots of land may soon be a thing of the past. My own personal lifestyle preferences will also keep me close to cities, as my desire for more space is not as large as my desire for convenience and location – no long commutes or spacious suburbs for me.

Some forward-thinking urban planners, engineers, designers and architects (including some whom I work with) are taking up our space challenge by designing sustainable communities[17] with shared community gardens, cars, water tanks and renewable power supplies, allowing apartment dwellers and other urban buildings to split the costs and benefits of green technologies. These communities are designed to not only improve the state of the environment, but also provide increased liveability by encouraging connections between individuals. Psychologists have long known that a strong sense of community is a factor in increased happiness, so designing our neighbourhoods in such a way to combat some of the loneliness and disconnectedness of our modern world, whilst being more environmentally sustainable, is great news all around.

Another eco-perk of living in a high-density area is that my individual footprint has automatically decreased. Although it may be easier to imagine countryside-living with your own garden, fewer people and less traffic as more natural and eco-friendly, high-density living is actually more sustainable. The International Institute for Environment and Development (IIED) released a report that shows New Yorkers have one-third the impact as the national average in the US, Barcelona is around half the national average of Spain, as is London when compared to the rest of the UK[18]. This is primarily due to decreased transportation emissions thanks to public transport, as well as less energy use from living in smaller spaces. So on the days when I feel cramped in my smallish apartment or I miss the ferry home from the city and have to wait another 30 minutes for the next boat, it helps to know that my urban lifestyle is helping me live a green life.

And I feel even better when I walk in the door of my fabulous eco-chic abode. I love that more than half of our furniture is used and has been refinished to suit our style. I love that I can breathe easy knowing that our paints and cleaning supplies are safe. More than anything I love that my home is a real reflection of its owners and our sustainable lifestyle.

Part Three

How to change the world

The green scene

"Congratulations! There are over *8,000* of you here today! *WE DID IT!*" exclaims an enthusiastic environmental activist atop a stage in Belmore Park near Central Station.

A roar of cheers and applause rumbles through the crowd as Ty and I hurry along the outer edge of the park, awestruck at the number of people in the crowd, to get near the stage.

"And that *other* rally on the *other* side of town only has 2,000!" he continues as the crowd explodes with excitement – including me, whooping at the top of my lungs (while Tyler coolly claps).

The *other* rally to which he is referring was organised by people who are fighting the proposed Australian carbon tax; the rally we're attending was organised in response to that rally. In one week Get Up, a grass-roots community advocacy organisation, with the help of a genius social media campaign, was able to pull together this huge crowd of citizens who are willing to pay a fair price for our goods (including the cost to the environment). The campaign absolutely put *Use Your Own Mug* to shame and is another successful example of the power of social media to influence social and political change.

As our train pulled into Central I'd seen the huge crowd out the window, and I'll admit I was surprised. Ty and I have arrived about

15 minutes after the listed start time and it seems we are *un*fashionably late to this event. Walking toward the park you can hear a distinctive hum of excitement that grows with every step we take toward the centre stage, and I have the distinct urge to run because we are missing it!

This is my third environmental rally in as many years, and I'm getting more and more comfortable with each one I attend. Thinking back to my first rally, arranged by 350.org (350 parts per million (ppm) CO_2 in the atmosphere is the level many scientists agree will stabilise the climate, currently we're sitting around 390ppm) a few months into my transition, I remember feeling totally out of place. My somewhat conspicuous attire and naivety about sustainability meant I couldn't completely relax. At the same time I remember feeling exhilarated as I marched through a crowd of people who I took to be diehard environmentalists.

There was a drum circle, hundreds of creative signs and placards, and at the end of the event there were musicians and booths set up in Hyde Park. The rally had opened my eyes to a whole world I didn't realise existed in my lifetime; I thought protests and rallies had been left in the 1970s and I felt incredibly empowered after attending my first one, knowing I was helping to shape history.

I attended the same event the following year, particularly wanting to show my support ahead of the approaching COP-15 meetings in Copenhagen (now I know those meetings didn't have the results we'd been marching for at the time, but meetings in recent years have made some progress ahead of 2015, when countries will have to publish their plans for cutting greenhouse gas emissions by 2020). I was there early and by myself, so I was able to really soak in the atmosphere. I remember a noticeable difference in the crowd compared to the previous year – it was bigger and also the demographics had expanded with an increased number of people in their 60s and above, many more families with small children, and a lower proportion of traditional hippies. In one year the event had transformed itself into a mainstream, multigenerational family event. There was still the core contingent of greenies and the drum circle from the year before, but there was also an a cappella singing group and more options for eco-friendly food and drinks at the end.

Simply comparing one year to the next, it was clear the green social network was expanding, and I was just one of many concerned citizens willing to step out for the cause.

Today's rally follows the same trend, and there is a beautiful mixture of diehard protestors, young families, old families, and people from all walks of life standing together, pleading for "Climate Action Now!"

I have brought my camera to document the rally, and I climb onto a bench to get a birds-eye view of the crowd. From atop my perch I spot a group of cheeky women dressed as the "Tuvalu Scuba Team". At their highest point the Tuvalu islands are only 4.5 metres in elevation and could be one of the first nations to be displaced due to climate change. Some reports suggest that within 100 years the islands will be underwater. The humour of this group reminds me of last year's Slow Moving Politicians who walked the entire march in slow motion – even in the face of frightening statistics and disheartening political movement it's nice to see the Aussies still have their sense of humour.

I also have a prime view of the various signs and placards people brought with them today with messages such as:

- Snowmen Against Global Warming
- There is No Planet B
- Action Not Anger
- End the Jargon. Tax Carbon
- Abbott: Fossil Fool
- 7 Billion Reasons to Go Green (accompanied by cut outs of a chain of people).

I have so much fun with my green dalliances in fashion, shopping and beauty products, but I never want to lose sight of the larger social, cultural and governmental shifts that need to occur to ensure the health of our planet for generations to come. This is precisely why I attend these types of events. I don't really consider myself an 'activist' – in fact when I hear that word I visualise folks carrying megaphones and occasionally being arrested – but I suppose now I am, just a different sort.

I couldn't protest everyday, it's simply not in my DNA, but I know that if I'm really serious about the environment, these events must be part of my life, too – if for no other reason than to support the amazing people who organise and protest and campaign on behalf of our cause day in and day out. Besides, it's not difficult to do, and I definitely get more out than I put in to these types of events. Words can't explain the energy rush I get from being part of this crowd, feeling the positivity and absorbing all the sights, sounds and emotions of the group. It's truly moving to be surrounded by a diversity of others who want the same thing I do for the planet, and instead of focusing only on my personal changes I can feel the strength and power of collective action.

As I continue to pan the crowd taking photographs I spot a familiar face from the Climate Institute, an organisation that shares office space with my company. It is an independent research organisation that works with community, business and government to influence and drive effective climate change solutions. They also support the Australian Youth Climate Coalition (AYCC), which shares our office space from time to time as well. This cohabitation of committed greenies ensures the atmosphere in the GreenHouse is always one of positive momentum for climate change action.

I can't really make my way over to say hello, the crowd is too dense to easily navigate, so I make a mental note to catch up with him on Monday.

It's not unusual for me to see someone I know at green events. In fact, it's been happening since my very first Green Ups event, which I attended soon after I started working at GBCA.

"Hey, I know you!" said this handsome, friendly American guy.

"Oh hi! Where do I know you from?"

He looked very familiar but I couldn't place him. I'd just arrived with Lillian at the Beauchamp Hotel in Oxford Street for an art-themed Green Ups event – Sydney's fabulous monthly networking group focused on all things green. Since Lillian's an artist and the Beauchamp is her favourite bar in Sydney, I had to invite her along.

"You were in my Green Star course a few weeks ago, I'm John."

"Oh that's right! Great to see you again, I'm Lisa, this is Lillian. So, have you been to a Green Ups before?"

"No it's my first one. I only moved to Sydney a couple months ago and a guy at work told me about it."

We chatted for a little bit longer, and it turns out he lived in Manly, too, so we agreed to take the ferry home together – I love meeting other greenies!

In line with the art theme for the night the organisers had requested we all bring the plastic bags floating around our homes, and there was a station set up at the billiard table where Lillian and I learned how to turn plastic bags into 'yarn' and then crochet with it. Her amazing creative skills (and some previous knowledge of knitting) meant she whipped together a cute flower-shaped broach in less than five minutes. I had less skill and even less luck creating anything aside from lots of 'yarn', but I did have a lot of fun.

There was a slide show running of environmental artworks from around the world, and towards the end of the evening the owner of the Beauchamp talked about how the pub ran on green power and was saving to install solar panels on their roof. A beautiful pub in a great location and it has a green conscience? I'll definitely continue frequenting the Beauchamp (as if I needed an excuse).

Following the speeches I looked at the time and felt a bit like Cinderella – I was going to miss my ferry home if I didn't leave immediately. I found John, but then we lost each other somewhere between the stairwell and the exit and I made a dash for the boat without him – each greenie for herself when faced with missing the last ferry home. Luckily when I came running full speed onto the boat there he was – he'd jumped in a cab from the pub when he realised how little time we had.

John and I had a great chat on the way to Manly, and I learned about his history with sustainability, including his recently completed Masters of Strategic Leadership towards Sustainability in Sweden and time spent volunteering in Zambia. He's only 25 but has such clear vision and direction. Hearing his story moved me, and reminded me of the chats I've had with members of the AYCC; I'm at once thankful for the passionate younger generation and slightly jealous that it took me so long to come around to the cause. At least I'm here now!

John works in the very exciting Life Cycle Assessment (LCA) industry, which delves into the total environmental impact of any product, looking at every step from its origins through to its uses and its endings, and evaluates the comprehensive impact. LCA is the future of understanding the true impact of goods on the environment, and I for one can't wait for the day when everything we buy has an eco-label including LCA data.

To give you an example of how it works, let's look at the LCA for a cup of coffee (as I was taught by John's colleague in a course I attended). A cup of coffee includes energy to plant the beans, the water to grow the beans, the energy required to harvest the beans, delivering them to be roasted, the energy to roast them, packaging them, delivering them to a store or café, and the water and energy needed to brew the coffee. This is without even considering the milk or the mug, or what will happen to all of those elements once they are done being someone's latte. It's a very detailed and meticulous process, and I'm so glad to have a connection into the LCA world for when I have questions on future purchases.

The sustainability circles used to talk about goods in terms of 'cradle to grave' and now it's being pushed further to 'cradle to cradle', encouraging items to be used, recycled, and used again to lessen their complete environmental impact – extending the life of materials. I am merely skimming the surface of a very complex concept. The book *Cradle to Cradle*[1] is a great overview of this type of thinking for those interested in more details.

"So what about you? What did you do before the GBCA?" John asked after telling me his story.

"Oh, um, I come from a really different background than you do," I started, feeling a bit apprehensive about confessing my past to this super-greenie, "I actually used to work for very commercial organisations in marketing and advertising."

"Really?!" he asked, looking surprised and sitting forward with interest (at that time I also noticed he was wearing TOMS, fantastic!).

"Yeah, I had a bit of an awakening a couple years ago that made me realise I needed to stop working for companies that only cared about money and use my skills for the environment instead."

"Wow, that's awesome!"

Huh? He seemed genuinely impressed. Up until that point I'd been explaining to people from my old world my change in attitude and was met with looks of confusion, now here was someone who seemed to completely understand why I did what I did. I was speechless.

"I think it's really great that you've made such a big step."

"Oh, uh, thanks. Truthfully it's not always been easy, I've sort of alienated myself from some of my friends and have felt out of place for a while. It was a bigger change than I realised."

"I've always been the environmentalist in my group, so I've never had to explain it to people, they just say, 'Oh that's John, he's a greenie' and move on. But, yeah, I can imagine it would be different if you've changed after people had known you another way."

We talked about Australia and the environment the rest of the way to Manly, and on my walk home it hit me that I was entering a whole new world. A world filled with people who believed in environmentalism as much as I did – and many of whom knew much more about it than I did. I was excited to be learning from them, and as an added bonus, it seemed they were excited to have me along. This wasn't an exclusive group; they were happily inviting new members to the cause, and seemed genuinely pleased that I'd joined the brigade, despite my questionable past. Perhaps even more pleased because of it.

I look back on that night as my official inauguration into the green social network.

Between the events I attend through my job and those I attend via the many email lists I subscribe to, I get around the green scene. It's great; I'm continually learning more about sustainability and its many facets. These events are also important because they motivate and inspire me on days when I may be getting bogged down in the details of day-to-day life. I never tire of hearing from the innovators, technicians and advocates themselves about how they developed a new technology or material for a building or a new way of thinking about financing a project. I've been in a presentation by a woman trained by Al Gore himself, I saw Bjorn Lomborg – the sceptical environmentalist I read oh-so-early-on in my environmental journey – and even seen Cate Blanchett discuss Sydney's sustainable 2030 plan. I've heard from ingenious architects, engineers and developers on how they planned and built some of the country's greenest buildings, from a health and healing expert on the importance of green spaces for hospitals and from local community leaders who are making huge strides within their neighbourhoods.

The speakers that resonate with me the most are the ones who have a message to bring to the mainstream – to the average Jane who isn't an expert in sustainability, perhaps not even interested in it, who needs something really unique to catch her attention and get her excited about the environmental campaign. Last year I attended a memorable event that did just that, featuring the leader of the Plastiki sailboat expedition, David de Rothschild.

The Plastiki was created out of 12,500 reused plastic bottles (the number consumed every 8.3 seconds in the US). It sailed all the way from San Francisco to Sydney in 129 days as a way of demonstrating our society's reliance on this non-renewable resource and to draw attention to the 'plastic island' in the North Pacific Gyre I described to Maryanne. The Plastiki used bicycle generators and solar panels for her energy requirements, and even used filtered urine to water the hydroponic garden growing food on board. An engineering marvel to say the least!

I had first read about the Plastiki before it departed from San Francisco, in the *Good Weekend* section of the *Sydney Morning Herald* (what can I say, I still revel in light news on the weekends). I remembered it because I liked de Rothschild's response to the journalist's question about what he says to people who don't believe in climate change. He replied that petroleum is a limited resource and we'll eventually have to live without petrol and plastic anyway, so let's start thinking about alternative solutions regardless of your take on climate change. I can still get somewhat fiery when climate deniers attempt to negate the scientific evidence regarding climate change, and appreciated his alternate logical response. When I saw the announcement that he'd be speaking in Sydney I wasted no time in getting a ticket.

The presentation itself was fun – he was very casual and relaxed as he showed us clips of video footage featuring the trials and tribulations of the Plastiki – the crew had just pulled in the day before and were still on a high from their completed mission. I also loved hearing that the boat was on display at the Maritime Museum; I can just imagine all the children, our future green generation, walking through it with their parents and being inspired by what they saw and making plans for their own Plastikis.

The event was held at a recently revamped reception centre on Sydney Harbour that touts itself as 'green'. I'd attended the opening a few months prior with my work colleague Sophie, and, well, the jury is still out on how green it is. They incorporated a number of great initiatives, but the scent of the new carpets and upholstery indicated they hadn't selected low VOC options, the chandeliers had lots and lots of sparkly lights, and the doors and some walls were covered in bright red leather. But the catering is based on a '100 mile radius' from the centre and they say they are installing solar panels and working with architects and engineers to lessen their impact on their surrounding environment – so at the very least the intent is right and I hope they follow through with their proposals. This is precisely why independent certification of buildings, like products, is so important. I appreciate they are taking steps in the right direction, and hope they decide to obtain certification to back up all their green claims.

While at the opening event I bumped into one of the partners of Republic of Everyone, a forward-thinking creative agency dedicated to sustainability and corporate social responsibility projects. Before I got my job at GBCA I was vying for a position there (shhh, don't tell my boss!). I had met the other partner at a seminar on 'Social Networking for Not for Profits', and so made introductions and we agreed to chat in the future about potentially working together on a campaign.

See what I mean? Small green world. I love it.

"Have you heard of the 1 Million Women campaign?" I ask, trying to get the attention of a group of ladies walking past the booth in the 'Fashion & Textile Hall' at the Royal Easter Show.

For every three or four groups of people who walk by one usually stops and allows me to continue my spiel:

"1 Million Women is about celebrating the power women have in the environmental movement."

And about every other group who make it that far stick around long enough for me to get to the good stuff:

"It's a free campaign, we just ask women to register on the website and make a commitment to reduce their eco-footprint over the course of a year. Our goal is to inspire 1 million women to get on with climate action by cutting a tonne of pollution from their daily lives. The website has tips on cutting your emissions and an online tool to help you track your progress."

I love this campaign. Not only is it easy to get on board and connect, but also I know from my previous existence marketing grocery items that women are responsible for over 70% of all household purchases. We are a very important group to get involved in the cause. I signed up to the group as soon as I heard about it and agreed to help get more ladies registered – hence volunteering today.

The interactive website includes suggestions for reducing your impact as varied as saying no to red meat to reducing air travel to using reusable food containers, so women can jump in and immediately start making changes regardless of their current level of eco-activity. The potential of this campaign is astounding – one million women all committed to fighting climate change (now *that's* a green social network). The campaign's reached over 85,000 women so far and the numbers increase every day. Who knows where it will be by the time you read this book. Sign up today if you haven't already – you'll be able to cut a tonne before you know it!

I'll admit that it hasn't been an easy day trying to talk to people about environmental responsibility while they are enjoying the festivities of the Easter Show, but the campaign's energetic and dedicated founder, Natalie Isaacs, is on site and provides constant encouragement. I've gotten about 30 people to register in a couple hours, not a bad effort, but I'm sure Natalie's recruited double that in the same amount of time. I've taken note of her dedicated yet compassionate and non-judgemental tone and try and work it into my own voice.

Volunteering today has reminded me that even though I'm in my happy green scene at work and with some new friends, there are still a whole lot of people at a different stage of environmentalism – and for plenty this means climate change is not even on their radar. No matter how deep into the movement I get I hope that I don't forget that not everyone is on the same page as I am. Everyone is on her own green journey and if I want to keep promoting environmental action I'll need to use the right voice, which is definitely not condescending, pushy, or holier-than-thou. Now *that's* a lesson I wished I'd learned better at the start of my eco-journey.

"Welcome to 30 The Bond – Australia's first green building," says the beautiful Maria Atkinson to the crowd, standing in her gorgeous fuchsia tweed suit. "If you have a headache, are feeling a bit congested, or your eyes are hurting after a long day in the office, just sit back and enjoy the benefits of breathing in 100% natural air."

Tyler and I are sitting in the lobby of one of Sydney's greenest buildings, one that really set the standard for green building when it was built back in 2005. I didn't realise Maria would be opening the event when I signed up to attend; she's one of the founders of GBCA and I'm thrilled to see her in the flesh and hear her speak so passionately about the benefits of green building nearly a decade after founding the organisation.

The venue is really stunning, too. An entire wall of the lobby is exposed sandstone, one of the city's longest and oldest remaining examples of hand cut sandstone from the age of convict labour. There are vibrant green plants sprouting from cracks in the wall where natural springs are trickling, demonstrating that life always finds a way. Based on the many photos I've seen of this building I know that during the day the area is flooded with natural daylight through the generous skylights running the length of the lobby.

We came to this beautiful space to celebrate the second birthday of 1 Million Women and hear from author (and activist, social entrepreneur and former Greenpeace CEO) Paul Gilding. His book *The Great Disruption* recently made headlines in the *New York Times* that found its way into my inbox, Facebook and Twitter accounts:

> "You really do have to wonder whether a few years from now we'll look back at the first decade of the 21st century — when food prices spiked, energy prices soared, world population surged, tornados plowed through cities, floods and droughts set records, populations were displaced and governments were threatened by the confluence of it all — and ask ourselves: What were we thinking?" [2]

Before Paul takes the stage I take in the crowd, observe the proportion of women to men (about 20 to 1), and search for familiar faces. I spot a few, including the co-founder of Clean Up Australia and another spunky greenie gal who works for the state government that I regularly run into at Green Ups events. A woman sits down in front of me, joining a row of her friends, and says, "Isn't it great to have such a large gathering of lower North shore mothers here tonight?" I love it! It's fantastic to see all these women pulling together to make change happen starting in their households, just as 1 Million Women encourages, and to see the different types of women who are getting involved in the movement. From the bush to the city to the leafy North Shore, women are pulling together for a greener future.

More people are joining the green fold every year, too. The market for consumers of green products (frequently called the LOHAS market – Lifestyles of Health and Sustainability) is continuing to increase in size and depth. Consumer spending on healthy and sustainable goods and services jumped from \$12 billion in 2007 to \$21.5 billion in 2010, and is expected to hit \$27 billion in 2012[3]. The research indicates that there is still a certain level of scepticism on green claims, but that price is no longer the barrier it once was to green living as price premiums on green goods continue to drop.

Mica Nava, consumer studies expert and Director of the Centre for Cultural Studies Research, writes about the power of voting with your wallet, which is precisely what the LOHAS consumers are doing. Nava explains the attraction and impact of green consumerism because it "offers ordinary people access to a new and very immediate democratic process: 'voting' about the environment can take place on a daily basis"[4] through our everyday spending. When we spend more on green goods and spend less overall, we send the message to government and industry that we don't need all this stuff, especially if it's made unethically and with no consideration for the environment. As I learned very early on, one of the greatest actions we can all take is to keep those credit cards in our handbags; it's a powerful message in our growth-driven world and is something we all can do everyday. Groups like 1 Million Women can help make the transition easier, because you know there are thousands of others out there who are learning to change their habits, too. I hope this green network continues to grow into many more communities, niches and demographics of people, because together we are making a difference.

In the words of the man I came to hear tonight, Paul Gilding:

> "… we need to stop waiting for someone else to fix it. There is no one else. We are the system; we have to change. Companies will respond when consumers and investors change their demands. Politicians will drive change when we make them do so. . . Now that we're all connected, if we all act together, we'll change the system." [5]

Paul is my kind of environmentalist – change starts with each one of us. As I've learned, once you start changing it is easy to make connections with other greenies and join the growing green social network. As a group we can motivate one another, and together our voice is so much more powerful than when we speak alone.

The internet also allows us to connect in ways previously unimaginable, enabling even greater change. We can now connect across towns, states, countries and oceans at the click of a mouse or touch of a button. I've never been one to prioritise building online relationships over nourishing in-the-flesh relationships, but being involved in online communities through 350.org, Green Thing, 1 Million Women, Get Up, NRDC, Greenpeace and many more certainly has opened my eyes to the size of the worldwide green social network. I've also recently started dabbling in Twitter and the blogosphere, connecting with new people and witnessing firsthand the millions of relationships being fostered online.

I truly love being part of this living, breathing, and most important, *growing,* organism that is the environmental movement. Compared to a couple of years ago, when my self-esteem plummeted after Beefgate, today my self-esteem is stronger than it's ever been in part because I'm part of a group that I'm proud of and feel good about. As a result of my improved self-esteem, I feel compelled to keep acting and keep speaking out about climate change action – it's a beautiful cycle that helps me feel good about myself and what I'm doing, and hopefully the end result sees me influencing positive change.

Aside from the great strides the movement has made for the environment, what I love most about this group is that it's totally blown my short-sighted perception about what it means to be an environmentalist. There are lots of different types of greenies out there who are living proof that environmentalism is just part of what creates an individual's image and identity. There are very business-like greenies, who look more 'corporate warrior' than 'eco-warrior', and very fashionable greenies, like the lovely designer Louise Olsen from Dinosaur Designs (and now Supercyclers), who is also a founder of Green Ups. There are techie-greenies, who have taken 'living paperlessly' to a whole new level with their committed relationships to their beloved iPhones and iPads. There are engineering and architect greenies constantly creating new green solutions. There are political greenies who know how to speak to politicians and fight the green fight on the front lines. There are artistic greenies who show their commitment through painting, creatively recycling materials or designing clothing and jewellery in sustainable ways. Of course there are plenty of my beloved hippy greenies; they aren't as high a proportion as I initially imagined – based on image alone – but I suspect many are hippies at heart.

I don't feel judged by environmentalists as I'd initially feared way back when I met with the editor – and knowing what I know now she probably wasn't judging me at all. Every now and then a traditional greenie will be surprised I'm as green as I am, but that's the exception more than the rule. I'm thinking of a specific incident when I was explaining to a super-greenie that my hairdresser was across the street, and I'd started going to them because of their eco-credentials; she looked at me quite seriously for a minute and then said, "I'm impressed". She may have assumed because I looked a certain way I only 'sort of' cared about the environment and *really* cared about my appearance. Come to think of it, she probably wasn't even judging me; she was probably genuinely impressed that I had taken that into account when I selected my hair salon.

If anything it's non-greenies who are most surprised when they learn I'm an environmentalist because I don't fit their description. I'll meet a trendy looking guy or gal, and we'll get to talking about fashion or design because I still look the part and it seems like subjects we can bond over, but eventually the conversation will turn and they'll learn I'm also an environmentalist. I love seeing the surprise on their faces when I tell them because I get it, I was like them a few years ago, thinking that you couldn't be stylish and be green; it had to be one or the other.

I hope that to those folks I'm an example that you can have it both ways, sustainability with style, and that I encourage them to start thinking about making more green choices in their own lives. The good news for them is they already have stylish-living down pat, so now they just have to incorporate eco-elements bit by bit, which is getting easier by the day.

After that, joining the green social network is easy – everyone's welcome as long as she comes with an open mind and hope for a greener future – not to mention supportive, encouraging and powerful.

Ripple effect

Trying a new greenie action of using coffee grounds from Starbucks to fertilize our grass and gardens. Thought you'd be proud – R

Proud?! Ecstatic is more like it! I love when anyone shares a green change with me, but because Rosie, my best friend in America, is still not 100% convinced about climate change, whenever I get an email about something green she's doing I get extra excited. Rosie's not your typical sceptic, though. She's made a conscious effort to lead a greener lifestyle, including diligent recycling and growing an organic garden (complete with chickens for fertiliser and pest control), so that she leaves a cleaner, less polluted world for her boys. She's one climate sceptic I'm proud to call a friend.

After the personal disaster of Beefgate, I stopped pushing my environmental message onto my friends. Encouraging green action within my social group had been a key motivating factor at the start of my environmental journey, but I simply couldn't take the rejection. Thankfully my relative silence didn't stop some friends from making environmental changes.

Lillian in particular has been a huge supporter since my first email about *Use Your Own Mug* – whilst her lifestyle hasn't changed as significantly as mine, she has always been open to change: using her cute vintage thermos, buying local products, telling me about Keep Cups and more recently about the community bookshelf in her neighbourhood where people can easily swap books. Our makeup shopping excursion and her phone call to me about *Gorgeously Green* oh-so-long-ago showed me her commitment to the cause and to our friendship, and really kept me motivated at a time when my energy was low and my doubts were high.

Maryanne also provided me much support, and a happy side effect of my becoming an environmentalist was that our friendship grew closer and deeper. We'd been good friends for a few years, but we didn't really have that much in common. I was the fashion-obsessed shopaholic she referred to as her 'personal stylist'; she was the sporty nature-lover with a unique curiosity and a care for others like I'd never seen. I never minded our differences; in fact, I cherished her perspective on life. But as she started calling me not to ask if a certain outfit was appropriate but to discuss something closer to her heart, I felt our friendship grow in a new, exciting direction.

Recently Geoff mentioned that watching Ty and me has reminded him to be more diligent in his environmental choices. As he put it:

"I'd become sceptical of environmental claims, especially when they don't take into account all elements of the product's life cycle, that whole cradle to grave concept. But listening to you two talk about green travel and buying stuff like those soap nuts, it's making me feel a lot less blasé about it all."

Just by living my greenest life I'd influenced Geoff, someone who has been interested in the environment for quite some time and initially influenced my green changes. And who, it turns out, needed some additional motivation of his own after suffering a little green fatigue.

And now, after seeing the power of the green social network and receiving Rosie's email, I'm more convinced than ever that friendships will help the environmental movement flourish.

It's been nearly three years since I flipped my environmental switch. I'm now a green-collar worker and have started a green-living blog to share environmental tips and tricks with my friends (and the world!). It seems like a good time to determine if my journey has inspired others to start their own, especially in light of Geoff's admission.

Even though I'm not consciously pushing my green message, over the past few years I have had lots of conversations about sustainability. The topic tends to arise naturally, when someone asks what I've been up to or how work is going, as it's increasingly difficult to separate the environment from the rest of my life.

Sam (he of the takeaway coffee cups) is becoming more interested in sustainability, especially from a business perspective as he completes his MBA. Lately we've been having really interesting conversations about companies' sustainability practices. It's really lovely to see a shift in his behaviour, particularly the way we can talk about environmentalism now as compared to when I would get frustrated if he forgot to use his own mug. I think it's partly because the environment has become an integral part of my life and I no longer apologise for that, and partly due to the fact 'green' is working its way into the mainstream business world, so it's not a personal judgment I'm making against him, but we're having a broader sustainability discussion.

My family has also come along on the ride to a certain extent. I receive frequent emails from them with links to interesting green companies in the US. My mom recently changed all the lights in her house to low-energy options and got more insulation installed in her home (those government rebates were an amazing motivator for many Americans, including Mom). And last Christmas, though some ignored my request for 'no gifts', everything I was given had a green angle. My sister-in-law made me wine bottle bags out of an old sweater, my mother-in-law wrapped all presents in reusable cloth wrapping paper, including the market bag she hand-knitted for me, my mom gave me a natural and organic salt scrub, and even my dad, who claims to not be convinced on climate change, gave me a reusable bag from his local grocery store.

I was also recently asked to settle a dispute between Naomi and Drake over whether they could recycle their pizza box. I typically don't get involved in other couple's domestic debates, but when I have the answer I must, and this time I sided with Naomi: generally-speaking, pizza boxes are not recyclable. Even though they are made of cardboard, the grease soaks in to make the box unrecyclable.

I have enjoyed becoming the resident environmentalist (Sarah recently introduced me to some of her friends that way), though at times I do feel pressure to not accidentally greenwash when giving advice. Being known as a greenie allows me to talk about eco-topics without feeling the need to apologise. Hey, it's what I do. And interestingly, it's the new people I meet who are most interested in any tips I can share – it's a very fun role to play, and I'm happy to be able help anyone who's keen.

Feeling bolstered by Rosie's email, Sarah's introductions, Geoff's admission and settling Naomi and Drake's debate, I decide to ask more of my friends straight out if I've influenced them to make any eco-changes. It's time I stop being afraid of talking about the environment with my friends.

In response I learn the following:

- On a 'water-sensitive' and slightly humorous note, Randall admits:

"This is sort of disgusting and maybe not the kind of thing you want to hear about, but, when I'm home all day alone, I don't flush the toilet if it's just urine in there. I might have to change that policy if the baby gets old enough to climb into the bowl or if my lady friend becomes repulsed."

I'm not repulsed; hopefully his wife's not either. I think it's great and relevant to Australia's water restrictions, and it's important to celebrate environmental changes large and small. His example also reminds me of a childhood poem:

If it's yellow, let it mellow. If it's brown, flush it down.

Wise words.

- Maryanne tells me all the stuff she and David already did before my green journey began – like using reusable bags, having energy saving light bulbs and eating natural food – and says that I have encouraged them to use Keep Cups. She also particularly likes hearing about natural beauty products that I've used or read about, and wants the information to keep on coming.

- Naomi shares that she's previously been sceptical of green claims on goods, putting them in the same category as 'lite' foods – sounding a bit like Geoff and his scepticism of green products. But seeing me live my green lifestyle and share my knowledge, she can put more faith in certain green products and services because "a trusted friend recommends them." I sure am glad I started that blog!

- Even Kate, who hasn't been terribly vocal either way about my green changes, now uses a Keep Cup and has bought adorable bamboo placemats (hard bamboo, not spun into a textile) for her new apartment. She's also taking the bus a whole lot more frequently than she used to and is looking forward to borrowing Naomi's bike while she's travelling. Go Kate!

Lest I give the impression that I'm converting people left and right, I'll come clean and admit that not everyone in my life is going green. Ewan admitted:

"Sorry Luv, I'm just too selfish to think about the environment all the time."

I appreciate his honesty (I still place honesty above greenness on the friendship scale), though I wish it weren't true. I know it was merely his way of saying he has so much else going on in his life that thinking about the environment isn't high on his list. A lot of people feel this way – it's not that they don't want to be greener, but they don't want to give up their entire lives to do it.

I also had a very frustrating conversation one night with Anil about changing to green energy. Here is a condensed version of the scenario:

Anil: "Hey, are you still into using your own mug?"

Lisa: "Yep – are you?"

A: "Umm, I guess not, but hey, do you eat beef?"

L: "Anil, I was the one who told you about beef!"

A: "Oh yeah."

L: "I've switched to green energy, though."

A: "You know you can't be sure you're getting green energy?"

L: "I know my exact house may not get it, but the total amount I use comes from a renewable source, whether it's my flat or a house out in the country."

A: "It's a total conspiracy. The big oil companies are making so much money out of that scam."

L: "What? I think you have misinformation."

Round and round we went. He wouldn't say he was a sceptic or that he didn't care about the environment, but he really wasn't giving the environment a chance, either. It wasn't until Tyler joined the conversation that Anil stopped debating and started listening – perhaps giving into peer pressure now that it was two against one? Though I suspect to this day he is not on green energy and probably doesn't use his own mug.

There are also the friends who still claim that it's society's fault / the government's fault / consumer culture's fault and choose to complain rather than act. I'm not saying all those things don't play a massive role – they do, we exist in a very growth-driven world that values money over environment – but instead of burying my head in the sand, I choose to work for change, from the smallest switch of using my own mug to bigger-picture initiatives like attending rallies and writing letters to my politicians. I don't have time to complain about whose fault it might be.

⌑∅👗👒👖👠💍👛💄👜💡♡

I meet up with Sarah at Opera Kitchen before the ballet – we have season tickets, which are so fabulous because we are guaranteed four beautiful ballets a year and four special nights out with each other – and as we sit awestruck by the gorgeous scenery of Sydney Harbour with the bridge and the Opera House I ask her,

"How did your Earth Hour party go?"

A few weeks ago she asked me for tips on hosting an eco-friendly dinner party for some friends who, as she puts it, "are not green *at all.*" I helped her come up with some gentle suggestions – like Keep Cups, bringing your own bag to the grocery store, changing your light bulbs and switching to green power – and steer clear of the 'no beef' suggestion (I'm glad someone can benefit from my mistake!). I know how important it is to suggest changes people can easily incorporate into their lifestyles to non-greenies so they don't feel attacked by the suggestions.

"Oh, it was great! I'm not sure how much everyone has taken on board, but they all were really great about listening to the tips as we ate by candle light, and I gave them each a cute reusable bag to take home."

"Well done," I'm so pleased to hear that she's taking the messages out into her social networks, "Everyone needs to start somewhere, and what a perfect opportunity to talk about it."

"You know that I religiously use a Keep Cup, too? Actually, I was devastated when I lost my original one because I'd have to waste resources getting another one."

"Tell me about it! Tyler lost mine and I felt the same way. You're supposed to use it over and over again – it's a *Keep* Cup!" I laugh, but truthfully I'm still cranky he lost my Keep Cup. My only hope is that it's being used by someone who didn't have one before and that it didn't get tossed in the trash.

"I've even given Keep Cups as gifts to co-workers who get multiple takeaway coffees a day. One gal liked hers so much that she gave one to her mum and claims it's the best gift she's ever been given."

And there is more...it's like I opened the floodgates of every green change she's made. She is excited to be telling me, and I am ecstatic to hear all about it.

"I've stopped buying books before checking with my other 'reader' friends to see if they already own the one I want. And if no one has it, I'll organise a trade – I'll buy this one if you buy that one, then we can swap. I can't yet bring myself to use e-books, but am even considering that option.

"Oh! And I'm now the proud owner of a Soda Stream, which means I'm no longer buying sparkling water. It saves at least six large bottles going into the recycling every week and turns out it's actually cheaper! Two couples I've preached to about this have now bought a system themselves...I'm so proud."

"You should be proud, that's fantastic. I love how you've looked at where you were having an environmental impact, with bottles of bubbly water, and figured out a way to green that activity. Such a clever idea!"

"You know Lise, a lot of it is because you've personalised 'green' for me. Seeing what you do has opened my eyes so much more than anything I've read or seen in the media, and makes me want to do so much more."

"Oh, wow, thanks," I'm feeling a bit embarrassed, but mostly touched by her openness and honesty.

"Between your green lifestyle and my simultaneous move to 'pescatarianism', I'm generally becoming a more conscious consumer - thanks in part to you. I'm nowhere near where I should be, so hopefully I'll continue adopting more practices as time goes on. Actually, I need a training session on green cleaning!"

"Ha ha, anytime. Happy to share my special cleaning recipe."

Sarah continues to tell me all the green initiatives she is taking with her upcoming wedding – it's a destination wedding in Mexico, which means everyone will be travelling to get there, so she wants to make everything else as green as possible.

Some of her green wedding choices include:

- RSVPs online instead of sending the traditional response cards and envelopes
- No disposable cups, plates, silverware, tablecloths or serviettes
- Use of local produce and flowers
- Renting decorations in order to avoid throwing things away afterwards, and donating anything that isn't rented to the wedding planner for use at a future event
- Guest hotels are within walking distance to the villa where the events are to be held and to the beach.

I'll be at her wedding in Mexico – I will offset my flights, of course – so I'll be able to appreciate her green initiatives in person.

Sarah's changes have been a lovely surprise, and a real highlight of my environmental journey. It's not that I ever thought she *wasn't* a potential greenie, I just hadn't been consciously trying to influence her over the past few years. But it seems that simply as a result of spending time with me as I became greener and greener I did inspire her – because in her words, I personalised 'green' for her, and she realized she could do it, too. I can't take complete credit, because Sarah is genuinely trying to make a difference in her life, but I'm honoured to have influenced her at all, and will be learning many lessons from her in the future, no doubt.

My discussion with Sarah really highlighted that you never know who's going to become your next environmentalist friend, or what path they'll take into environmentalism. I feel privileged to have been able to inspire so many of my friends to incorporate green living into their routines, and can see a glimpse of the power of social networks to change the environment.

It's what Sophie Uliano of *Gorgeously Green* suggested through her 'Green Goddess' evenings, and it's what social movement expert Stuart Barr suggests about creating successful social movements:

getting in at the community level and understanding people's lives so that change can be sustainable for them.

Barr argues that environmental changes will work best if implemented within social networks, and discusses the importance of embedding sustainable lifestyle options into everyday practices; instead of calling for radical shifts in behaviour, encouraging environmental policies to "focus on how people live their everyday lives, the lifestyle groups within which they are situated and the aspirations they have" in order to encourage sustainable actions from the ground up[1]. As I've been living my greenest existence and finding my personal green balance, I've learned what's easy and not so easy about the changes required of me; it seems those around me are learning through my example.

In his book Barr argues for the mainstreaming of sustainable lifestyles as the only way to effectively engage people in the environmental discussion. And here I am, seeing it work right before my very eyes. Sarah and her Soda Stream and green wedding, Rosie and her garden patch with coffee grinds for fertiliser, me finding my balance between sustainability and style by using eco-beauty and fashion items – these are all examples of incorporating environmentalism into our everyday lives and shifting green to a regular lifestyle.

I truly believe most people want to do right by the environment – you don't tend to hear anyone say they want to trash the Earth – but they can't always identify means of doing so that are appealing or fit with their lifestyle. Some aspects of one's lifestyle must change to really live eco-aware, and seeing friends successfully living 'green' provides reassurance that you don't have to give up your identity to become an environmentalist; it seems I've provided that example to some of my friends and they are now starting to pass on the message.

As more individuals from my group incorporate green actions in their lives, we influence each other and others, shifting the collective identity of our social group into a greener direction. A mob that once valued shopping and dining as pleasure-seeking activities is evolving into one that also finds pleasure in shopping for ethical goods, eating eco-wise and taking steps to combat climate change. Word is spreading that you can still be cool, hip, trendy (insert whatever words you'd like to define yourself with here) and an environmentalist. While I don't think 'environmentalism' will ever be a key defining aspect of the group, the number of individuals who are incorporating environmentalism into their self-identification and even better, sharing the news with others, demonstrates to me a real chance for positive change in the future.

"Lisa, you'll be so proud of us!" exclaim Shelley and Noel at Anika and Randall's little boy's first birthday party.

Oh good – another green story coming my way!

"We used an ad that Smiggle handed us in the shopping centre to wrap the little guy's present!"

"That's awesome!" I say – I love creative reuse of materials; I made the birthday boy's card out of scraps of card and ribbon I had lying around my flat.

"I don't think you realise how much you inspire us," says Shelley, "the other night Noel and I went to the shops to get stuff for his film shoot, and all three times we stopped somewhere I made him go back to the car to get the bags – we kept forgetting them but I then I'd think of you and wanted to make you proud, so I kept telling Noel, 'We have to go back for our bags, think about Lisa!'"

"Oh, I love it! Thanks for sharing that with me," I laugh a bit – it's very sweet, though I hope I'm not too scary!

Maryanne pipes up, "Look what we gave the birthday boy!"

She shows me a cute sign made out of coloured paper in the shape of a train; it is an invitation for the birthday boy to ride the Bronte Beach train with Maryanne's little boy.

"This way we aren't giving him more toys, but an experience instead, and time together." Frequently the best green gifts are the most thoughtful and relationship building ones, too; it's lovely to see it happening starting at age one.

"See Lise, you're having a ripple effect on us," says Noel.

"Yeah, because we think of you when we're doing everything, wanting to make sure we do the right thing. Then we'll have a ripple effect on others – think of all our friends we'll influence," exclaims Shelley.

"Yeah Lise, imagine the possibilities of all this!"

Yes, just imagine.

What will be possible if we keep this up? What other social networks will my friends reach? What other changes will we inspire?

I have goose bumps just thinking about it!

Finding balance

I'm sitting in the Opera House with one of my best green friends, Bjorn, listening to this year's winner of the Sydney Peace Prize, Dr Vandana Shiva, explain the importance of keeping genetically modified (GMO) foods out of India. I got tickets early so we're in the eighth row and have a clear view of the award-winning eco-feminist (how fabulous is her title? I can't wait for the day 'eco-feminist' is on my business card). In her poetic narrative Shiva, a physicist who also has a PhD in Philosophy, passionately explains how genetic modification is war on food – gene guns and plant cancers are the weapons of choice for changing food genetics. These weapons disturb the metabolism of plants and the side effects include the creation of super-weeds and super-pests that are resistant to herbicides and pesticides. She further points out that the names of herbicides also conjure up images of war – Round Up, Machete, Lasso, Pentagon, Prowl, Sceptre, Squadron, Lightning, Assert, Avenge. She's right, this is certainly not the language of sustainability or nourishment for our bodies.

Shiva says that nature has already created drought- and flood-proof seeds – we don't need GMOs to do it. Working with communities through the Navdanya organisation, a "women centred movement for the protection of biological and cultural diversity"[1], she has seen biodiversity produce more food than when crops are isolated. In these communities there is more nutrition per acre, more food per acre, and more income for farmers per acre when food is grown organically and without GMO seeds.

Throughout her career 'earth rights' have driven Shiva as a means of protecting human rights, and she provides example after example of human lives at risk as a result of environmental issues. For example, in one decade India lost 200,000 farmers to suicide after finding themselves trapped in debt; not only are GMO seeds high priced, but there is also a high cost of chemicals to combat the super-weeds and pests that GMO seeds have brought about. Shiva calls this massive loss of life genocide, not suicide, because of the role the Monsanto seed company has played in creating this trap[2].

She also describes toxic red mud flooding through the streets of Hungary that killed nine civilians, calling it the "blood of the earth"; it came from an aluminium smelter that uses boxide. For every one million tonnes of aluminium produced, there are 100 million tonnes of toxic runoff, which led to this particular disaster. If the price of aluminium included the environmental cost, Shiva doesn't think aluminium production would continue at current levels because no one could afford it.

She cites other examples of human rights being impacted by environmental crises: the Pakistan floods, Indian flash floods and the oil spill in the Gulf of Mexico. She concludes that artificial processes and climate change have led to the devastation not just of the planet but the people living on it – this is why earth rights are human rights.

Shiva brings us a hopeful message, though: the power of people can stop these things. She has seen it first hand in India through the work of Navdanya, which has helped set up 54 seed banks and trained over 500,000 farmers in seed and food sovereignty and sustainable agriculture. She has also been involved with other Indian communities that have protested and stopped unsustainable mining initiatives in rural villages. She encourages us all to act so that we can prevent future devastation.

After she concludes her speech, two opera singers enter the stage to sing songs of gratitude in Shiva's honour.

Their voices are breathtaking, but opera's never been able to hold my attention and my mind wanders. I reflect on how much I've changed over the past few years. Who would have imagined three years ago that I'd be sitting in this audience? I didn't even know about the Sydney Peace Prize let alone have an interest in GMO foods, yet here I am. Present, engaged and informed of all the issues Shiva's speaking about tonight.

Today I have a greater understanding of challenging concepts that I barely knew existed before starting my environmental journey. In addition to climate change and other environmental concerns, I've learned a lot about human rights including human trafficking, food shortages, education inequity, disaster relief and poverty, including measures that can help in each case. I appreciate more than ever just how fortunate I am to be sitting in this amazing theatre in one of the most beautiful venues in the entire world in this spectacular city in a free and democratic society. Add to this appreciation the fact that I'm surrounded by hundreds of people who value the same things I do – this is the green social network expanded into the ethical social network – and tonight I can't help but be filled with immense hope for the future. There is plenty of work to do, but I believe we'll all pull together and improve the state of the environment, and human rights, around the globe.

I also reflect on how much I *haven't* changed. I've been able to maintain the part of my identity I was most afraid of losing when I first joined the movement – my sense of style – even as I've become greener and greener. (Though I must admit, the longer I'm in the movement the less importance wearing each trend as it appears seems to hold.) Tonight, for instance, I'm wearing a gold sequined bolero jacket, my glittery platinum-gold stilettos, a black halter and my skinny Veronika Maine pants; the pants are newest at about six months old, and everything else is over three years old and still looking fabulous. Once again I'm reminded of the importance of quality over quantity in my fashion. I'm definitely channelling more 'glamour' than 'greenie' tonight, but feel appropriately dressed for a special night at the Opera House celebrating the awe-inspiring achievements of Dr. Vandana Shiva.

Many of tonight's attendees are channelling more 'greenie' than 'glamour' and, in my opinion, are completely under-dressed – the number of people in jeans and other casual wear is shocking. At first I felt self-conscious and overdressed, then I thought to myself, "This woman has empowered thousands of impoverished people and fights to protect the food source of India for goodness sake. No one needed to buy a new dress or suit for the occasion, but show her some respect." Shiva herself looks radiant in a crimson, maroon and gold sari, and I feel by dressing up I'm honouring her and her work.

I guess I haven't changed that much – still striving for the perfect look for any occasion.

I'm definitely still on my eco-journey and not 100% green (if that is even achievable in this day and age), but I am managing the pace so that I don't feel I've lost myself in the process.

There have been the occasional setbacks, too. For instance, about a month ago I made the decision to start colouring my hair again – that's right, using chemicals and energy and water, and generally increasing my environmental impact, all in the name of vanity.

Of all the green changes I have made I really didn't think I would succumb to hair dye – I'd been quite happy with my natural brunette for a couple of years – but then one day I met Lucia and everything changed. . .

Ty and I were on the ferry home when a lovely family of Italian tourists starting speaking to me.

"Lei è italiano?" asked the mother.

"No, American, uh, Americano," I replied with a smile and a shrug; with my naturally dark hair and dark eyes my Italian heritage is apparent and this type of thing happens from time to time with tourists from Italy (and Greece and Turkey – gotta love having a Mediterranean background).

We all smiled at each other and then the gorgeous little girl decided to practice her English on me.

"What is your name?" she asked in her sweet Italian accent.

"Lisa. What is your name?"

"Lucia. How old are you?"

"30. How old are you?"

"9. What is your favourite colour?"

"Red."

"Lavender?" She points to my handbag, smiling.

"Um, yes, lavender. Or purple."

"Purple."

We smiled at each other. Oh the world was a wonderful place, and we were enjoying talking colours and numbers, feeling the joy from making a connection with a stranger. So delightful.

"Leeza?" She scrunched up her face and inquired, "Why brown?" pointing to the top of my hair, "and yellow?" pointing to the bottom of my hair.

Her mother looked slightly more mortified than I felt inside, and Tyler started laughing. Then I started laughing, too, and shrugged my shoulders – how do you explain to a nine-year-old the concept of bad hair dye regrowth? Her mother shushed her even as I insisted it really wasn't a big deal, and we rode the rest of the way home in silence.

As soon as I got home, though, I rushed to the mirror; when a nine-year-old girl asks what's up with your hair, you know it's been neglected for too long. Upon inspection I could see the colour had faded so that the old highlights starkly contrasted what was coming out of my head; I hadn't realized it was so noticeable. It wasn't a lovely balayage effect, just neglected regrowth. Maybe I was turning into a hippy after all. I used to spend hours each week in front of a mirror, examining the size of my pores, the colour of my roots, the whiteness of my teeth and the shape of my eyebrows; somewhere between the all-over colour and learning new eco-beauty routines I'd stopped paying attention to my once-gorgeous locks.

How had I let this happen?!

I needed to get my hair back to beautiful, and quick, so I started researching my options immediately.

The first eco-hair products I uncovered left much to be desired. Henna dyes seem to have been around for a while; one brand in particular had a dated-looking illustration of lions in front of Egyptian pyramids on the box. Is this because henna has been used since the time of the pharaohs? I understood the 'mane' connotation, but I'd prefer to see a picture of someone who used the product on her hair. Another eco-hair colour range had an illustration of a water droplet on the packaging, and another featured extremely poor photographs that gave no indication whatsoever of the colour that would end up on your hair.

On the one hand, since I've worked in the advertising industry I know that the quality of packaging does not necessarily equate to the quality of the product; on the other, I couldn't trust a company that didn't care about aesthetics enough to hire a model, professional photographer and stylist to promote their *hair colour range*. This wasn't some eco-cleaning product I was buying; this was something I would use to enhance my appearance. The fact that I am purchasing hair colour at all should tell you I'm at least a little bit vain. You've got to give me more to work with!

The Tints of Nature brand was more promising, and based on some books and blogs I've read it is well liked amongst greenies. Unfortunately they claim to cover only 70% of grey hair – would that be strong enough to sort out my two-tone situation?

I inevitably came across a few websites touting the 'natural look' as the best look, filled with comment after comment from women who have forgone hair colour and embraced their grey tresses. I thought to myself, *well, maybe once I'm older I'll consider going grey, but I don't have to worry about that now.*

Famous last words if I ever saw any.

I'd been delaying a decision to address the two-tone problem when one day, as I was getting ready for work, I spotted one – a long silver strand, sprouting up near my temple where I should have seen it long before now. Where did it come from? I leaned close to the mirror, contorting myself to get a better look. Are there more?! Why hadn't anyone told me? I slowly went through my scalp section by section, plucking as I went. 20 minutes, and 12 hairs later, I was in shock. How can this be? I am only 30 years old, how can I have a dozen grey hairs? Is it a rebellion?

Ha ha! You burned us with chemicals for years, now we'll show you who's boss!

I'm lucky little Lucia didn't point out three colours in my hair: brown, yellow and silver.

I was mortified.

And motivated.

I want so much to live a natural lifestyle, but this was hitting below the belt. With the heightened seriousness of the situation there was no way I was trusting henna or '70% coverage'; I needed a stronger guarantee. I went to work researching salon-quality hair colour and found a potential saviour – Aveda.

I was already familiar with the brand because my stylist in the US used Aveda products. Essential oils make them smell so fresh – the Shampure line of shampoo and conditioner is particularly divine and minty. Aveda's hair colour products use 97-99% plant-derived ingredients, which makes it even more appealing. I'm comfortable knowing that 1-3% of the product is synthetic; colour won't last if you don't use a chemical to open the hair shaft for the colour to bond (most 'natural' hair dyes also use a small percentage of unnatural products to achieve this outcome – greenwashing abounds everywhere you look). Besides, what's the point of colouring your hair with a sub-par product if it means you have to do it more often?

Aveda has other impressive eco-credentials, too. They use 100% wind power to operate their manufacturing plant, have stringent sustainability guidelines, including giving back to the communities in developing areas where they source ingredients, and have hired LCA *Cradle to Cradle* guru Michael Braungart as a consultant to ensure they continue to improve their practices. Other greenies criticise Aveda, mostly for selling their green credentials when not everything is 100% green, but if I compare them to other mainstream, salon quality beauty brands they are leaps and bounds ahead of the curve. I personally think there is space to celebrate them even as we encourage them to continually improve their sustainability practices.

As I continued my research, however, I heard buzz around some stylists that a recent formula change veered further from natural ingredient list. There are rumours that the range now includes Ammonia, a known allergen, and p-phenylenediamine (PPD), another known allergen and likely carcinogen. Neither are ingredients I want on my scalp, nor do I want stylists putting their personal health at risk for the sake of my beauty. The bulk of Aveda's range is top-notch by sustainability standards, but the fuzziness around the ingredients in the hair colour makes me apprehensive.

But what to do about my silver sparklers? I'm definitely not ready to accept my greys at the ripe old age of 30.

Enter Original & Mineral (O&M), developers of Clean Colour Technology, designed right here in Sydney. This professional hair colour range is free from Ammonia, PPD and Resorcinol (another toxin commonly found in hair colour), and still achieves amazing, professional results. It's used in salons across Australia and at select salons in the US, New Zealand and Singapore.

Hallelujah! I phoned the flagship O&M salon and promptly made an appointment.

As I walked down Oxford Street toward the salon, I felt a bit apprehensive. It'd been so long since I'd been in a salon. Was I really doing the right thing for the environment? My hair had long been an important aspect of my identity and I'd taken great pride in having beautiful, luscious locks. Being alerted to my less-than-ideal hair situation had shaken my confidence, but once I saw those greys my youth was at risk, too, and this is one aspect of my image I am definitely not ready to give up yet.

As soon as I stepped inside the salon I forgot all my worries. The scent of natural essential oils, the music, the natural light. I let the decadence of the moment wash over me as I was guided to a chair and given an aromatic scalp massage and cup of tea while I awaited the arrival of my consultant. Oh how I'd missed these moments.

After much soul searching I've come to the personal decision that I can get my hair coloured every few months with the greenest products around and it won't be the end of the world; I do so many other things for the environment, so on this one I'm giving in. Maybe in the future I will have reached a stage of enlightenment where I don't crave such trivialities, but that day is not today. I shall not go quietly into middle-age complete with a head of grey hair, and I will enjoy feeling beautiful.

And sitting in the Opera House tonight, listening to an award-winning eco-feminist, with my newly coloured head of hair, in a gorgeous, glittering outfit, I feel fantastic.

⟿ ∅ 👗 🎎 🍜 🎵 👁 🍲 💡 ♡

Knock knock knock!

My heart jumps and I rush to the door to find a tall, dark and handsome courier holding up a garment bag. He says, "I have some dresses for Lisa to try on?"

"Yes! That's me!"

"How long do you think you'll need?"

"Oh, um, is that how it works?" I ask as I take the bag from him, "I guess about 10 or 15 minutes?"

"Take your time, I'll be waiting by the van until you're done," he gives me a knowing smile.

I shut the front door and rush to my bedroom, nervously unzipping the purple garment bag. I audibly gasp as I see two immaculate designer dresses hanging in front of me.

Hello Versace. Hello Dolce & Gabanna. Welcome to my boudoir.

It's a fashion dream come true.

I slip the Versace off the hanger and try it on first – when I saw it on the website I fell in love. It's a black goddess dress with divine gold embellishments that cross one strap and spill down the waist and then disappear amongst lovely draping layers. It is very beautiful and feels extremely light and luxurious. Unfortunately once it's on I see it's not doing my body any favours. My feminine curves are enhanced in all the wrong places with this particular cut, and I sort of feel like a figure skater with the combination of the mini gold sequins and short flared shirt.

I take off the Versace and look at the D&G dress with hesitation; it certainly doesn't look like anything special on the hanger. I almost didn't order this one, but thought I should try on at least two if I was going to the trouble of arranging a fitting. As soon as I pull the pale silver silk over my hips and lift the straps over my shoulders, the genius of the dress reveals itself. I zip up the mesh back and soak in the fitted, hourglass perfection. It has enough stretch to hug the curves I want accentuated and disguise the ones I don't, and generally makes me feel like the most beautiful woman on the planet. So *this* is why people pay thousands of dollars for couture dresses (not that it was ever anything but the price that kept me away before, but now I feel I have more proof about why certain designers are so coveted).

The main body of the dress, which goes just to the knee and has a thin strap of 'belt' cinched around the waist a lá Rouland Mouret's covetable Galaxy dress, is the lightest hint of silver, with dark grey mesh and gun metal silver leather details on the bodice to give it just a bit of an edge. Sweet little darts touch the upper edges of the derriere – what a divine detail. It's the perfect mixture of sexy and classy, and thanks to the amount of yoga I've been doing on my lunch breaks (instead of shopping) I am totally rocking this tight little number.

With the dress on I realise I already have the perfect shoes and handbag to complete the look – even better! I dig the shoes out of my closet, slip them on, and take a quick pic on my iPhone, messaging Tyler for a second opinion. He promptly replies, "You're not wearing THAT to any party if I'm not there."

I have found my dress.

I change back into my casual sundress, which seems so inadequate now, and go outside to the waiting courier who whisks them away.

I ring Michele from *Can I Borrow That?*, the ingenious designer dress rental company that will loan me the D&G number for a week at a tiny fraction of the retail purchase price; as per the online contract I must ring within the hour to advise if I will rent either dress I tried on.

"Hi Michele, it's Lisa Heinze, I just tried a couple dresses."

"Oh hi Lisa, how'd you go?"

"Yeah, great, thanks, I'd like to rent the Dolce & Gabana dress."

"The silver one?"

"Yes."

"That one is so *gorgeous*," she oozes, dropping her professional tone to a more personal one.

"I know! It's *fab*ulous! I can't wait to wear it!" I gush, feeling like I'm talking to an old friend.

We arrange the rest of the delivery details and hang up.

I've been working in my green-collar job for over a year now, and we have a Gala Dinner in a few weeks. Since GBCA has a number of events each year (saving the planet and they know how to party – I told you it was my dream workplace) I have already worn my party dresses a couple of times each, and I really wanted something different. I didn't want to buy a brand new cocktail dress for this one dinner, though; I don't have any other upcoming events so it seems wasteful to buy a new dress just for one night.

I thought about buying vintage, but in the lead up to the Gala dinner I've been swamped and had no time for an afternoon hunting through the stores, let alone to schedule any tailoring required. I remembered reading ages ago in *Vogue* of websites that allowed you to borrow designer shoes and handbags, so I took a gamble and was thrilled to discover a few different websites that also rent designer dresses. In addition to being able to wear dresses I couldn't afford to buy if I wanted, I don't have to worry about the dry cleaning, being seen in the same dress twice or buying something that I'll only want to wear once. It's an eco-fashionista's dream come true.

Renting this designer dress is collaborative consumption at its finest, at least for me. Collaborative consumption is the movement that describes, "traditional sharing, bartering, lending, trading, renting, gifting, and swapping reinvented through network technologies on a scale and in ways never possible before"[4]. Thanks to the internet and social network technologies, instead of buying things new for one-time use, we can easily borrow them or swap them for something we have and no longer use. Collaborative consumption enables people to fulfil their desires in a more sustainable way than traditional consumption practices allow. And as Rachel Botsman, one of the authors, said in her TED talk, it helps make eco-purchases more "hip than hippy" – what a great phrase.

I'm ecstatic to have found this unlikely accomplice for environmentalism in designer dress rental. I suspect the business was probably created for the budget-conscious rather than the eco-conscious fashionista, but I'm happy to reap the rewards and thrilled about finding a creative solution that allows me to be both green and glam.

This has got to be my favourite eco-experiment yet.

⭕⌀👗👖👟👠✨👛💡❤

"Babe, can you turn on some music before everyone arrives?" I shout from the bedroom as I hurriedly take stock of my closet because we have five guests due to arrive for dinner any minute now.

Hmm. It seems like every time I look in my wardrobe there are fewer and fewer clothes. Even more surprising, this brings me a sense of calm. The remaining pieces are timeless designs and in great condition, and for the first time in over a decade there is air between items on the rack. Happy, beautiful clothes with space to breathe!

Let's see, I love this bright chartreuse top from Morrissey. I bought it a few years ago as a back-up top for a wedding, and the vibrant colour is highlighted by golden beading and shiny squares of oversized lime sequins running across the top edge that really bring it to life. I also love the floaty pleating all the way around the blouse; it makes me think I should be boogying at Studio 54, swishing the fabric back and forth to a disco beat. I usually wear it with skinny pants, but tonight it's too warm for that. I wonder if this will go with my coffee-coloured fitted mini? Maybe if I tuck it in, the skirt is high waisted. Perfect! I love the creativity that occurs as a result of limited resources.

"Hellooo?" Ewan sings through the screen door just as I zip myself up.

"Hello! Come in!" I rush out into the front of the apartment to welcome Ewan, his partner Leo and our friend Thomas – I'm happy to see they carpooled.

"Oh Love – this looks delicious," says Ewan as he gives me a kiss hello and takes a look at the entrée emerging from the oven, "what are we having?"

"Roasted organic baby carrots, beetroot and spring onion with goat cheese, pistachios and fresh herbs," I reply as I pour everyone a glass of Tamburlaine organic Verdehlo, picked up on a recent day trip to the Hunter Valley with Kate. Actually, we went up there on another green adventure – I'd purchased a gorgeous antique outdoor table set on eBay and thought I may as well pick up some local organic wine while I was there.

"Oh of course, I should have guessed you'd have a green theme!"

Ewan and Leo, the consummate hosts, graciously invited Tyler and me into this very exclusive dinner party circle for the last event. Their dinner was Mediterranean-themed, and was held in their fabulous Waterloo flat overlooking the city. Every detail from the welcome cocktails and nibbles in the living room to the tea lights and elegant seating arrangements on the enormous balcony were perfect – and I haven't even mentioned the food! With Leo in charge of the menu it was a gastronomical extravaganza featuring ingredients such as endive, fig, prawns and a range of beautiful cheeses.

Two parties preceded Ewan and Leo's, and apparently each dinner surpassed the one prior in terms of menu and presentation – no pressure! We knew what we served our guests would have to be sustainable – we're experts at greening our own groceries now so it only makes sense to share our natural, healthy food skills with our friends. Everything on tonight's menu is either organic, local or package free (all three if we're lucky!), I even used homegrown chillies in the pasta sauce.

"Yum. Those veggies look really good for organics, we have a hard time finding them in our shop," says Leo.

"My grocery store is hopeless, too," I commiserate, "but a girl at work told me about a company that delivers organic produce. Best name ever, too – Lettuce Deliver!" We have a chuckle over the fantastic pun.

After Sara and Tom arrive and we're sitting at the table, Ty raises his glass for a toast to welcome everyone and thank them for coming to our sustainable dinner party, complete with bamboo salad plates, cloth serviettes and beeswax candles.

"So, is everything organic?" asks Sara.

"Not everything, but all the produce. We tried to do as much organic and package-free as we could, and we're not serving any meat. I wrote down all the details on our 'menu'," I explain, pointing to my chalkboard wall *cum* menu board.

Ristorante Biologico

Roasted organic carrot, beetroot, spring onion & green beans with local goat curd and pistachio.

Organic radicchio & gorgonzola with Hunter Valley organic olive oil.

Baked organic spaghetti arrabiata with local blue swimmer crab & homegrown chillies.

Organic coconut & lemon semifreddo with raspberries & macadamia.

The items that raised the carbon footprint of the meal the most are the two cheeses because dairy is part of the greenhouse-heavy livestock industry. I was happy to find organic and local goat's cheese and gorgonzola – the gorgonzola is even an award-winner, so I know I'm not compromising on taste in my low-carbon menu. The goat's cheese is divine, too, it's Meredith Dairy brand and is hand-formed, so requires less energy as compared to cheeses that are formed with machinery.

"This pasta is so delicious!" exclaims Sarah, "and thanks for making something without meat, I hate to be the picky one."

"Honestly don't even think about it! You know how I feel about beef and lamb anyway," none of these folks were on Beefgate weekend, but most have heard about my issue with ruminants, "plus, it was a good excuse to learn more about sustainable seafood."

"So crab's okay to eat?"

"According to the sustainable seafood guide this blue swimmer crab is fine."

The Australian Marine Conservation Society produces a very useful seafood guide on their website and an app to help consumers determine what options are sustainable, which is so important in light of today's over-fished oceans[5]; tonight's crab is local, sustainably caught and not currently at risk of overfishing.

The sustainable dinner party is great fun - I love being a hostess and we have plenty of laughs over our four courses and I-won't-confess-how-many bottles of organic wine (don't worry, I'll be recycling all those bottles). I think we've struck the right balance of sharing sustainable food without talking about the environment all night – I'm dedicated to being green but I'm still as aware as ever to not be irritating or pushy if I want to keep my friends.

"Well, you did it," Ty toasts me with some organic Syrah once the guests have left and we begin to clean the dishes.

I know he means the dinner party, but tonight has shown me so much more. I see now how capable I am of being myself and living sustainably. I can dress up, have fun, socialise with (non-greenie) friends and still lead a green lifestyle. I'm confident that as I continue to practice living my environmental values it will only become easier, too. Now that deserves a toast.

$$\sim \oslash \, \mathring{\curlyvee} \, \mathring{\curlyvee} \, \mathring{\rotatebox{90}{\Rightarrow}} \, \Lambda \, \mathring{\curlyvee} \, \ddot{\circ} \, \dot{\ominus} \, \mathring{\curlyvee} \, \heartsuit$$

Lying in Savasana, my final meditation after an amazing yoga session with my inspiring instructor Bella, my mind is wandering. I'm trying to stay focused, but it's hard because I've just had a realisation so exciting that I can't stop thinking about it. Besides, the realisation has stemmed from my yoga practice today, so I should be allowed to think about it.

Yoga literally translates into 'to yoke' or 'to unite' and is about striking that perfect harmony between yin and yang, your body and mind, breath and movement, the earth and the heavens. Today was filled with crow pose, tree pose, eagle pose and half moon pose – a balance-filled practice that required a combination of focus and relaxation. As I'm meditating on the practice I've just completed, a thought clearly comes to me: it is easy being green – you just have to find your personal balance of sustainability, and I have finally found mine.

See why I'm so excited?

When I first started my journey into environmentalism, I wanted to change immediately into the perfect example of living green. I've always striven for perfection – from top grades in school to being head cheerleader to personifying a glamorous image and succeeding in a desirable career – it only makes sense that I wanted to be the perfect greenie right from the start, too. Obviously that didn't work, because I freaked out about how much was changing, became irritating to some friends, and nearly gave up on the whole thing. As a result of slowing my pace and finding personal balance I finally feel at peace with the sustainable woman I have become.

And without being too irritating to you, my kind reader, I really love the person I'm becoming. I love learning about new issues and talking about things besides fashion or the latest bar opening – though I still enjoy those topics, even more so if said fashion label or bar has a green angle. Though it was terribly painful, I'm so happy I peeled back the layers of the woman I'd created to see who really existed underneath the image. It turns out she's intelligent, caring and determined, as well as fashionable, and she's committed to working towards positive environmental change.

I'm certain that my job in the green industry helped immensely in my transition – instead of adding to the problem of overconsumption as in my previous job, I am working towards the solution. Also, because I have been welcomed into the growing green social network, my self-esteem and confidence have returned because I'm in a strong social group, and I'm constantly rewarded for performing good eco-behaviour. Knowing that I'm working for positive change also helps put my setbacks into perspective, like realising colouring my hair a few times a year doesn't have to mark the end of my green lifestyle.

Reflecting back on all the changes I've made over the past couple years I must say I'm pleasantly surprised my complete identity wasn't lost when I surrendered my addiction to stuff. Compared to my previous habit of (at least) weekly purchasing I've made great strides in reducing what I buy and substituting reused or borrowed pieces (with the occasional new piece tossed in) to keep feeling stylish and trendy. I'll admit I do sometimes crave the latest catwalk trends and still love the artistry of high fashion and the creativity coming from the cutting-edge labels; luckily these days there are so many amazing eco-aware fashion labels that I don't have to sacrifice my values for my style. And when all else fails, I can borrow a fabulous designer outfit and share the ownership amongst many other fashion lovers.

So what is my image now? How do I express myself as a green fashionista? Or more broadly, as an aware citizen of the world? I still have plenty of things that I use to create my image, but more and more of the things are green, and I consume fewer things overall. For now I create my image with a reduced wardrobe including plenty of hand-me-downs, vintage goods, seasoned pieces from the back of my own closet and sustainable fashion labels; eco-friendly makeup and hair colour; pride in environmentalism; a love of nature; a sense of community and global responsibility; and most important, a sustainable balance.

A balance of green and fun. A balance of looking glam and living green. A balance of love for my friends and love for myself. A balance of mind and body. A balance of living in today's world and working toward a greener one in the future. A balance of sustainability and style.

I'm sure my eco-balance will shift over time – if I check back on myself in another couple of years I suspect (and hope!) I'll be even greener – but learning to make changes that I can sustain has given me the strength to persevere on my green journey, and that brings me so much joy I can't sit still.

We are the change

As I was thinking about how to wrap up my green story I came across this quote:

Live simply so that others may simply live.

First I thought, "Oh, that is so beautiful."

And then I thought, "Oh, wait. No. That is wrong. That is so, so wrong."

If I think about the Lisa of a few years ago, that statement would never have inspired her to join the movement; more likely it would've irritated her. It's condescending. It's judgmental. It tries to incite action through guilt. On top of all that, it's unrealistic. It's a beautiful sentiment with well-meaning intentions, and has probably even converted a greenie or two, but after what I've experienced I believe that statement belittles people and our complexities, and ignores the larger cultural setting in which most environmental changes must take place.

My mate Geoff was right all those years ago – the climate dilemma isn't a scientific one, it's a human one, and encompasses all the complexities that accompany human life. So to say to people 'live simply' for the sake of the environment is like a slap in the face. We are not simple people, these are not simple times, and the solution to combating climate change is not that simple.

So I guess that can't be my eco-living mantra.

Instead, the quote that keeps my eco-juices flowing day in and day out is:

Be the change you wish to see in the world.

Governments are not moving fast enough, and there are plenty of interested parties (like deep-pocketed oil and coal companies) working hard to maintain the status quo. It's up to us to start changing, and we can do that right now.

I'm not naïve enough to think that my individual changes are going to stop climate change in its tracks – there is enough research out there telling me this is not the case[1]. What I am saying is that when all of us make our own personal changes *and* we work together for broader societal and political changes, we will beat this thing.

When I set out on my environmental journey it was with a hope of becoming greener whilst remaining myself; I think it's safe to say I've failed miserably. Sure, on the surface I may look the same – I maintain my interests in fashion and design, and manage to look more 'trendy' than 'traditional hippy'. But scratch the surface and the real results of my green makeover are revealed; that's the bigger story. I've changed more than I ever imagined possible – from superficial things like the brand of makeup I wear, to larger shifts like swapping careers, and the deeper change of taking responsibility for my actions as a citizen in our global community – and to my delight I'm truly happier and more fulfilled than I have ever been before.

It certainly took me awhile to get to this place, though, and I learned so much along the way. I hope that by sharing my story I can help ease your transition into a more sustainable lifestyle, because we need you on board. In fact, as soon as you got started, we all got a whole lot closer to a truly sustainable future, so keep up the great work!

As one of my favourite environmental groups, 1 Million Women, reminds us – one woman isn't just one woman (and for you fellas reading this, one person isn't just one person), we all have social networks where we can share our stories far and wide. As we lead our greenest lives we can influence our friends, family, colleagues, people at the gym or places of worship, and more. When you join the climate revolution, you gain the power to bring hundreds more along with you, and truly change the face of climate history.

Everyday it's getting easier to make sustainable choices and lead a more sustainable life, and everyday more options become available to help us do so without sacrificing our personal style (check out the Sustainable Shopping Guide in the next chapter for my personal shopping tips).

Throughout this book I have explored sustainable choices in fashion, beauty, food and so much more. Beyond these choices, though, is an overall adjustment to the way I view the world and the way I live my life with greater environmental awareness. I've compiled my advice here as a set of guidelines to help steer you toward your most sustainable self. Once you embrace these guidelines to sustainable living you'll find that sustainable choices become easy to make – practically second nature.

Anytime you feel stuck or overwhelmed, don't fret, simply come back here and re-focus – even world changers like you and me need advice from time to time – and remember, we're all in this together.

Lisa's guide to living sustainably with style

Jump right in

There will always be reasons to *not* get started – time, money, convenience, fear of risking your image – but just jump in and see where your journey takes you.

Vote with your wallet

This is a phrase that goes back to the origin of the environmental movement, but it's never been truer than today. Each time we make a purchase we support the practices of the company from which we are purchasing. Make your vote count for the planet, human rights, and a sustainable future. And remember, sometimes the most important vote is not taking your wallet out at all.

Research first, shop second

I know, this is counterintuitive to we shoppers of the world, but it will save you from eco-buyer's remorse. Thank goodness for smart phones for research on-the-go. Not every single purchase I make is eco-friendly – I don't think that is possible – but I make a conscious choice each time I make a purchase, and that's a huge step in the right direction.

Quality, not quantity

Avoid fast fashion, as well as trends you suspect will have a short shelf life, and purchase well-made pieces with timeless style. Opt for high quality pieces, made with fine craftsmanship that will last for years to come. Try not to focus on a slightly higher price – spending more now will mean spending less in the long run, and is infinitely better for the planet.

Embrace online shopping

I still enjoy window shopping to get ideas and stay up on the latest trends. I also love discovering mainstream labels that are starting to incorporate sustainable pieces in their ranges, and that typically is done while I'm 'on the ground'. But for now many of the best eco-items are only available online, so get comfortable clicking – and remember to check for customer-friendly return policies.

Sleep on it

Long known as a money-saving shopping tip, this is equally, if not more, important as an eco-shopping tip. Regardless of how 'green' something is, sleep on it. If you still need that item the next day, go for it. You'll be amazed at how many things get left behind.

Remember your R's

No eco-list would be complete without these cornerstones for sustainable living.

Reduce
I used to purchase fashion or something for my home every week; sometimes it was just a small purchase, other times it was big, but it was always something. These days I refrain from impulse purchases, and limit the amount I buy altogether. I've been pleasantly surprised to find I still feel stylish and fashionable without the myriads of options I once had.

Reuse
I've kindled a flame with vintage shopping and used furniture – even pieces I find on the street (I still can't believe I've done this. Three times.) I've also had great fun dabbling in collaborative consumption – borrowing tools and dresses instead of buying something new for a single use. Clothes swaps are also a fantastic option for fashion reuse.

Recycle
Learn what is recyclable at your home, and where to recycle things that don't get picked up at your kerbside, like batteries, light bulbs and old oil and paint. Take things home to recycle if you can't find a recycling bin while you're out and about, and choose items wrapped in recyclable packaging.

Repair
Dishwasher broken? Repair it instead of buying a new one – even if it will cost the same amount of money. Heel tip break off your stiletto? Get it fixed, and you may as well get them re-soled at the same time. You still feel like you have a brand new object once it's repaired and back to tip top shape, but your inner eco-warrior will feel even better knowing you saved an item from the landfill.

Be a frequent shopper at your local health food store

Discovering my local health food store was life changing. All the natural products I need are in one place – beauty supplies, natural cleaning products, essential oils and unprocessed food. And if your store is as great as mine, they'll have a frequent shopper discount and will special order items in at your request.

Go back to basics

I wish my grandmothers could see me now that I'm learning to go back to basics; I suspect they would also teach me a few more tricks! I've had so much fun making my own cleaning supplies, soups and sauces, and growing my own produce. Next on my list is learning how to sew – it's about time this eco-fashionista gained this skill, don't you think?

Experience life, don't consume it

I find there is so much joy to be had from the delicious experiences in this world, and I encourage you to embrace those experiences instead of collecting things. Take the time to drink your coffee amongst the buzz of your favourite café. Give the gift of time by taking your friend to lunch, or having an adventure in the park with the little ones in your life instead of buying them the latest toy. Things will break or get worn out, but memories of a beautiful experience only get better with time.

Demand eco-labelling

I wish it wasn't so difficult to know the true environmental cost of products I buy or so easy to be greenwashed. Researching and purchasing would be so much easier if everything we bought had an eco-label. To encourage this change make sure any products that claim to be organic, Fairtrade, ethical or green have certification labels, and write to your favourite brands asking them to certify their eco-claims if they haven't done so already.

Celebrate your free-ride

Free-riding is the term social movement scholars give to entry points into a movement that don't cost a thing, not even the cost of moving out of your comfort zone. I started free-riding when I learned how easy it was to buy natural beauty products. Lillian was able to free-ride because of her existing love of vintage goods. You will find your own way of free-riding into environmentalism, and this should be celebrated! Just don't stop at the celebrating. Far from being the end of an environmental transformation, free-riding is your ticket to enter the movement.

Don't rush it.

Not all eco-changes will come easily, and for me they were hard for reasons I never considered. Take things slow and remember that green changes will be more sustainable if you work at a pace you can maintain.

Don't ignore your (or anyone else's) emotions

I didn't realise at the time that I needed to grieve the loss of some aspects of my identity. It's sad to give up the things you love even if they are 'bad' for the environment or as 'trivial' as shopping. It's just as important to have compassion for others transitioning into green living even as you celebrate their positive eco-changes, because that person may be saying goodbye to a previously important part of herself. Climate change is a moral dilemma, and many people also experience strong emotions as they learn the impacts climate change will have on the planet and the people on it. Acknowledge these emotions, understand what you are feeling, and talk about it; don't be embarrassed or ashamed, these emotions are part of your journey.

Speaking of journeys . . .

Acknowledge that everyone is on her own green journey

Start with yourself, and lead by green example. I shouldn't have worried about changing everyone around me until I was comfortable with my personal changes. Little did I know that eventually I would inspire those around me just by living my greenest life. I no longer question anyone's environmental commitment; I merely speak of my own and make suggestions when appropriate. Most importantly, I encourage green changes without forcing them onto people who are not interested.

Be confident

I now approach my green lifestyle with the same level of commitment and self-confidence as I do my fashion choices. This confidence has helped make the end result of green living appealing to those around me. I don't appear to be doing without; I maintain a fun, social lifestyle and my unique personal style. My confidence and comfort in my green skin enable me to provide an example to others they can stay themselves and go green, too.

Make the biggest impact

I get asked all the time for my number one tip to live a greener life; it's nearly impossible to answer because it depends on your current lifestyle. I made the biggest impact by reducing how much new fashion I purchased, but Sarah didn't shop as much as I did, and made her biggest impact by using Soda Stream and avoiding excessive packaging. Others will make this impact by cutting back on their meat or taking public transportation. Have an honest look at your life and determine where your biggest impact can be made.

Connect

Being surrounded by likeminded individuals has made me feel I am not alone in this fight for the environment; it also rebuilt my self-esteem after it was shattered as a result of Beefgate. Sharing knowledge and learning from others who are on an environmental journey is very fulfilling and motivating, and our collective identity for environmental action enables us to work together for real change. As Paul Gilding says, we are the system, and if we want change, we must be the change (taking us back to my favourite eco-quote!).

Consider the global community

Everything is connected. Not just you to me, or us to environment, but climate change to overpopulation, food shortages, poverty, sweatshops, human trafficking and public health issues. We live in a time with huge potential to make immense positive change to our world, and that change begins with caring about the global community. Climate change is just one piece of this increasingly complex puzzle, but as we work towards solving the climate dilemma we can positively influence these other issues as well.

It's not what you give up, but what you get in return

I used to think that becoming an environmentalist was about all the things I had to give up: shopping, clothes, shoes, holidays, cars, my identity, my friends, and my carefree lifestyle. But what I've received in return for my eco-efforts is invaluable: a new definition of success that values well-being and equality over financial achievement; deeper, more meaningful friendships; a green social network to keep me informed and motivated; new skills; an environmental education; greater self-awareness and self-esteem; increased happiness.

All those psychologists are right when they say that money can't buy happiness – it's not always easy to believe when you're standing in a designer boutique wearing a beautiful dress or test-driving a hot new car, but living with less has turned out to be happy, relaxing and blissful.

Huh. Look at that. It turns out living simply is great for the environment and for your personal happiness.

But getting to this place of living simply? Well, that wasn't so simple.

⌣⌀👕👚👖🎀♀💡📷💡♡

I am more optimistic than ever that we will create the change we need. I've been able to forge the unknown territory of environmentalism and not only survive, but thrive. I'm more inspired than ever about the potential of people-power after taking stock of my friends' changes and the way they've incorporated green into their personal lives, including sharing the message with their other friends. I also know there are smart, talented and passionate people working up numerous ingenious solutions to our climate dilemma, and I've been fortunate enough to meet and work with many of them. It doesn't mean we are done working for the planet, but we are well on our way, and there is no better time to get involved than right now.

You will no doubt learn your own lessons on your environmental journey, and I hope you feel inspired to share your story. I hope I've been some help along the way or, if nothing else, provided some entertainment as someone who didn't exactly transition gracefully into environmental living, but who has safely come out the other side.

If you remember nothing else from my book, here are my parting words to help you attain (and maintain!) sustainability with style:

Live your greenest life. **Lead by example. Never stop learning.** Involve yourself in green communities. **Reduce, repair, reuse, recycle.** Be patient with yourself, but not too patient. **Buy a Keep Cup.** Visualise our greener future. Go outdoors and love nature. **Switch to green power.** Embrace natural beauty. Encourage those around you. **Choose natural over synthetic.** Make your change sustainable. **Remember all things are connected. Love pre-loved items.** Talk about the environment. **Research first, shop second.** Bring your own bags. **Contact politicians.** Connect with fellow greenies. **Keep hope alive. Be the change.**

Oh, and don't worry too much about becoming a hippy – it's really not that bad.

Sustainability with Style
Shopping Guide

Sustainability with Style Shopping Guide

Consider this guide a behind-the-scenes look into my wardrobe and beauty cabinet. Here you'll find my favourite fashion labels and shops, beauty products I have personally used, and general tips for shopping sustainably. I just know you'll discover your own favourites, too, so I've left space for you to make notes at the end of the guide.

This guide is not designed as the be-all and end-all of sustainable shopping. New sustainable fashion brands and beauty products are being launched all the time (lucky us!). And there are plenty of brands I haven't yet uncovered or experienced personally.

I also don't want to imply you should completely ignore all other brands. You never know what company will be next to join the green movement with an organic line or Fairtrade certified clothing, and I believe we should support these eco-efforts. So thank you (and well done!) for using this guide – it's through making sustainable choices that we communicate the type of fashion and beauty we want now and in the future. Happy shopping!

♡

Sharing is caring! I'd love to hear about the brands you come across in your eco- and ethical-shopping adventures. Share with me anytime on Twitter or Instagram: @lisa_heinze

All listings and claims are current at the time of publishing. Please do your own research before making a purchase.

Fashion : Guidelines

Okay, I'm going to level with you. I can't ignore the fact that reducing the amount of new things we buy has the most positive impact on the planet. Most of us need to adjust to living with less, and this is certainly the area of my life I had to concentrate on the most. So before I promote my favourite eco-fashion labels, I have one final suggestion for you to ask yourself the following questions before purchasing anything new:

- Do I really need this?
- Is there something similar in my closet already?
- Are there any clothing exchanges coming up, so I can swap instead of shop?
- Can I find something similar in a secondhand shop?
- If this is a special or one-off occasion, can I rent or borrow something instead?

Of course there are times when we really do need something new. Secondhand items don't always look professional enough for work, and many consignment shops are filled with last season's fast fashion pieces that were not made to last. Not to mention items we always need new, like exercise gear and undergarments. When the time comes to splurge on new items, I find these three principles go a long way toward creating and maintaining a sustainably stylish wardrobe:

- **Research first, buy second** : do your homework before hitting the shops to save yourself time and energy seeking the best options
- **Choose quality over quantity** : don't be afraid to spend a little extra money on a timeless item that has been made well and will last many seasons

- **Get comfortable making online purchases** : become adept at buying online, ensuring to review exchange and return periods, and enjoy the time you've freed up as a result of avoiding the malls.
- **Read labels, seeking sustainable fibres and ethical production** : refer to the table below for fabrics to prefer and avoid, and what certifications you should look for to back up claims

Prefer		Avoid
Organic cotton	Tencel/Lyocell*	Viscose
Hemp	Peace Silk/Wild Silk	Rayon
Modal*	Upcycled or Recycled fabric	Polyester
Cupro*	Reclaimed or Surplus fabric	Bamboo*

Organic certifications	Ethical certifications
GOTS : global-standard.org	Fairtrade International : fairtrade.net
USDA : ams.usda.gov	ECA : ethicalclothingaustralia.org.au
Australian Organic : austorganic.com	Made in the USA : madeintheusabrand.com
Ecocert : ecocert.com	

- **Take good care** : Did you know that the majority of our clothing's eco-footprint occurs after we take it home? You can keep your sustainable fashion green by:

  - Treating your clothing with respect – store it neatly in clean, dry wardrobes and shelves
  - Laundering less frequently, and spot cleaning as much as possible
  - Washing in cold water
  - Line drying
  - Gently handwashing 'Dry Clean' pieces of clothing, or seeking green dry cleaners that use safer chemicals

* Modal, Cupro, Tencel/Lyocell and Bamboo can all be 'toxic' unless they are produced in closed loop facilities that reuse chemicals and don't emit polluted wastewater. For the most part Modal, Cupro and Tencel/Lyocell are 'safe', but it's always best to do your homework before purchasing. I've left Bamboo in the 'Avoid' column because it is the fabric most widely used to greenwash unsuspecting fashion lovers in the form of a 'wonder fabric', its growth and manufacturing is largely unregulated, and the majority of bamboo fabric is not created in closed loop facilities.

Fashion : Shopping Guide

Okay, now onto the good stuff – an insider look into my world of sustainable fashion.

E : Ethical   **S** : Environmentally Sustainable

Fashion brands

Ace and Jig aceandjig.com E		Unique and bold womenswear, designed to outlast trends, using beautiful, textured woven fabrics from an ethical weaver in India.
Afia shopafia.com E		Sustainable women's line sourced and sewn in Ghana, West Africa. I love the colourful prints and on-trend silhouettes from this label.
Amour Vert amourvert.com E S		Paris-chic meets Cali-cool, all made using a zero-waste design philosophy and sustainable materials. I love nearly every piece on their site.
Auralis auralistudio.com E S		Sustainable resortwear designed and manufactured between Puerto Rico and New York. Uses only organic and ethically produced materials. Their convertible jumpsuit has it's own cult-following.

Bhalo bhaloshop.com E	Ethical fashion label working with rural Bhangladeshi women to create casual-cool handmade, Fair Trade, limited edition pieces.
Carlie Ballard carlieballard.com E	Chic clothing made of natural fibres in an ethical Indian factory. Perfect for the travellers and dreamers out there – and also where I got some fabulous woven Ikat trousers.
Chinti & Parker chintiandparker.com E S	Super-soft jumpers, dresses and cardigans made ethically from sustainable materials. These flattering pieces don't shy away from fashion-conscious colours and patterns, either.
Choolips choolips.com E	Beautiful, fashion-forward pieces made fairly in Ghana using traditional practices, including head-turning scarfs, dresses and jackets. Many pieces are printed and stitched once ordered – brilliant.
Cue cue.cc E	Trend-driven and affordable Australian fashion, much of my corporate wardrobe comes from Cue. All items made in Australia are accredited by ECA, so look for the tag.
Deborah Lindquist deborahlindquist.com E S	A trailblazer at the forefront of the eco-fashion movement, Deborah Lindquist uses vintage cashmere, hemp blends, organic linen, and even the odd recycled military parachute to create couture and everyday fashion. Made in the USA.

Ecoology ecoology.es **E s**	Dresses, tops, skirts and jackets made ethically from sustainable fabrics from a small factory in Spain. A great mixture of classic styles with some current trends.
Eileen Fischer & eileenfisher.com **E s**	The '&' collections by Eileen Fisher have a larger story to tell beyond the easy and elegant style synonymous with the label, like sustainable materials, female empowerment, Fairtrade and more.
Feral Childe feralchilde.com **E s**	Modern and playful womenswear produced ethically in New York's garment district. Created primarily from sustainable materials like natural fibres and upcycled fabrics, Feral Childe also has an impressive sustainability policy.
Frock LA frockla.com **E s**	Feminine and flirty dresses, tops and skirts made in the USA from comfy, eco-luxurious blended jerseys. FrockLA is designed to help you feel like a super-sexy eco-warrior.
Ginger & Smart gingerandsmart.com **E**	Australian fashion at its best, and accredited by ECA. Some of the most beautiful, fashion-forward pieces I have seen.
Goodone goodone.co.uk **E s**	Ethical, sustainable, and (fabulous!) award-winning design, based in the UK. Goodone use a mixture of sustainable fabrics, including upcycled materials, and share their ethical manufacturing knowledge with other labels through their 'One Good Factory' project.

H&M : Conscious hm.com E S	A continually growing collection of the latest fashions created out of sustainable materials. Here's hoping that in a few years all their on-trend fashion pieces are created ethically.
Heidi Merrick heidimerrick.com E S	Marvellous ready-to-wear fashion made ethically in Los Angeles, featuring a number of luxe vegan leather pieces. This label is just my style.
Honest By honestby.com E S	Fashion-forward clothing and a 100% transparency policy from manufacturing through to pricing. Fabrics are environmentally friendly, protect animal welfare and are skin-friendly, too. Honest!
I Owe You iouproject.com E	Unique casual-wear handmade in India. Each item has a barcode you can photograph and upload into the website to learn more about the person who made your piece of clothing. If you love plaid, this is a brand for you.
Kissin Cussin kissincussin.com.au E	Bohemian, feminine and playful women's fashion made ethically in Sri Lanka. This label began with its founders' (cousins, of course!) ambition to help get a village back on its feet following the 2004 tsunami.
Kowtow kowtowclothing.com E S	Cutting edge basics from a New Zealand label that uses 100% certified organic and Fairtrade cotton in its line. A staple for any eco-fashionista's wardrobe.

Lalesso lalesso.com E	Vibrant and carefree summer fashion inspired by East African khanga fabrics. Produced in Kenya, the business creates employment for a fair wage in an area plagued by poverty. I am constantly complimented when wearing my Lalesso skirt.
Lemlem lemlem.com E	Lovely handcrafted women's and children's casual clothing produced in Ethopia, creating jobs and preserving the traditional art of weaving. Created by supermodel and former World Health Organisation Goodwill Ambassador, Liya Kebede.
Manning Cartel manningcartell.com.au E	Modern, cutting-edge fashion label from Australia, recently achieving ECA accreditation. I love the innovative textures and shapes in these beautiful, artful pieces.
Minna minna.co.uk E S	Stunning vintage, handmade and ethical clothing, including a lovely range of bridal gowns. This eco-luxe line features a lot of gorgeous reclaimed lace and other sustainable materials, and always has me swooning.
Nearfar nearfar.myshopify.com E	Ethical, artisanal fashion created in Sierra Leone by tailors practising traditional processes. Those afraid of vibrant colours and prints need not apply.
Partimi partimi.com S	I really love Partimi's nature-inspired prints on fluid silhouettes. All pieces are created with sustainability at the heart of the practice, and the timeless designs are sure to last endless seasons.

People Tree peopletree.co.uk E S	Pioneers in sustainable and ethical fashion, working for over 20 years with Fairtrade artisans and farmers. This fashion is always playful and on trend.
Pure Pod purepod.com.au E S	Australian-made, ethical and sustainable womenswear, these retro- and urban-inspired pieces are designed by Australian eco- and ethical-fashion pioneers.
Reformation thereformation.com E S	Environmentally sustainable fashion brand that uses vintage and surplus materials to create on-trend fashion. Manufactured ethically in New York and Los Angeles, and popular among all the bright young things.
Rosel roselwear.com E S	Eco-chic, fair trade, urban-knit collections inspired by the clean lines of 1960s and 1970s American sportswear. I am totally digging the strong colours, bold shapes and the occasional stripe.
Sail the Seven Seas sailthesevenseas.co.uk E S	Stylish yet utilitarian clothing made from repurposed military and vintage fabrics. Manufactured fairly in Corsica, with many limited edition and custom-made pieces featured in the collection.
Sara C sara-c.com E S	Feminine tops, dresses and scarves with bold prints. Produced ethically in the UK using an eco-friendly dye-process and sustainable fabrics. This unique label is definitely one-to-watch.

Scanlon & Theodore scanlantheodore.com E	This sophisticated and timeless Australian label has ECA accreditation on its Australian-made pieces. A great excuse to pop into their gorgeous space next time you're in Paddington or near the Strand in Sydney.
Sindiso Khumalo sindisokhumalo.com E	Contemporary textile design created by working with non-profit groups around the globe, empowering communities through economic activities. The bright graphic prints make my head spin (in a really good way).
Studio Jux studiojux.com E S	Contemporary-cool designs created by Nepalese 'rockstar' tailors who are paid fairly for their work. Eco-materials such as hemp, recycled PET and organic cotton are used, and something about the website makes me know the designers and I would be great friends.
The Social Studio thesocialstudio.org E S	Melbourne-based label making ethical garments from upcycled and reclaimed materials. The Social Studio offers unique pieces created by some of the most creative Australians, who also happen to be refugees.
The Sway theswaynyc.com E S	Edgy and cool handbags, clutches and biker jackets made of excess leather. There is nothing else to say but that I am in love.
Titania Inglis titaniainglis.com E S	Striking yet wearable pieces made of sustainable materials, based on the designer's philosophy of lush minimalism. Manufactured ethically in New York from innovative, low-impact fabrics.

Tluxe tluxe.com E S	Luxe basics lovingly made in Australia from sustainable materials including organic cotton, silk and wool. These sophisticated pieces are perfect for layers, and offer the occasional statement piece as well.
Veronika Maine veronikamaine.com.au E	Classy, classic dresses and separates, and a real favourite of mine for the office. Based on the few pieces in my wardrobe, I can attest Veronika Maine stands the test of time in terms of both style and quality. All items made in Australia are accredited by ECA.
Zoologie! zoologie.com.au E S	Modern crafted clothing produced locally in Melbourne in small batches. Zoologie is designed to outlast trends, and made to high quality standards. They hope to become vintage classics in many decades to come – I think they are well on their way.

Basics & Denim

A question of aquestionof.net E S	Sustainable street style made of GOTS certified organic cotton. The edgy statement tees and cool sweatshirts and jackets are a great addition to your casual wardrobe.
American Apparel americanapparel.net E	The brand led the charge for renewed interest in Made in America and paying workers a fair wage, and has some solid sustainability commitments including an employee bike rental program, energy efficiency adjustments to the factory and material reuse.
Betty Browne bettybrowne.com.au E S	All about tees that make you feel sexy, and what's sexier than made-in-Oz organic cotton tees? My black Betty Browne tank/singlet is an integral part of my wardrobe.
Good Society goodsociety.org E S	GOTS certified organic cotton denim, and a passion for creating positive social change by donating 25% of their profits to charity. I have a pair of their indigo skinny straight leg jeans and always feel amazing when I wear them.
Kuyichi kuyichi.com E S	With a claim like "The first conscious fashion brand" you know this label is serious about sustainability. An impressive range of organic denim and streetwear, including the world's first closed-loop denim options.

Loomstate loomstate.org E S	Environmentally and socially sustainable casual apparel using certified organic cotton, Tencel and other sustainable materials. I particularly love the look of the V-neck t-shirts and beachy totes.
Nudie Jeans nudiejeans.com E S	In 2012 Nudie achieved 100% organic cotton for its denim. Hooray! Nudie stores offer free repair of your jeans, and have rugs available made from recycled jeans. Oh, and they look amazing, too.
One Teaspoon Salvage oneteaspoon.com.au S	A little bit rock & roll, a little bit glamour, One Teaspoon's Salvage denim shorts and mini's are the epitome of rebellious cool. I always feel eco-hip in these salvage denim cut-offs.
REUSE Jeans reusejeans.com S	Using 80% recycled denim, this sustainable label creates denim jeans, shorts and skirts in a variety of stylish fits and colours. I particularly love the bright neon and pastel skinny jeans.
Sosume sosumeclothing.com E S	An Australian brand with a major social conscience that led the charge for sustainable practices in this country. They use only the most sustainable fabrics, produced ethically, to create their cool, covetable basics.
Threads 4 Thought threadsforthought.com E S	Fun, casual and ethical clothing made with sustainable materials like organic cotton, Tencel and recycled polyester. They've started branching out into playful leggings and dresses, too, so I'll be keeping my eye on this brand.

Activewear

Lululemon lululemon.com E	Strong sustainability and ethical values, and as transparent in its business practices as any large brand comes. Some products are made from sustainable materials – like my running shorts made from recycled polyester.
Nike nike.com E S	Leader in fair labour and sustainable business practices, and continually setting the bar higher – I love seeing the athlete/competitor mentality applied to sustainability. With great aesthetics, too, this is definitely my running shoe brand of choice.
Patagonia patagonia.com E S	A real standout, this outdoor company has sustainability at its core – materials, production and corporate ethos are all centred around a healthy planet. Among other things they have a transparent supply chain, are 1% for the Planet members, and have Common Threads program encouraging consumption reduction.
Teeki teeki.com E S	My beloved yoga pants! Made in the USA from recycled PET bottles and featuring bright, eye-catching designs made from zero-waste printing. I am a Teeki gal for life.

Sleepwear & Lingerie

ALAS alasthelabel.com E S	Beautiful and playful sleepwear and loungewear, produced with GOTS certified or Fairtrade accredited organic cotton and safe dyes. All pieces are made ethically in India, and I can attest to these uber-comfy PJs bringing nothing but sweet dreams.
Augustine augustinelondon.com E S	Elegant, delicate and feminine lingerie. Made in France from certified organic cotton and Tencel. Augustine also has a carbon-limiting strategy, including minimising distances in the supply chain, and requires certifications from its suppliers. Just lovely.
Clare Bare clarebare.bigcartel.com E S	This eco-lingerie brand has you covered from the "oh-so-cute" side of the spectrum to the "oh-so-sexy". It is all eco-friendly and made-to-order in the USA from sustainable fabrics and vintage materials.
LuvaHuva luvahuva.co.uk E S	Stunning nighties, negligees, bras and undies handmade with love in the UK. The fabrics include organic cotton, soy fabrics, vintage lace and end of line remnants. I love their celebration of feminine style.
Madonna Bain madonnabain.com.au E S	Beautiful eco-intimates range made fairly in Indonesia and Australia from GOTS certified organic cotton. All pieces are made to spoil and delight, and bring a little more luxury and romance into your life.

Accessories

Colin Leslie Eyewear colineslieeyewear.co.uk E S	Eyewear label specialising in fashion-forward frames using organically-sourced bamboo. Handmade in the UK. The Aviator sunglasses are especially cool, and this brand has quite a celeb following.
Eco Optics eco-optics.com S	This eyewear label features an Eco range made from 95% recycled materials and part of 1% for the Planet – returning 1% of sales to environmental charities. One tree is planted for each pair sold, and they are nearing their one-millionth tree!
Hovey Lee hoveylee.com E S	Eco-friendly and ethical jewellery line using 100% recycled materials. Any gemstones are sourced from Fair Trade suppliers, and all pieces are made in Los Angeles. It's great to have some guilt-free eco-bling in your life.
Nancybird nancybird.com E S	An Australian label specialising in handbags, scarves and belts. These artistic pieces are created from natural fabrics including cotton, linen and vegetable tanned leather, and the design studio has some solid sustainability practices in place.
Proof iwantproof.com E S	This eyewear company makes sunglasses out of sustainable wood sources and plant-based plastics. For each pair of glasses sold, one person receives sight-saving surgery in India.

Raven & Lily ravenandlily.com E S	A long-time favourite of mine, Raven & Lily employs marginalised women in Ethiopia, India, Cambodia and the US at a fair wage. Featuring eye-catching jewellery made with reclaimed bullets and a new line of upcycled skirts and tees.
Sass & Bide Made w/ Love sassandbide.com E	This iconic Australian brand has teamed up with the International Trade Centre's Ethical Fashion Initiative to create handbags with East African Women. Now onto their third collection, I'm looking forward to even more pieces Made with Love.
Solo Eyewear soloeyewear.com E S	Stylish handcrafted sunglasses made of recycled bamboo. The founder was also inspired when learning that approximately 1 billion people on the planet don't have access to eye care, so for each pair of Solo purchased, eye care funding is provided for people in need.
UNA Fashion unafashion.com E S	Fairtrade and sustainable leather bags made in a sustainable factory in Kolkata using organic cotton and eco-leather, which is biodegradable and free from chrome, heavy metals and other harmful chemicals. I particularly love the belt bag.
WeWOOD we-wood.com S	Wooden wristwatches made from reclaimed, recycled and offcut wood. For each watch purchased, one tree is planted. Clever initiative tied to great design.
Yellow 108 yellow108.com E S	Very cool, very chic sustainable hats and accessories made from salvaged and recycled materials. Based in LA, Yellow 108 helps factories minimise waste by using eco-material offcuts, and donate 2% of all sales to local charities.

Shoes

Funkis funkis.com S	Clogs and sandals made from sustainably-sourced timber and leather in Sweden. Timeless and quality footwear designed to outlast trends while ensuring you always look fashionable.
Guava Shoes guava.pt E S	Contemporary, geometric-inspired footwear destined to turn heads. All shoes are created by Portuguese artisans using sustainable materials, and they are definitely pieces of wearable art.
Kamik kamik.com S	A range f gumboots/wet weather boots made from recyclable materials. Most boots can be sent back to the manufacturer for recycling at their end of their useful life (which should take awhile, these boots are made to last!).
Love is Mighty loveismighty.com E S	Beautiful and stylish, this handmade and vegan footwear line is created by artisans in rural India. I have my eye on a sparkly pair made with old gum wrappers – don't let that description fool you, they look just like sequins!
Nisolo nisoloshoes.com E	Stunning sandals, loafers, and oxfords, as well as the occasional bag and bracelet. Nisolo was created as a means to provide much-needed regular work to talented artisans in Peru, providing these entrepreneurs access to a global market.

Osborne shoposborn.com **E S**	A footwear company that combines artisanal fabrics and practices with eco-materials and fair trade production. These cool booties and oxfords are produced in small batches, and are sure to keep the hippest hipsters happy.
Roma boots romaboots.com **E**	This "Buy One Give One" rain boot company provides boots to impoverished Romanian children. Boots come in a range of glossy and matte colours, keeping your feet dry and your style in tact on the rainiest of days.
Tom's toms.com **E**	The pioneer in one-for-one retail, Tom's specialises in shoes and eyewear. Some of these casual shoes are made of sustainable materials like hemp, organic cotton and recycled polyester, and for each pair sold a pair is given to a child in need. Working with Tom's Giving Partners, the program also helps children in developing nations stay in school and gain opportunities for a better future.

Fashion : favourite shops

O : Online   **N** : New   **V** : Vintage   **R** : Rental

C's Flashback 316 Crown Street, Sydney V	A classic stop on the op-shop trail in Sydney's Crown Street. If you have the time and inclination, you can uncover many affordable treasures!
Dear Gladys deargladys.com.au O V	A fantastic online vintage shop specialising in delightful dresses. Dear Gladys donates its proceeds to Fitted for Work, a not-for-profit organisation that helps disadvantaged women obtain and maintain work. I've found a couple of my most noteworthy vintage pieces on this site.
Dressed Up dressedup.com.au R	Designer dress rental featuring frocks for any occasion. Why buy when you can borrow? I love wearing couture gowns for a fraction of the price.
Eco Bird ecobird.net O N	Online store specialising in sustainable fashion pieces from Australia and New Zealand. I got a fantastic Kowtow asymmetrical top from here that always makes me feel oh-so-chic.
Ekoluv ekoluv.com O N V	Conscious, sustainable fashion and accessories, and you can shop by which ethics appeal to you most (Fairtrade, sustainable, vintage, and more).

Fashioning Change fashioningchange.com O N	One of the first online shops for sustainable fashion, following the founder Adriana's "Promise of 5" – Style, Quality Construction, Protection of Health, Protection of the Earth and Protection of Human Rights.
Fire & Shine fireandshine.com.au O N	Exercise and leisure wear, sourced and produced through ethical supply chains. Many made from sustainable materials, and it's so great to have a one-stop-shop for a mixture of ethical yogawear brands.
Grandma Takes a Trip grandmatakesatrip.com V	Hands down my favourite vintage shop – from the clever name to the beautifully curated collection to letting me borrow a gown for my book launch – don't pass through Sydney without stopping here.
Green Horse greenhorse.com.au O N	Fun, eclectic fashion and accessories with a sustainable focus. They also sell a limited range of cosmetics and bodycare.
Helpsy shophelpsy.com O N	Founded on the belief that design-forward fashion can have a positive social impact 100% of the time. You can shop by the ethics you seek, and find many memorable pieces.
Hunter Gatherer bsl.org.au V	Fantastic op shop with 3 locations in Melbourne managed by the Brotherhood of St Laurence. Never has an op shop had such style. Hunter Gatherer has a special place in my heart because this is where I scored my vintage poncho and a favourite vintage dress.

Indigo Bazaar indigobazaar.com.au O N	A favourite online retailer of mine featuring ethical pieces from around the globe. You'll find African and Indian prints mixed with modern Australian and New Zealand labels. Every piece has a story.
Master & Muse masterandmuse.com O N	A collection pulled together by supermodel Amber Valetta, featuring clothing and accessories that are both fashionable and socially responsible.
Modavanti modavanti.com O N V	The destination for socially conscious fashion lovers, this site offers new sustainable fashion mixed with carefully selected pre-loved pieces. You're certain to find something for every style.
Zady Zady.com O N	Online retailer combating the fast-fashion craze by offering pieces of timeless style and solid construction. They favour ethical, Made in USA and sustainable pieces, and part of the profits go to the Bootstrap Project, helping artisans in the developing world.
Zoo Emporium 180 Campbell St, Surry Hills, Sydney V	Another favourite vintage-haunt of mine in Surry Hills. Make sure to check out the bargain basement! I found an amazing mauve dress here for $30, complete with on-trend broad shoulders.

Beauty : Guidelines

We are completely spoiled by the ever-increasing number of eco- and ethical-beauty brands available today. I never feel like I am doing without my pampering! Most of the items I use can be picked up at my local health food store or nearest Whole Foods (when I'm in the US), and all are available online.

I know that to some natural beauty means avoiding makeup and styling products altogether, but that's a discussion for another day as far as I'm concerned. I love makeup, I love doing my hair, and whether I doll-up for myself, my spouse or my friends (who can really say who it's for?), I feel amazing when I've spent the time to make myself look my best. If you're like me and enjoy a little glamour in your life, you can rest assured that there are many options available to keep yourself beautiful, naturally.

When it comes to shopping, the two areas I tend to focus my attention are ingredients and packaging.

Ingredients

Anything we put onto our skin, our largest organ, is absorbed into our bodies. Much of what we put on our bodies gets washed into our water supply. This is why avoiding toxic ingredients is a key consideration for greening your beauty routine. I can't emphasise enough the importance of reading all the ingredients in a product before making a purchase, and I urge you to consider if you really need all the potions vying for space in your beauty cabinet.

Over the past few years I've found a number of ingredients checklists to help me shop for beauty products:

Ingredients to avoid

Diethanolamine (DEA)	Para-aminobenzoic acid (PABA)	Phthalates
Lead	Parabens	Propylene Glycol
Mineral Oil	Paraffin	Sodium lauryl/laureth sulfate (SLS/SLES)
Palm Oil	Petrolatum	Synthetic fragrances

If you're interested in learning more, I suggest the Skindeep Database managed by the Environmental Working Group. But beware – this addictive website may keep you reading for hours at a time, and cause you to throw away many of your beauty and body products once you read the ingredients. **www.ewg.org/skindeep**

Like fashion labels, beauty products can be guilty of greenwashing, so check for certification of any eco-claims.

Organic certification	No animal testing certification	Palm oil free certification
USDA : ams.usda.gov	CCIC : leapingbunny.org	Green Palm: betterpalmoil.org
Australian Organic : austorganic.com	Go Cruelty Free : gocrueltyfree.org	
Ecocert : ecocert.com	CCF : choosecrueltyfree.org.au	
NASAA : nasaa.com.au		

Packaging

Finally, I always consider the eco-footprint of my beauty product packaging. Ever since my days working at the design agency and learning how certain companies willingly manipulate shoppers, I've been very considerate of the packaging of my beauty products. I adhere to the following guidelines as much as possible:

- Avoid excessive packaging
- Choose products in recyclable packaging
- Prefer packaging made of recycled materials, and look for FSC certification on paper packaging
- Seek brands that take back and/or refill containers
- Buy the largest size possible

Ingredients and Packaging

Creating your own beauty 'potions' is really fun, and helps you take care of ingredients and packaging in one hit. There is no shortage of internet tips and 'recipes' to help explore this aspect of green beauty. Some of my favourite homemade options include a baking soda facial, using almond oil as eye makeup remover, and coconut oil as a hydrating hair treatment. I'd love to hear what other homemade products you create in your kitchen!

Beauty : Shopping guide

Here it is! A sneaky peek into my medicine cabinet and makeup bag, and why I love each product listed.

B : Body care   **F** : Facial care   **H** : Hair care   **M** : Makeup

Aloedent aloedent.co.uk **B**	Natural toothpaste, mouthwash, dental floss and lip balm, using Aloe Vera (aka 'The First Aid Plant'). I've been using this brand for years, and no cavities!
Andalou Naturals andalou.com **B F H**	Natural, Fairtrade and organic ingredients are used in Andalou's "Fruit Stem Cell science". This is my current skincare regime, and my skin has not looked this great in many years.
Avalon organics avalonorganics.com **B F H**	All products are made with certified organic ingredients, no fragrances, phthalates, harsh sulfates or parabens. I especially love the Lavendar shampoo – leaves my hair naturally silky clean without stripping it of moisture.
Aveda aveda.com **F H M**	Though slightly contentious among hardcore greenies, Aveda has a rich history of natural ingredients and a decent sustainability policy. Ingredient sourcing is also designed to help the communities from where the ingredients originate. 89-90% of organic raw ingredients are used in the products, and I love the amazing scents from the essential oils.

Be Genki begenki.com **B**	Luxurious products that avoid the 'bad' ingredients, and come packaged in recyclable bottles, jars, and boxes (made from 100% recycled paper). Be Genki also donates 5% of its profits to environmental sustainability campaigns.
Burt's Bees burtsbees.com **B F**	A real pioneer in triple bottom line business practices. Burt's Bees uses a high percentage of natural ingredients and a supplier code of ethics including audits, third-party certifications and site visits. The Milk & Honey body lotion is a real fave of mine.
Butter butterlondon.com **M**	Best known for their amazing nail polish – fantastic colours and quality, made without Formaldehyde, Toluene or DBP. Butter has expanded to makeup free from phthalates or parabens. They stand Rock & Roll, Great Britain, and Fashion – and the environment.
Dr. Hauschka drhauschka.com.au **B F H M**	I'm so in love with the Pure Care Cover Stick – it corrects blemishes like magic while also working as a great concealer. The company sources the highest quality natural ingredients, and all herbs used by the company are grown in biodynamic farms.
Earth science earthsciencenaturals.com **B F H**	This company makes my favourite deodorant (Mint & Rosemary, oh-so-fresh). All products are made of natural ingredients, and they offset, too. Bursting with eco-appeal.
Ecotools ecotools.com **B M**	A makeup tool/brush company, with products made with bamboo handles, recycled aluminium ferrules, and cruelty-free bristles. This is what I use to put on my makeup. If it's good enough for co-founder Alicia Silverstone, it's good enough for all of us.

Ere Perez ereperez.com **M**	Australian-owned cosmetics brand that uses only natural ingredients. The mascara is award-winning, and I especially love the Rosehip Oil Lip Bars (I wear the colour 'Life') and the Olive Oil lipstick.
Everescents everescents.com.au **H**	Plant-based haircare featuring certified organic ingredients. This company donates 5 cents from every item sold to Camp Quality, helping children with cancer. I use the hairspray and can attest to its holding power.
Grown grownalchemist.com **B F H**	Beautiful products made with organic ingredients and no harsh chemicals. Grown harnesses the natural properties of plants, turning them into effective beauty. The gorgeous recyclable packaging will also have you fooled that this is an 'eco' brand at all, as luxurious as it gets.
INDAH indah.com.au **B F**	Australian-owned and produced certified organic skincare, body care and perfume balm, as well as Extra Virgin Coconut Oil. INDAH also works with Borneo Orangutan Survival Australia, working to protect the habitat of these amazing animals.
Josie Maran josiemarancosmetics.com **B F H M**	Luxury with a conscience, featuring star ingredient Argan Oil. Using Fairtrade practices, sustainably-sourced ingredients, and much charitable giving, there's a lot to love about Josie Maran, including GOGO mascara which sales support City of Hope cancer survivors.
Jurlique jurlique.com.au **B F**	Over 25 years of experience from this coveted luxury Australian skincare brand. Jurlique uses many organic and biodynamic ingredients, and is the only Australian beauty brand with its own certified biodynamic farm.

KORA koraorganics.com **B F**	An organic skincare line created by Australian supermodel Miranda Kerr. Luxurious and hydrating, and full of natural and certified organic ingredients. Noni fruit, rosehip oil, aloe vera and lavender feature strongly in the line.
Korres korres.com **B F H M**	One of my favourite makeup brands; the eyeliner, lip gloss and blush are commonly found in my makeup bag. Using natural ingredients like wild rose and pomegranate, Korres works with small farms, agricultural unions, and schools to cultivate the ingredients.
Kosmea kosmea.com.au **F**	Skincare as nature intended, formulated around organic rosehip oil and other plant extracts. This home grown Australian company now offers its products around the globe. I particularly enjoy the Clarifying Facial Wash.
MOP mophair.com **H**	MOP strives to bring together technology and nature, and many ingredients are certified organic – not frequently found in salon products. Mostly paraben-free and sulphate-free, but check the labels before purchasing. The C-system shampoo smells particularly divine.
Musq musq.com.au **F M**	My go-to mineral makeup brand, and my all-time favourite mascara. Musq was Australia's first 100% natural luxury skincare and makeup brand, and the high-quality items make your skin look and feel divine. It's no wonder they are regulars on the runways at Fashion Week.
Nature's Gate natures-gate.com **B F H**	Not many natural brands can claim to have begun by adding hand-collected rainwater to herbs to make shampoo – these guys are the real deal using organic and local ingredients. They have a complete range of products, and I love their crème de peppermint toothpaste.

Nourish nourishorganic.com **B F**	The Wild Berries organic body lotion is the highlight of my morning – so thick and moisturising with a delightful scent. The first company to work with USDA to create body products that meet organic food criteria. Also cruelty-free, gluten-free, and mostly vegan.
Original Mineral originalmineral.com **H**	The company behind my preferred hair colour line, Clean Color Technology. No ammonia, resorcinol or PPD – safer for me and my hair stylist, and results that can match, or exceed, any other salon colour.
People for Plants peopleforplants.com.au **B F**	Certified organic Australian skincare with none of the nasties, brought to us in part by the dreamy Jamie Durie. Great prices, lovely (recyclable) packaging, and intensely moisturising hand lotion. This is a fairly new brand, and one that I'll be keeping a close eye on.
RMS Beauty rmsbeauty.com **M**	Thanks Mom for sharing this magical find with me! Featuring non-toxic, raw, food-grade and organic ingredients, allowing living properties to impact the skin. I definitely have fun with the Living Luminizer product, which adds a delightful glow to my complexion.
Skinny Skinny skinnyskinny.com **B F H**	I love this organic dry shampoo! Sprinkle it in, let it sit for a couple of minutes, and comb through. Amazing results, saves water and time. Bath soaks, soaps, scrubs, and moisturizers are also available, all made with certified organic ingredients.
Stem Organics stemorganics.com.au **F**	Australian-made organic skincare, featuring native ingredients like Kakadu Plum. I rely on the exfoliant and toner as part of my skincare regime. In addition to gorgeous, recyclable packaging, Stem is carbon neutral and supports the Butterfly Foundation and WWF.

Sukin sukinorganics.com.au **B F H**	An old favourite of mine, I religiously use the hair conditioner (I love the mandarin scent.). Natural, affordable, carbon neutral, and offers jumbo sizes of shampoo and conditioner. Sukin's certified organic rosehip oil is Australia's #1 selling natural beauty product.
Suvana suvanabeauty.com **M**	The best organic Paw Paw salve to make those lips shine (among the myriad other uses for Paw Paw ointment). Ecocert certified, and the honey is a nice addition to the product, too.
The Body Shop thebodyshop.com **B F H M**	An eco-pioneer in the beauty industry. In addition to no animal testing, The Body Shop supports small communities with Fair Trade work, actively protects the planet through various practices and activism campaigns, and promotes self-esteem amongst its customers.
Tints of Nature tintsofnature.com.au **H**	Natural hair colour for those who prefer to colour their hair at home. I have not tried this brand, but it is frequently listed as the best at-home natural hair colour range. Let me know if you use it, and how well it works.
Weleda weleda.com.au **B F**	Practising sustainability since 1921, Weleda are eco-experts. I really enjoy the face moisturisers, and the Rose deodorant has a lovely, feminine scent. Producing its own organic ingredients when possible, and using Fairtrade farms for all other ingredients.
Wotnot wotnot.com.au **B F**	Eco-friendly, biodegradable and organic products. This company makes my sunblock of choice, and when I do need facial wipes (like when camping) this is an amazing natural and biodegradable option. They have a lot for babies, too.

My sustainable fashion discoveries

Designer	Why I love them

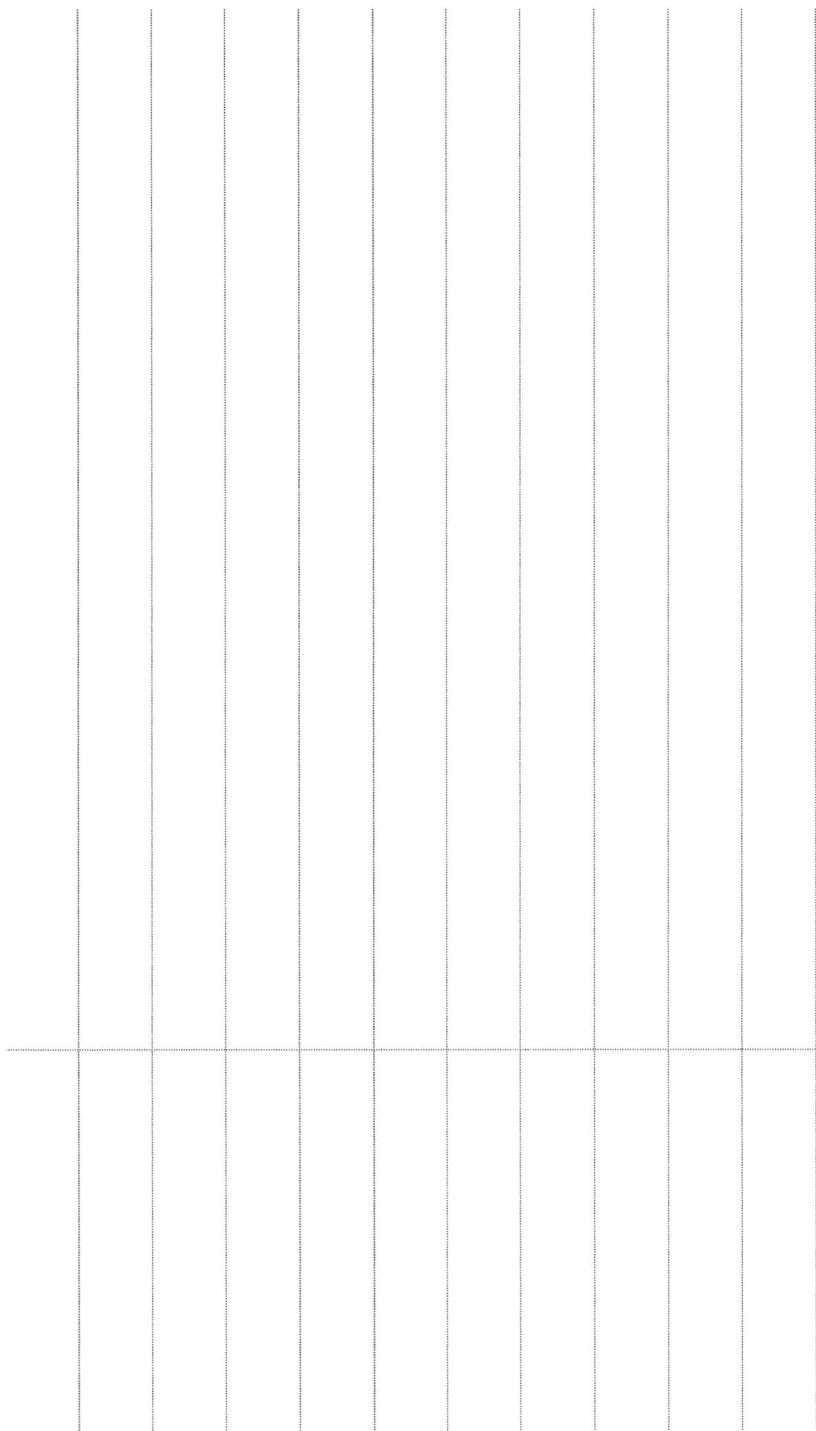

My natural beauty discoveries

Brand	Why I love them

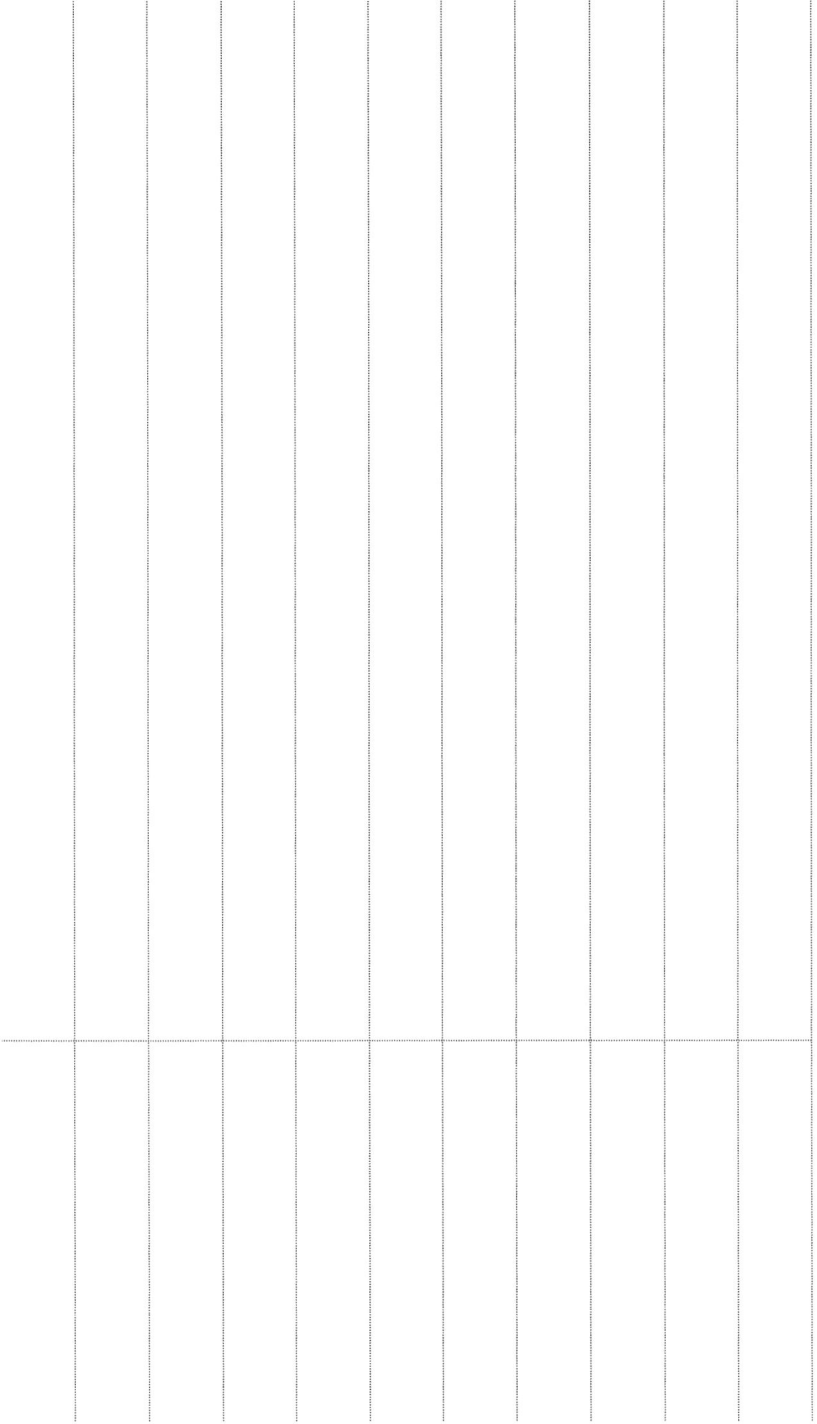

Appendix: Cultural and social analysis

This idea for this book originated from my Master's thesis in Cultural Studies. It was written as an ethnography, and within my thesis I analysed much of what happened internally as I made changes, how this related to the wider culture in which I live, and the complexities that arose between my friends and I as I spruiked environmentalism. The scenario referred to as Beefgate was real and happened as described within this book, and was a real turning point in my eco-journey.

In this appendix I have included highlights from my academic analysis to shed light on an area that I feel requires more attention by the world of environmentalists – the cultural and social setting in which eco-changes must take place. We can no longer afford to only consider the scientific and rational aspects of climate change. It is time to better understand people and our responses to climate change, and I've endeavoured to add to this important discussion.

This analysis was included within the body of the book in the First Edition, as chapter 5 entitled *Beefgate*.

Beefgate was a personal disaster, there is no getting around it. How did I manage to make such a mess for myself? All I wanted to do was make the world a greener place and instead I felt like I completely lost the plot and alienated my friends in the process. I seriously considered throwing in the sustainability towel.

The conversation I had with Geoff at the start of my journey keeps springing to mind – the science is in, now's the time to better understand people in order to encourage real action. It's time I put my Cultural Studies degree to good use, and there's no better place to start than with me and my friends. As the editors of *Hop on Pop* (a cultural studies anthology masterpiece named after the Dr. Seuss book) put it, we need to study the details of our own corner of the world because "we can neither engage in meaningful conversations with other segments of our society nor can we act with political responsibility until we have a realistic understanding of the culture around us[1]." I feel that the people in my corner of the world have the potential to make great positive environmental impact if we can simply channel our energy in the right direction.

I suppose I'll start with some self-reflection.

Clearly I experienced an identity crisis. Okay, so I abandoned my dream career and forfeited my shopping habit, but I think the problem lies deeper. I wanted to quit that job for ages and I do have other interests; I'm not totally one-dimensional. No, I think it had something to do with why Randall had a hard time using his own mug, and everything to do with the mantra I'd long lived my life by: *Image is Everything.*

For years I spent a lot of time and money maintaining the right image, which for me meant looking beautiful, wearing the latest designs and participating in trends as they occurred, whether in fashion, dining, socialising or art. I'm also not too proud to admit that I thrived on embodying my ideal of a successful, beautiful woman. I was not perfect, but boy was I trying to be. Having the right shoes, the right clothes, the right makeup, the right hair, the right man, the right interests and the right job all helped create this perfect image. Part of me hated it – the pressure to live up to this ideal can be exhausting and even seems to go against the progress of feminism[2], which I also identify with – but mostly I loved it. I also seemed to succeed because of it, even winning my design agency job partly because of my image.

I was selling an ideal image, but I also embodied that image, and it was fabulous.

It isn't just me, or other fashion lovers, who identify with an image created by material possessions. People throughout our society express themselves through things they buy and how they spend their time. Scholars in consumer and cultural studies have long described the way people create their identity and lifestyles through buying particular goods and participating in certain activities[3].

As a true fashionista things like my hairstyle, wearing the latest season's shoes and denim, having subscriptions to a range of fashion magazines and even the act of shopping itself created my identity. I wasn't simply filling a need, I was cultivating a persona who knows all the trends and maintains a desirable personal style. The same can be said of an athlete who only wears Nike, communicating that she is serious about her performance and only trusts in the best athletic gear companies, or a corporate lawyer who wears serious suits and works serious hours, signifying her serious profession. These days my reusable coffee mug is not just a receptacle for holding a hot beverage; it also demonstrates that I care about the environment.

Even those who reject shopping, as many within the environmental movement may endeavour to do, are creating their identity through their lack of consumer goods. When I immersed myself amongst a group of these hard-core greenies at my first eco-march I had to admit I was nowhere near identifying with the many heads of dreadlocked hair and countless cork-sandaled feet – would those people ever really be my people?

We give meaning to some of these signifiers ourselves, and frequently the media and advertising have played a role in defining them; Apple products are a prime example. Apple has an amazing marketing machine that hooked us with the iPod, reeled us in with the 'I'm a Mac' ad campaign and eventually pulled us on board the Apple mother ship, even convincing diehard fans to line up outside their shops ahead of the release of the latest products. Between iPods, iPhones, iPads and desktop and laptop computers, Apple is *the* must-have tech brand for the hip and trendy and technically savvy. I'm not disputing the power of the technology or the skills of their innovators – I'm in love with my Macs (yes, I have two) and my iPhone – but there are plenty of other musical devices, smart phones and tablets that don't have the cult following of Apple products. Marketing has a lot to do with the perceived value of these devices.

It seems we can't escape marketing if we try[4]. Messages about goods and brands are constantly being spread through advertising, magazines, movies and the Internet, helping to define what styles are 'now' and what our life experiences 'should' look like; we only have to consider fashion trends sparked by *Sex and the City* or *Gossip Girl* to see how Hollywood gives goods added appeal or a covetable meaning. And speaking as one who knows, marketers are always on the lookout for new channels to spread their messages, so there's no telling where or how we may be influenced about particular brands.

I'm not going to go so far as to say that all marketing is evil, but plenty of it is sneaky and designed to out-smart the consumer, and for awhile I was adding to the problem. Throughout my early career I encouraged people to buy goods that are not necessary. Goods that require energy to produce, treat, package, transport and promote. Goods produced without considering sustainability practices. And perhaps worst of all, sold in such a way that insinuated one needed this particular item to be a good mother, a good Australian, healthy, or beautiful – as if the act of buying something can give you any of those traits.

Advertising messages are designed to make us feel that we need to improve ourselves, and we can do so by buying what is being advertised. Even though I know how it all works, I still wasn't immune; in fact, I seemed to buy into the machine more than anyone, purchasing many, many goods to create my identity.

Further complicating our relationship with goods and image is learned behaviour based on our society and upbringing[5]. Growing up in the 1980s and 1990s in beautiful suburban America, I'd long been encouraged by the capitalist consumer society I inhabited to work hard, earn lots of money, and spend it proudly on the biggest, best and most glamorous things I could find. There was rarely a mention of concern for where the things came from or where they would go when I grew tired of them, the important thing was to own them. It was here that my values and tastes were formed and became well entrenched, and it's within this norm that I was been rewarded; I achieved a perceived status of success exemplified by my career, my home, my clothes, my jet-setting lifestyle, and all the other things that create my image.

And while I could go on and on about the perils of convenience culture as it relates to the environment, poverty or personal happiness (there are plenty of books that do just that), instead I'll admit that this world I inhabited was really fun. For the most part it wasn't a lifestyle that I really wanted to give up – I knew I needed to if I was serious about the environment, but to say I wouldn't miss it would be a complete lie.

No wonder I felt so bad. The environmental movement caused me to question everything I used to create my personal identity – my job, my shopping, my beautiful hair, my stylish wardrobe – and it all came as a complete surprise. In short, it's all I feared when I decided to go green – that I'd have to become a hippy who doesn't colour her hair, wear high heels or care about money.

Identity crisis, meet Lisa.

Lisa, say good-bye to your self-esteem (and you can't even use your old pal 'shopping' to buy your way out this time around).

Glad I sorted that one out.

👄 ⌀ 👕 👝 ⚷ ⚔ 🜊 💍 👛 💡 ♡

And as if examining my personal self-esteem problems wasn't painful enough, now I have to sort out where I went wrong trying to convert my friends to the cause.

Self-reflection has uncovered part of the problem – my friends have lifestyles similar to mine, so when I questioned their choices, I was actually attacking their identity – not a very 'friendly' activity. It's also likely they foresaw the personal challenges or witnessed my struggle with environmental change and so said 'no thank you' to that path. Based on the 'grace' with which I was pulling it off at the time, I can't say I blame them for not wanting to join my green brigade.

But things really blew up for me around Beefgate, and I suspect it was about more than just image concerns. I've decided to bring in some big-guns of social behaviour to help me sort this out and hopefully identify where I went wrong with Beefgate. My friendships are important to me and I don't want to throw them away, even in the name of the environment.

Erving Goffman was an award-winning sociologist responsible for groundbreaking research in human behaviour, particularly as it relates to group settings, and his descriptions of group behaviour are as true now as when he was describing 1950s cocktail parties. In 1959 Goffman wrote *The Presentation of Self in Everyday Life*[6], and in it he explained that people seek knowledge about others in social situations, taking clues from conduct and appearance, in order to understand how to relate to them, and then present themselves in the best possible light to the other person/people. In 1963 he followed up this work with the release of *Behaviour in Public Places,* in which he elaborated that individuals' self-presentation is either 'approved' or 'disapproved' depending on the specific social group and situation within which the behaviour takes place, and that people can be 'punished' for performing unapproved behaviour within the group setting. He recognised that various occasions and settings require varying behaviour, but "the rule of behaviour that seems to be common to all situations…is the rule obliging participants to 'fit in'"[7].

After I read this major light bulbs switched on in my head. He was so right! For example, my friends have picked up the clues that I'm passionate about the environment, and so present themselves in a way they think will please me. Early on when I asked them about their environmental behaviour and they avoided straightforward answers, they were trying to present themselves in a way that 'fit in' with my green ideals and ensure our get togethers were pleasant. This happens with people I meet for the first time in social situations, too; when they learn I'm a greenie they are cautious what they say around me, talk only about environmental topics, or apologise if they say something they think isn't green-friendly. Similarly, Randall found himself pulled in two directions: he wanted to 'fit in' with his colleagues and so decided not to carry a reusable mug to work; when he was with me he wanted to 'fit in' and agreed to use his own mug. In a way it's nice that we all want to please one another, but it does not help the environmental movement that the dominant culture is still a consumer culture that rewards 'fitting in' via consumption rather than environmentalism.

There is another widely accepted phenomenon of group behaviour that complements Goffman's theory of 'fitting in' and further explains my friends' behaviour: social identity theory[8]. The theory contends that self-esteem is directly linked to group belonging and that the better you feel about your group, the better you feel about yourself. From this perspective, my friends' perceived desire to appear environmentally aware could stem from a desire to maintain their own self-esteem through maintaining strength and unity (and therefore a positive feeling) of our group.

So then how did I go from people trying to please me to feeling like an outcast?

Goffman would tell me that I performed behaviour 'unacceptable' to the group when I requested a beef-free weekend, so I was punished. No one wanted to 'fit in' with me when I made my beef-free request, not even my own husband. What exactly did I do wrong? Why was beef so contentious?

Social psychology experts tell us that groups have established collective identities based on shared values and interests[9]. Our group had come together because we each identified with something within the group and were able to continue as a group because of this collective identity. In layperson speak – we have things in common, which is why we are friends, and these shared interests define our social group.

Just as individuals create their lifestyles with particular goods and activities, groups also have signifiers that identity them. The concept is called homology, the link between a lived culture (or subculture) and the objects and activities that surround it. Dick Hebdige famously explained this concept through his analysis of Punk Culture in 1960s London and the various signifiers – like safety pins, chains and coloured hair – that helped identify that subculture as a distinct group[10]. Similarly, my university friend Rosie and I used to joke that we 'checked each other out' for a couple of weeks before we attempted a friendship. We read signs from each other's clothing and personal style to determine if the other had the appropriate level of fashion acumen and street smarts to 'fit in' with our existing circle of friends. This is not to say friendships don't go deeper than these visible signs; of course they do, but these external clues can be a great starting point for social relationships.

Some characteristics of my "Aussie family's" collective identity include working hard and playing hard, participation in consumer culture and enjoying a carefree existence – we really are a pleasure-seeking group. Whether it's a surf trip up the coast or a cleverly themed house party, we like to have a good time. And based on the results of Beefgate, it seems that beef on a beach weekend is a signifier for the group. Beef, or more likely the freedom to eat it, represents the Aussie Good Life, which we identify with; by threatening that signifier I was threatening the group identity. Just as I felt personally attacked by environmental condemnation of my fashion addiction, members of the group felt attacked by my threatening to take away the freedom to eat beef on a beach weekend because it represents a defining aspect of our group.

My request for a beef-free weekend was probably also considered unapproved behaviour because I was taking a moral stance. Beefeater's email says it best, he/she felt I was forcing my ideals upon others by limiting dietary choices through my request. Maybe this perception relates to connections between environmentalism and religion, as both have moral dimensions, and the concept of imposing one's religion upon others is totally taboo in the socially liberal circle we inhabit. Taking a moral stand was against the rules in our group – a rule that apparently only I didn't know, because everyone else stayed out of the discussion. I hadn't quite made the link between environmentalism and morality, and as a result I was perceived as a zealot.

There also appears to be a clear distinction between work and play within the group. When you're playing you shouldn't have to think about anything hard, like money or the environment, because you've earned your time off to do whatever you please – including renting an expensive beach house with your hard-earned cash and enjoying any food you choose. Our group is not unique in encouraging the use of money and free time to create a world of pleasure; it's common practice in our capitalist society to promote the accumulation of things as a reward for hard work. This logic is also frequently applied in advertising – any number of advertisements insist "You're worth it", to "Have a break" or "Have it your way" all because you've earned it.

This is the world in which we've all been raised and have thrived. To turn our backs on our goods and activities means going against the norm of our society – it's not easy or attractive. So just as I, as an individual, find it challenging to change my behaviour, so does each group member – and it wasn't even his or her idea to change in the first place!

Now I can see that by requesting a beef-free weekend I was questioning the Aussie Good Life, taking a moral stand and challenging our modus operandi of 'work hard to play hard', therefore attacking the identity of the group. This in turn challenged the strength of our group and ultimately threatened everyone's self-esteem. It endangered everything our group stood for and what held us together, so I had to be punished for the sake of the group. I was reprimanded by those who disagreed, and also punished by those individuals who agreed with my eco-action in principle but didn't openly support me because they thought it might harm the group. I felt further punished on the weekend because it was barely green; my requests had been ignored and I had to sit there quietly. The e-mail exchanges left me reluctant to express my ideas further, because they didn't fit with the characteristics of the group.

Ironically, my exclusion further threatened the group because, as social identity theory explains, when individual connections within a group are weakened the entire group and self-esteem of the other individuals within it are also weakened[11]. This explains why people try and keep the peace for the good of the group, and why no one supported the 'controversial' no beef idea in a public e-mail. Everyone naturally wants to maintain the strength of our group out of collective love and respect, and also for the sake of their own self-esteem.

After considering all of this it's really no wonder I was punished for my threatening behaviour. I wish I'd had the foresight to know it was threatening behaviour, but then I wouldn't have this story to share. Live and learn, eh?

Now I know that if I want to get out of this thing with any friendships intact, I need to make my future activism attempts emotionally and socially sustainable so that they actually work and I don't give up in frustration. I need to ensure they have enough of a kick to jolt people into action, though, so my friends start thinking about environmentalism on a more regular basis. Social movement scholars identify the need for collective identity to embrace a cause in order for social movements to occur[12]; my attempts to date have not managed to incorporate sustainability into our groups' collective identity at all. After Beefgate I'm not certain this is even a reasonable goal.

Perhaps my future activism attempts can take a page from Lillian and her vintage thermos. Social movement scholars would explain her quick take-up of a reusable thermos as 'free-riding' activity. Free-riding is defined by having little time or financial commitments associated, and I'm going to extend the definition to include identity commitments, too. In Lillian's case, she already enjoyed vintage goods; now they have the added benefit of also being sustainable, and she can retain her existing lifestyle whilst participating in the environmental movement[13]. I, on the other hand, had never previously embraced vintage into my personal style, so I couldn't free-ride into vintage shopping because my identity that included having the latest trends was threatened.

Similarly, the suggestions I made to the group did not fall into this free-rider category. By asking people to give up takeaway coffee cups or beef on a beach weekend I asked them to give up an aspect of their carefree lifestyle and identity, and the common values that brought our group together in the first place. I'll have to keep looking for other free-rider options that will help ease the way into environmentalism for all of us if I really want to influence change within my social group.

I was amazed at the questions and dilemmas I faced as I strived to embrace environmentalism. I thought it was just a matter of living with increased awareness, but I eventually saw how many aspects of our lives are tangled up with the environment in ways I never imagined. Geoff was right, climate change is not a scientific dilemma – it's a cultural one, a psychological one, a deeply emotional one, a personal one, as well as a collective one.

And now I also understand that it's not just that we consume lots of stuff – although the statistics shock me, the claims are not new. Many environmentalists have long argued the need to learn to live with less and that our culture's capitalist mentality encourages growth and accumulation of stuff. The central issue is that we use this stuff to define our identity. If we take away these signifiers, these objects and activities, who are we left with? When questioning our consumption habits undermines our identities, it's no wonder people aren't rushing out to join the movement. Why sign up to something that makes you feel bad about everything you believe in and the things that define who you are?

This is not a concept I've come across in my research on sustainability to date. There is certainly an undercurrent of knowledge that mainstream culture is not attracted to a hippy lifestyle, but no one has specifically identified that it's because all these *things* we surround ourselves with are being used to create our identities. If people are asked to give up their favourite items or activities for any reason they will put up a fight in order to protect their identity, and the environmental movement is not immune to these defences. If mainstream society is to begin a climate change journey, environmentalism needs to enable people to retain their identity and free-ride into the movement.

I was personally dealing with these painful realisations when my already fragile self-esteem took a hit because I felt 'out' of my group and hurt by their attitudes. I then questioned whether it was a group I really wanted to be in anymore, which wasn't fair to anyone. Add to this feelings of identity loss from leaving my job and forfeiting my passion for fashion, and it's no wonder I cracked.

Even though it was a lot to take in, I'm glad I have a better understanding about why I initially struggled with environmental changes. Learning this allowed me to be a bit more patient with myself and others, because I realised it's about more than just convenience, money, selfishness or greed – some of these changes are very personal and internalised, and take time to embrace. I am glad I was stubborn enough to stick it out and learn how to go green and not completely lose myself. I'm also glad I learned an appropriate way to communicate with my friends about the environment, and that simply by living my greenest life I demonstrated that not everything had to change – I could live sustainably, with style, and so could they.

Notes

_____

My Coffee Cup Moment

[1] Nixon, S. (2003). *Advertising Cultures*. London: SAGE, 159

Learning from the Experts

[1] Oreskes, N. (2004). Beyond the Ivory Tower: the scientific consensus on climate change. *Science* 306 (5702), 168.

[2] IPCC. (2007). Climate Change 2007: The Physical Science Basis. *Contribution of Working Group I to the Fourth Assessment Report of the Intergovernmental Panel on Climate Change.* IPCC.

[3] Lomborg, B. (2001). *The Skeptical Environmentalist: measuring the real state of the world.* Cambridge, Mass: Cambridge University Press.

Lomborg, B. (2007) *Cool it: the skeptical environmenalist's guide to global warming.* New York: Random House.

Lomborg, B. (2010). *Smart solutions to climate change,* Cambridge, Mass: Cambridge University Press.

[4] IPCC Press Release, 27 September 2013 "Human influence on climate clear, IPCC report says"

[5] Andresen, S., and Shardul A.(2002). Leaders, Pushers and Laggards in the Making of the Climate Regime. *Global Environmental Change* 12, 41-51.
Barr, S. (2008). *Environment and Society: Sustainability, Policy and the Citizen.* Hampshire: Ashgate.

Kollmuss, A., and Agyeman, J. (2002). 'Mind the Gap: Why Do People Act Environmentally and What Are the Barriers to Pro-Environmental Behaviour?'. *Environmental Education Research* 8.3, 22.

Oskamp, S. (2000). Psychological Contributions to Achieving an Ecologically Sustainable Future for Humanity. *Journal of Social Issues* 56.3, 373-90.

Thompson, G. D., and Kidwell, J. (1998). Explaining the Choice of Organic Produce: Cosmetic Defects, Prices, and Consumer Preferences. *American*

Journal of Agricultural Economics 80.2, 277-87.

Sterman, J. D., and Sweeney, L.B.(2007). Understanding Public Complacency About Climate Change: Adults' Mental Models of Climate Change Violate Conservation of Matter. *Climatic Change* 80, 213-38.

[6] Potter, E. and Starr, P. (2008 March). Australia and the New Geographies of Climate Change. *Australian Humanities Review online.*.

[7] Walker, G. and King, D. (2008). *The Hot Topic: how to tackle global warming and still keep the lights on.* London: Bloomsbury

Learning to be an environmentalist

[1] www.climatesmartsolutions.com.au

[2] IBISWorld Bottled Water Manufacturing in Australia, January 2010
West, D. (2007). *Container Deposits: The Common Sense Approach* 2.1, Boomerang Alliance. February.

[3]www.nytimes.com/interactive/2009/04/19/opinion/20090419bottle.html

[4] A report from the National Toxicology Program at the National Institute of Health in 2008 outlined the many health risks from BPA and the reusable water bottle market has never been the same! http://www.niehs.nih.gov/news/sya/sya-bpa/

Eco-shopping excursion

[1] Siegle, L. (2010). *To Die For: Is fashion wearing out the world?,* Harper Collins

[2] Cline, E.L. (2012). *Overdressed: the shockingly high cost of fast fashion,* Portfolio Hardcover

[3] www.nikeresponsibility.com

[4] www.ftc.gov/bcp/edu/pubs/consumer/alerts/alt160.shtm

[5] www.ejfoundation.org

[6] www.terrachoice.org

[7] www.innovationintextiles.com

[8] www.sustainability.lululemon.com.au

[9] www.americanapparel.net/contact/legalizela

[10] www.acfonline.org.au/consumptionatlas

[11] EPA Office of Solid Waste

[12] www.defra.gov.uk/environment/business/products/roadmaps/clothing/action-plan.htm

[13] Fiscal 2005 statistics from the Ministry of Economy, Trade and Industry's 3R Policy homepage http://www.itochu.co.jp/en/news/2009/090415.html

[14] Hamilton, C., and Dennis, R. (2005). *Affluenza: when too much is never enough,* Crows Nest NSW: Allen & Unwin

[15] Claudio L 2007. Waste Couture: Environmental Impact of the Clothing Industry. *Environ Health Perspect* 115, A449-A454.

(In)Activism

[1] www.acfonline.org.au/consumptionatlas

[2] *Livestock's Long Shadow* www.fao.org/docrep/010/a0701e/a0701e00.HTM

[3] www.worldwatch.org/node/6297

[4] *Tackling climate change through livestock*
www.fao.org/ag/againfo/resources/en/publications/tackling_climate_change/index.htm

[5] Two independent comprehensive studies, each analysing around 40 published studies comparing the differences between organic and conventional foods, have concluded there is overwhelming evidence that organic food is more nutritious.

Heaton, S. 2004. *Australian Organic Journal*, Issue 59, Biological Farmers of Australia.

Worthington, V. (2001). Nutritional Quality of Organic Versus Conventional Fruits, Vegetables and Grains.*The Journal of Alternative and Complementary Medicine*, 7(2), 161-173.

[6] The certification mark varies from country to country; make sure to check what the correct symbol is for your country.

[7] www.climateactionprogramme.org

[8] Weber, C.L. and Matthews, H.M. (2008). Food-Miles and the Relative Climate Impacts of Food Choices in the United States. *Environ. Sci. Technol.*, 42(10), 3508–3513.

[9] ACF Consuming Australia

[10] Uliano, S. (2008) *Gorgeously Green: 8 simple steps to an earth-friendly life,* New York: Collins.

[11] Uliano, S. (2008) *Gorgeously Green: 8 simple steps to an earth-friendly life,* New York: Collins.

[12] *Livestock's Long Shadow*

[13] Reijnders, L., and S. Soret (2003) Quantification of the environmental impact of different dietary protein choices. *Amer. J. Clin. Nutr.,* 78 (Suppl.), 664S–668S.

[14] www.news.cornell.edu/releases/Aug97/livestock.hrs.html

[15] www.epa.gov

[16] *Tackling climate change through livestock*

[17]www.independent.ie/farming/global-beef-output-to-top-60m-tonnes-this-year-1396111.html

[18] USDA, www.ers.usda.gov/Data/FoodConsumption/
Victorian Department of Primary Industry, www.dpi.vic.gov.au/

<u>Natural beauty</u>

[1] If you're looking for it in store, Grown has since changed its packaging to appear more premium, even using gold embossing.

[2] www.thedailygreen.com

[3] Environmental Working Group, Skin Deep Cosmetics database www.cosmeticsdatabase.com

[4] *Gorgeously Green* 'Most Dangerous' ingredients list can be found in Chapter Two, Green Goddess.

[5] www.ewg.org/reports/teens

[6] www.ewg.org

[7] www.cosmeticsdatabase.com/

[8] www.ewg.org/reports/teens

[9] Routledge E.J., Parker, J., Odum, J., Ashby, J., Sumpter, J.P. (1998). Some alkyl hydroxy benzoate preservatives (parabens) are estrogenic. *Toxicology and applied pharmacology* 153(1), 12-19.

Oishi S. (2002). Effects of propyl paraben on the male reproductive system. *Food Chem Toxicol* 40(12), 1807-1813.

Byford J.R., Shaw, L.E., Drew, M.G., Pope, G.S., Sauer, M,J., and Darbre, P.D. (2002). Oestrogenic activity of parabens in MCF7 human breast cancer cells. *The Journal of steroid biochemistry and molecular biology* 80(1), 49-60.

Darbre, P.D., Byford, J.R., Shaw, L.E., Horton, R.A., Pope, G.S., and Sauer, M.J. (2002). Oestrogenic activity of isobutylparaben in vitro and in vivo. *J Appl Toxicol* 22(4), 219-226.

Darbre, P.D., Byford, J.R., Shaw, L.E., Hall, S., Coldham, N.G., Pope, G.S., et al. (2003). Oestrogenic activity of benzylparaben. *J Appl Toxicol* 23(1), 43-51.

Darbre, P.D.,Aljarrah, A., Miller, W.R., Coldham, N.G., Sauer, M.J., and Pope, G.S. (2004). Concentrations of parabens in human breast tumours. *J Appl Toxicol* 24(1), 5-13.

Gomez, E., Pillon, A., Fenet, H., Rosain, D., Duchesne, M.J., Nicolas, J.C., et al. (2005). Estrogenic activity of cosmetic components in reporter cell lines: parabens, UV screens, and musks. *Journal of toxicology and environmental health* 68(4), 239-251.

Pugazhendhi, D., Sadler, A.J., Darbre, P.D. (2007). Comparison of the global gene expression profiles produced by methylparaben, n-butylparaben and 17beta-oestradiol in MCF7 human breast cancer cells. *J Appl Toxicol* 27(1), 67-77.

[10] www.wholefoodsmarket.com/products/premium-body-care.php

[11] Darbre, P.D., Aljarrah, A., Miller, W.R., Coldham, N.G., Sauer, M.J., Pope, G.S. (2004, January–February). "Concentrations of parabens in human breast tumours". *J Appl Toxicol* 24 (1), 5–13.

Darbre, P.D. (2009). "Underarm antiperspirants/deodorants and breast cancer". *Breast Cancer Research* 11 (Suppl 3), S5.

[12] www.cancer.gov/cancertopics/factsheet/Risk/AP-Deo#r1

[13] Wolf, N. (1991) *The Beauty Myth*

Green groceries

[1] Hunt, R.G., Sellers, V.R., Franklin, W.E., Nelson, J.M., Rathje, W.L., Hughes, W.W., and Wilson, D.C. (1990). Estimates of the volume of MSW and selected components in trash cans and land fills. Report prepared by the Garbage Project and Franklins Associates Ltd. for the Council for Solid Waste Solutions, Tucson, Ariz.

[2] www1.eere.energy.gov/industry/intensiveprocesses/pdfs/ energy_use_loss_opportunities_analysis.pdf

[3] Kenner, R. (Director). (2008) *Food Inc [Motion Picture]* United States: Magnolia Pictures.

Spurlock, M. (Director). (2004). *Supersize Me [Motion Picture]* United States: Kathbur Pictures.

Schlosser, E. (2001). *Fast Food Nation: The dark side of the all-American meal.* New York: Houghton Mifflin.

Pollan, M. (2006.) *The Omnivore's Dilemma: A natural history of four meals.* New York: The Penguin Press.

4 Pimentel, D. (2006). *Impacts of Organic Farming on the Efficiency of Energy Use in Agriculture.* The Organic Center.

5 Baker, D., Fear, J., and Denniss, R. (2009 November) "What a waste: An analysis of household expenditure on food." The Australia Institute, Policy brief 6, . www.apo.org.au/node/19598

6 Pimentel, D., and Pimentel, M. (eds.). (2008). *Food, Energy, and Society*: Third Edition. CRC Press: Boca Raton.

7 Total Environment Centre, Packaging Waste Overview, www.tec.org.au

8 My local food Co-op is in Manly and its guiding principals include working toward better health of the planet and their customers. Since writing this my beautiful husband has also become a volunteer at the Co-op. www.manlyfoodcoop.org

9 I must give credit to Qantas – since this conversation took place they have implemented very stringent recycling guidelines (and not because of any letters that I wrote). Well done flying Kangaroo. www.qantas.com.au/travel/airlines/domestic-onboard-recycling/global/en

10 I can't urge you enough to watch this – free online. www.vbs.tv/watch/toxic/toxic-garbage-island-1-of-3

11 http://www.asbec.asn.au/news/asbec_media Australian Sustainable Built Environment Council

Sustainable fashion

1 http://www.fscaustralia.org

[2] For some real insight on all the elements that go into all our stuff check out http://www.storyofstuff.org/

Home green homes

[1] Brown, S.K., Sim, M. R., Abramson, M. J., Gray, C. N. (1994). 'Concentration of volatile organic compounds in indoor air – a review', *Indoor Air*, 4 , pp.123 134.

Environment Australia. (2001). State of Knowledge Report: Air Toxics and Indoor Air Quality in Australia, Department of the Environment, Water, Heritage and the Arts (DEWHA), Commonwealth of Australia,

US Environmental Protection Agency (US EPA) (no date), An Introduction to Indoor Air Quality: Organic Gases (VOCs), www.epa.gov/iaq/voc.html

[2] Westpac are a founding member of the Australian Business and Climate Group and in 2014 was listed first in the World Economic Forum 'Global 100 Most Sustainable Corporations' listings.

[3] National Appliance and Equipment Energy Efficiency Program, Appliance Standby Power Consumption Store Survey 2005/06 – Final report; www.energyrating.gov.au/library/pubs/200609-storesurvey.pdf.

[4] Nriagu, J.O. and Kim, M.J. (2000, April **24**). "Emissions of lead and Zinc from candles with metal wicks", *The Science of The Total Environment.* 250,(1-3), 37-41

Wasson, S.J., Guo, Z., McBrian, J.A., and Beach,L.O., (2002 September 16). Lead in candle emissions. *The Science of The Total Environment* 296(1-3),159-174

[5] *Candles and incense as potential sources of indoor air pollution: market analysis and literature review*, EPA January 2001.

[6] Krause, J.D. (1999 August). *Characterization of scented candle emissions and associated public health risks.* Department of Environmental and Occupational Health, College of Public Health, University of South Florida.

[7] Romantic, candle-lit dinners: An unrecognized source of indoor air pollution, www.sciencedaily.com/releases/2009/08/090819153913.htm

[8] McKenzie, K. (2010 September). "Painting Australia Green" *Green Living*.

[9] *www.reversegarbage.org.au*

[10] www.openshed.com.au

www.friendswiththings.com

[11] Toxic algal blooms – a sign of rivers under stress www.science.org.au/nova/017/017key.htm

[12] 16 states ban phosphate-laden dishwasher soap www.content.usatoday.com/communities/greenhouse/post/2010/06/16-states-ban-phosphate-laden-dishwasher-soap/1

[13] www.choice.com.au/reviews-and-tests/household/laundry-and-cleaning/washing-and-drying/video-washing-machines.aspx

[14]Blaser M.J., Smith, P.F., Cody, H.J., Wang, W.L., and LaForce, F.M. (1984 January). Killing of fabric-associated bacteria in hospital laundry by low-temperature washing. *J Infect Dis.* 149(1), 48-57. www.sciencedaily.com/videos/2007/0810are_your_dishes_clean.htm

[15] *Gorgeously Green*

www.inhabitat.com/how-to-make-your-own-green-cleaning-products

www.cheap-and-easy-recipes.com

www.abundanceofwellness.com/blog/make-your-own-cleaning-products

www.gmagazine.com.au/video/574/how-make-your-own-eco-cleaning-products

[16]www.energysavers.gov/your_home/water_heating/index.cfm

[17] www.oneplanetcommunities.org

www.greenstarcommunities.org.au

www.livable.org.au

[18]www.iied.org/climate-change/media/cities-produce-surprisingly-low-carbon-emissions-capita

The green scene

[1] An excellent book on the subject is McDonough, J. and Braungart, M. (2002). *Cradle to Cradle*. North Point Press.

[2]Friedman, T. L. (2011, June 7) The Earth is Full. *The New York Times.*

[3] Mobium Group, Living LOHAS 4 study. http://www.mobium.com.au/

[4] Nava, M. (1991). Consumerism Reconsidered: buying and power. *Cultural Studies,* 5(2), 170.

[5] Gilding, P. (2011). *The Great Disruption: how the climate crisis will transform the global economy.* Bloomsbury, London, 263

The ripple effect

[1]Barr, S. (2008). *Environment and Society: Sustainability Policy and the Citizen.* Ashgate, 248-249

Eco-balance

[1] www.navdanya.org

[2] Monsanto is the company that owns the patents on GMO seeds, for more detailed insight into the questionable practices of Monsanto, and a thorough examination of the industrialisation of our food systems in general, I highly recommend watching the film *Food Inc.*

[3] I'm devastated to report that this rental service is no longer in business. For a similar experience, try DressedUp.com.au

[4] www.collaborativeconsumption.com/the-movement

[5] www.amcs.org.au

<u>We are the change</u>

[1] Among others, a report by WWF brings together research on the importance of moving beyond small individual changes to actively pursuing governmental changes. World Wildlife Fund (2009) *Simple and Painless? The limitations of spillover in environmental campaigning*

<u>Appendix : Social and cultural analysis</u>

[1] Jenkins, H., McPherson, T. & Shattuc, J. (Eds.) (2002). *Hop on Pop: the politics and pleasures of popular culture,* Durham: Duke University Press, 10.

[2] Wolf, N. (1990) *The Beauty Myth: how images of beauty are used against women,* London: Vintage.

[3] Just to name a few...

de Certeau, M. (1984) *The Practice of Everyday Life,* Berkely: University of California Press.

Douglas, M. and Isherwood, B. (1996) *The World of Goods: towards an anthropology of consumption,* London: Routledge.

Hebdige, D. (1979) *Subculture, the meaning of style,* London: Methuen.

Willis, P. E. (1978) *Profane Culture,* London, Henley and Boston: Routledge & Kegan Paul.

[4] If you're interested, the widely-read books *Affluenza* and *No Logo* discuss the reach of marketing and the damage it can cause our health, finances and self-esteem.

Hamilton, C. and Denniss, R. (2005) *Affluenza: when too much is never enough,* Crows Nest: Allen & Unwin.

Klein, N., Garner, K., Jhally, S., Alper, L., Klein, N., & Media Education Foundation. (2003). *No logo: Brands, globalization, resistance.* Northampton, Mass.: Media Education Foundation.

[5] Known as the theory of habitus.

Bourdieu, P. (1977). *Outline of a Theory of Practice,* Cambridge: Cambridge University Press.

[6] Goffman, E. (1959). *The Presentation of Self in Everyday Life,* New York: Doubleday.

[7] Goffman, E. (1963). *Behaviour in Public Places: notes on the social organisation of gatherings.* New York: The Free Press, 11.

[8] Tajfel, H. and Turner, J. (1986). The Social Identity Theory of Intergroup Behaviour. In Worcehl, S. and Austin, W. (Eds.) *Psychology of Intergroup Relations,* Chicago: Nelson Hall.

[9] Klandermans, B. and Weerd, M. D. (2000). Group Identification and Political Protest. In Stryker, S., Owens, T. J. and White, R. W. (Eds.) *Self, Identity, and Social Movements,* Minneapolis: University of Minnesota Press.

[10] Hebdige, D. (1979). *Subculture: The meaning of style,* London: Methuen.

[11] Tajfel and Turner (1986).

[12] Klandermans and Weerd (2000).

[13] Stern, P. C., Dietz, T., Abel, T., Guagnana, G. A. and Kalof, L. (1999). A Value-Belief-Norm Theory of Support for Social Movements; The Case of Environmentalism *Human Ecology Review,* 6(2), 81-97.

About the Author

Lisa Heinze was born in Salt Lake City, Utah, and has lived in Sydney, Australia since 2004. In 2009 she completed a Master's degree in Cultural Studies at the University of Sydney with research on cultural barriers to climate change action, and in 2014 she commenced a PhD examining sustainable fashion. She is co-founder of Clean Cut, a collective of sustainable fashion advocates bringing about greater awareness and celebration of the future of Australian fashion. She lives in Manly Beach with her husband.

Follow Lisa's latest eco-adventures online at www.lisaheinze.com.

www.ingramcontent.com/pod-product-compliance
Lightning Source LLC
Chambersburg PA
CBHW031426270326
41930CB00007B/589